Connect Your Amiga!

A Guide to the Internet, LANs, BBSs and Online Services
Revised Second Printing

by Dale L. Larson

D1732703

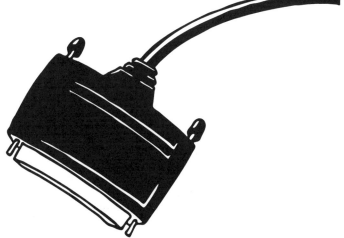

Published by Intangible Assets Manufacturing
in Drexel Hill, Pennsylvania, USA

Connect Your Amiga!
A Guide to the Internet, LANs, BBBs and Online Services

Published by:

Intangible Assets Manufacturing
http://www.iam.com
info@iam.com
828 Ormond Avenue
Drexel Hill, PA 19026-2604, USA
orders only: +1 610 853 4406
fax: +1 610 853 3733

Cover and cover art by Jefferey A. Litz.
Illustrations by Al Mackey and Joe Divalerio.

ISBN 1-885876-02-5
Library of Congress Catalog Card Number 94-078012

Lorem ipsum dolor sit amet, consectetuer adipiscing elit, sed diam nonummy nibh euismod tincidunt ut laoreet dolore magna aliquam erat volutpat. Ut wisi enim ad minim veniam, quis nostrud exerci tation ullamcorper suscipit lobortis nisl ut aliquip ex ea commodo consequat. I'm pink, therefore I'm Spam. Duis autem vel eum iriure dolor in hendrerit in vulputate velit esse molestie consequat, vel illum dolore eu feugiat nulla facilisis at vero eros et accumsan et iusto odio dignissim qui blandit praesent luptatum zzril delenit augue duis dolore te feugait nulla facilisi. "You're an idiot." - Mehdi Ali, as reported in the July 19, 1994 Philadelphia Inquirer. Lorem ipsum dolor sit amet, consectetuer adipiscing elit, sed diam nonummy nibh euismod tincidunt ut laoreet dolore magna aliquam erat volutpat. Look, ma, I'm huge. Ut wisi enim ad minim veniam, quis nostrud exerci tation ullamcorper suscipit lobortis nisl ut aliquip ex ea commodo consequat.

Second, Revised Printing: May, 1996, (First Printing: August, 1994)
Printed on Recycled Paper

Preface

There is a vast land to be explored out in cyberspace. Whether you are just beginning such a journey or are looking for exciting new areas as your next destination, welcome!

A wide variety of loosely related technologies make up what the mass-media is calling the Information Superhighway: modems and bulletin board systems, Ethernet and local area networks, TCP/IP and the Internet. For various reasons, understanding BBSs and modems will make it easier to understand LANs (or vice-versa). Understanding LANs and BBSs will make it easier to get around on the Internet. Knowing some of the underlying mechanisms will also be helpful, even when you'd rather ignore them. You might not even know which of these things you are interested in, just that you are missing out on something. Or you may know what you'd like to do, but you aren't sure what hardware and software you need, or where to get it for your Amiga. Either way, this book is here to guide you.

I choose the word "guide" carefully. This book provides pointers to many interesting things, and explores them in varying amounts of detail. If you want to actively explore, this book will be a great tool to help you. It will help you figure out what the differences are between the different kinds of technologies, and which you may be interested in learning more about. It will give you a lot of general and background information. It will help you find the Amiga-specific information which might not be available anywhere else. It will help you get unstuck. It will tell you where else to look for details about the various topics which aren't Amiga-specific. This book is a good place to start, and to turn back to later, but you may want to go many other places in-between.

Networking and related technologies are often made out to be difficult and mysterious. These reports are exaggerated. You can understand and use these technologies without joining a computer monastery.

I hope that your reading of this book will be active. I hope you'll have a good look at the table of contents, that you'll refer to the glossary frequently, that you'll skip around. If you feel like you already know something, skip it. If you know what you are interested in, go straight there (you can always jump back if you feel like you've missed something). When you want more information, look at the suggested reading list to find some of the books which have been important to me and which I think might interest you. I hope you'll take advantage of the Amiga resources in cyberspace to supplement what you find here. If you do these things, there will be no limits to your learning and you will be successful in your exploration.

A note about terminology. The standard wisdom is that terminology should be used consistently by a technical writer -- that one should pick one word for one thing and use just that word. I have intentionally used several interchangeable words in places throughout this book. This has the disadvantage of forcing you to do a little more work (figuring out whether I'm talking about something new or something you already understood), but it exposes you to the language you will have to know in order to get along well in the online world.

You must be flexible with the terminology you use. In this field, perhaps more than in the better established areas of computing, different groups of people use different terminology to refer to the same things. For example, people who are most familiar with UUCP speak a different language than people who are most familiar with FIDO. Some people call everything (including UUCP) the Internet. Some people insist that their terminology is Right and that all others are Wrong. The terminology I am most comfortable with is oriented more toward UUCP and TCP/IP and Unix and the Internet than toward other protocols running on other systems on different networks.

This book could easily have been more a textbook than a guide, 1024 pages long instead of 256. I would have had to spend more time writing it, and you would have had to spend more time reading it, but I don't think you would have gotten more out of it. If it had been 1024 pages, I might have led you around more, perhaps leaving you curious or puzzled less often. However, you would probably have learned less, in the end, because you would have done less. Perhaps I would have provided more details, and you could have spent more time reading about things that don't matter to you. This book acknowledges and advances your intelligence, rather than assuming that you are a dummy and would like to stay that way.

All the best to you as you connect your Amiga and explore the networks!
     -d.l., August 15, 1994

Update

Wow! So much has changed in less than two years. The world wide web has become an incredible phenomenon, and everyone wants to join. Where the Amiga had only one web browser in 1994, now it has more than a dozen! Where modems were once mostly used by businesses and the dedicated computer hobbyist, now everyone is buying one.

Still, much has remained the same. Even if you've tried to avoid learning much about the way your computer works and you say "all I want to do is get on the web, just tell me how to do that," you're still going to be much better off learning a little about how all this stuff works. It's still going to make it easier to know how this technology has evolved and what some of the less advanced options are.

-d.l., May, 1996

Acknowledgments

To Jan, for everything, thanks. For their artistic contributions, many thanks to Al Mackey, Jeff Litz and Joe DiValerio. For typographic advice and additional proof-reading, thanks to Mike Rivers. For converting the original book to Frame Maker 5.0 on SunOS, thanks to Al Mackey. For reading several early draft chapters and for asking (every other day) "how much more did you get done today?" thanks to Claudio Dosio. Thanks also to Ed Gee and to Adam Edwards for their reading and comments. For a wonderful list of corrections to the first edition, special thanks to Peter Jones.

At Commodore, Martin Hunt, Dale Luck, Greg Miller, Ken Dyke, Randell Jesup and Brian Jackson all made significant contributions to Amiga networking. Many developers outside Commodore provided numerous important contributions. To those who've furthered the availability of the many commercial and freely redistributable networking hardware and software products for our favorite machine, thank you!

To the dozens of those who've helped give the Amiga such an extrodinary presense on the World Wide Web, especially the webmasters and the browser authors, thank you for keeping the Amiga from becoming road kill on the information superhighway.

-Dale L. Larson

Part I. The Networks

The first part of this book deals with the general background information you need in order to make use of various networks and to make your Amiga a part of them. This information is, for the most part, not specific to the Amiga but is common to most computers.

Here we'll look at computer telecommunications (BBSs, modems, terminals, fax), store-and-forward networks (like FIDO and UUCP), local area networks (like Ethernet), and internets (including the Internet). Knowing something about each of these technologies makes knowing about any one of them easier.

As with the rest of this book, there will sometimes be more detail than you are interested in, and sometimes there will be less. You can skip details or pursue the further references under Appendix C: Recommended Reading.

Telecommunications

A BBS is not a network and an online service is not a network. (Sometimes they give you access to one.) So why talk about them here? Because a BBS or online service might satisfy all of your computer communications needs. And because many of the common features of computer networks are similar to more primitive features of BBSs and online services. If you are already familiar with BBSs, understanding the basics of networking may be little easier. If you aren't familiar with BBSs, perhaps you should be. You may be missing out on some good stuff.

This chapter provides an introduction to BBS systems and services. Some of the material is very basic, so skim any sections you are already familiar with.

BBSs and Online Services

A computer bulletin-board system (BBS) is a computer system used for exchanging public and private messages and files between people.

They are central systems used by many people, most of whom are usually geographically distant from the BBS. Some companies, schools, or other institutions have private, internal BBSs. Many BBSs are available for public access. Some BBSs charge a fee for some (or all) services, others are wholly commercial enterprises which charge for any level of access. These are frequently called online services rather than BBSs. In addition to files and messages, some BBSs offer access to databases, computer games, networks or other features.

Many BBSs are a single computer attached to a single telephone line with a single modem (see below). These are called single-line BBSs. Even though only one user at a time can use the system, hundreds may share the system by taking turns.

Other BBSs have multiple telephone lines and multiple modems. These are called multi-line BBSs. Some large BBSs and online services actually consist of multiple computers. The user of these systems generally cannot tell whether it is one large computer or several smaller computers running the BBS. Some BBSs can handle dozens of simultaneous users, and the big online services can handle thousands.

To understand the use and features of BBSs, you will need to understand some of the underlying technology. The sections ahead provide an overview of the technology, and, in general terms, the features. Other chapters explain the details of some of that technology, as well as how to find and select BBSs and online services.

Modems

A modem is a device which allows computer data to be sent over ordinary voice telephone lines. It encodes (modulates) computer data into audio signals and decodes (demodulates) audio signals back into computer signals.

Most modems are external peripherals
that use a serial port to communicate
with the computer. Some are internal
expansion cards. Some new high-speed
modems use a parallel port and special
driver software, but no such drivers
exist for the Amiga at the time of this

writing. So in a typical setup, a serial cable connects the computer
and the modem, and a telephone line connects to the modem as
well.

Modems usually have features to dial telephone numbers, answer
a ringing phone, etc. Modems are frequently used with terminal
emulation software which usually has several features to control a
modem.

For two computers to connect via modem, each must have a compatible modem. Most modems are compatible at some speed. As of
this writing, the most common modems follow the v.32bis/v.42bis
standard and can connect to similar modems at a rate of up to
14.4kbps. They can generally connect to older modems at a speed
of 9600 or 2400bps. A new modem standard is called v.34. It operates at speeds of up to 28.8kbps. For more information about
modem standards and capabilities, see the chapter on 'Buying and
Using a Modem.'

Terminal Emulation Software

Once upon a time, computers couldn't fit on a desk, and they lived
in large computer rooms. Most computers could be shared by
more than one person. To use the computer, you sat at a terminal.
Terminals looked like many of today's desk top computers -- a
screen and a keyboard. The terminals were usually connected to
the computers via serial ports at 9600 baud. Most could display
only text. Though they looked like computers, they had no compu-
tational or storage capabilities. They were strictly I/O (Input/Out-
put) devices -- they displayed the characters given to them by the
computer and they sent characters entered into their keyboards to
the computer.

The terminal is a very convenient interface to remote computers.
Even if the computer room and terminal are separated by thousands of miles, two modems and a phone line can connect them,
allowing the same access a user might have by being in the same
room with the computer.

Some large computers still live in computer rooms. Now that desk top computers are common, it is frequently convenient to use one instead of a terminal to access remote or shared computers. "Terminal emulation software" (sometimes called a "terminal program" or just a "terminal") is a program which makes a computer pretend that it is a mere terminal. It displays input (usually from the serial port) as characters on the screen, and sends keyboard input out to the connected computer.

There are many kinds of terminals, each with their own special codes to place characters at particular places on the screen, to clear the screen, etc. Two common types of character terminals are the DEC VT100 and the ANSI standard terminal. Some terminals even use codes which allow the display of graphics. Many computers require a particular terminal type or one of a few types. Consequently, there are many types of terminal programs, each of which may emulate one or more specific types of terminal.

Even desktop computers may need to be accessed from a remote location. By accepting connections from terminals, a computer can be accessed from the widest number of other places. Terminals and other desktop computers with terminal emulators can be used. For this reason, BBSs, on-line services and other computers which require remote access usually accept connections from character-based terminals. While it makes it possible for Amiga, Mac and PC users to access the same BBS, this has the disadvantage of making most users suffer through interfaces which don't take advantage of modern GUI (Graphical User Interface) technology.

There are "terminals" which support graphics and which are designed especially for BBS interfaces. RIP is one such standard. So if you log into a BBS which supports RIP, you might try getting a RIP-capable terminal emulator to see for yourself. The easiest way to get one is probably to download it.

Uploads and Downloads

Since terminal emulation programs are running on real computers instead of dumb hardware (simple terminals), they often include many features not found on the actual terminals they emulate. For example, they can capture long text to a disk file, automate repetitive tasks with macros that enter commands, send and receive binary files, etc. This last feature is probably the most important -- the ability to send and receive files. Most BBSs and on-line services thrive on the exchange of files between users --

picture files, text files and freely-redistributable software are made widely available.

In a terminal emulator, when you send a file to the remote computer, you are "uploading" the file. When you receive a file from the remote computer, you are "downloading" the file. Terminal emulators usually have built-in functions to make uploading and downloading possible. The upload function reads a file from your disk and sends it out to the remote computer, while the download function takes input from the remote computer and writes it out to your disk. There are usually many options available for the "protocol" to be used in the up/download.

A "protocol" is the agreed upon method for transmitting the file. The least common denominator protocol is ASCII -- the remote computer sends or receives the file as plain text, as if it were any other terminal input or output. Other protocols are more complicated. ASCII uploads and downloads are useful for capturing messages or email, or for uploading a message that you composed offline with a text editor on your Amiga. Composing messages offline lets you save time and money on phone bills while using features like spell checkers which aren't available (or convenient, anyway) on most remote systems.

Serial lines are not always error free. Many modem connections are not error free. Random noise is sometimes introduced into terminal sessions. Some characters are dropped, others are received incorrectly. When you are reading messages, this usually isn't a problem -- an extra character here and a dropped character there doesn't prevent you from reading the message. When you transfer a binary file, however, one character makes all the difference between a program that you can run perfectly and one that crashes. Most file transfer protocols are designed to detect and correct errors (like those caused by noise). X-Modem is the least-common denominator error-correcting protocol, but it is old and slow. Z-Modem is a good error-correcting protocol for use with today's equipment. Both are available on most systems and in most terminal emulators. Kermit is a common protocol on many systems which aren't necessarily designed for online access. Some online services use protocols unique to the service, such as CompuServe's B protocols.

For more information about the kinds of files you might download and how to use them, see "Freely Redistributable Files."

Offline Readers

An OffLine Reader (OLR) is a program which lets you read and respond to messages while you are not online. This means that you call in and get messages as quickly as your modem can transfer them (usually much faster than you can read), then hang up. The OLR lets you look at the messages one at a time, and may let you compose replies or create new messages. Once you've finished, you again call in and log on, sending the replies and new messages as fast as your modem can (usually much faster than you can type). This saves time and reduces your phone bill.

Some OLRs are complete, self-contained programs. Some are stand-alone programs that work with files you capture from your terminal program. Others are really just scripts for a terminal program. Depending on the BBS or online service, the OLR may use a special feature for OLRs or may have to work through messages much like a human would, only faster. The latter tend to be somewhat fragile and to break when the layout of the BBS changes. The well-supported ones, however, are still much better than nothing.

QWK is one system designed for BBSs which works with OLRs. You can use a terminal program to log into a QWK-supporting BBS and select an option to download a QWK packet. The BBS then creates an archive with all of your new mail and messages. It lets you download the archive with a standard protocol (such as z-modem). Then you log out and exit your terminal program. You run the QWK reader which will dearchive the packet and present each individual mail item or message to you. If you create any replies or new messages, a reply packet is created for you to upload to the BBS. QWK works well, and there are other, similar systems. The BBSs you call which support OLRs are likely to have freely redistributable OLRs available for download.

Freely Redistributable Files

There are lots of computer files you might like to have. Pictures, sounds, text, programs. Maybe you'd like the Mona Lisa as a backdrop on your screen, or you want to hear a foghorn when you make an error. Perhaps you want to be able to do a computer search of the full text of the United States constitution or the Christian Bible. Certainly you would like to have more software. You might be able to get these by walking into your local software store, or by copying disks from a friend or a user's group. Many files are copyrighted and may not be legally copied -- the only way that you can get them is to purchase them. Other files may legally be copied. The latter are freely redistributable.

Most files are, by default, copyrighted and not freely redistributable. Files can get to be freely redistributable in many different
ways. As a result, there are several types of freely redistributable
files. Public domain and shareware are two common types.

Many programmers do their work because they enjoy it. They
often write small programs which they think might be useful to
someone else. They decide to be generous and share the fruits of
their labors. They may do this by releasing their program (and the
source code for it) into the public domain. This means that they
abandon any copyright or other legal claim to the program and
that you can do anything you like with it. Programs and other
works also enter the public domain after a specified period of time,
so that many classics of art, literature and music are public
domain.

The programmer who wants to share his work but also wants to
maintain some control over it may keep his copyright but specifically grant the right to copy and distribute the work. He may
impose other restrictions, so you need to read the text files that
come with the work to determine exactly how you may use the
files. Some of these files are freeware -- you can use them all you
want, but you can't change them. There are also copyleft files,
those covered by the GNU public license (don't worry if you don't
know what a GNU is -- you'll eventually find out about the Free
Software Foundation). You need to read that license (which will be
included with the archive) to understand it. Copyleft is a whole
issue unto itself, and we're not going to examine it further here.

With shareware, the owner of the copyright grants permission for
you to copy the file but requires you to pay for it if you continue to
use the file beyond some trial period. This is the same as any other
commercial software, except that you can get the software without
paying at a store and you can try before you buy. Its a great policy
which benefits both parties, and if only for this reason, it should
be supported. It is also morally and legally necessary for you to
pay the shareware fee on software you use. Failing to pay for
shareware is the same as walking into a store, grabbing a software
package, and taking it home without paying.

When you download a file, look for a copyright statement or other
legalese. Make sure that you may legally use the file.

File Compression (arc, lha, uuencode, etc.)

It can take several minutes to transmit files over telephone lines,
sometimes much longer. To reduce this time, and to reduce the
amount of storage the files require, you can compress the files.
Most files that you will encounter on the Information Highways
will be compressed. Their filenames will end in extensions like
.arc, .lzh, or .lha.

How does compression work? In a text file, for example, several
words may be used many times. To save space, replace each such
word with a code which is shorter than the word. Actual compression programs use tricks like this (though usually more complex)
to create compressed files which are significantly smaller than the
original (often less than half the size of the original). The compressed files are not usable until they are decompressed.

To this point we've talked about files in the singular. In practice,
most software programs and other interesting files come in packages or groups. A program, for example, might have several auxil-
iary programs, text files with documentation, data files, etc. It is
often important that all of these files be kept together. Most compression programs will group several files into one file at the same
time it compresses them. When the compressed file is decompressed, it is split back up into its individual files.

A compressed file (which may contain several files) is usually
called an archive. The process of compressing files may be referred
to as archiving, the process of uncompressing as unarchiving.

There are several compression utilities which each use their own
compression algorithms. Some utilities know how to unarchive a
few different types of files, but none knows how to unarchive every
type. To use archives, you'll have to unarchive them with the corresponding archive utility. Most archive utilities are freely redistributable. Sometimes you'll get a new download utility which has
been compressed by another utility, sometimes they come as a
single executable file. You'll have to get at least one utility as an
executable file in order to unarchive the others you'll need. The
archive utilities are available on Fred Fish disks and on most
BBSs, online services and networks. Here are some of the common
Amiga archive utilities and the file extensions they handle:

LhA	.lha	Shareware
uuencode	.uu	Mostly used on Unix systems, actually makes files larger but converts them to ASCII only.

		Some email systems can only send ASCII.
lhunarc	.lzh	Obsolete, perhaps more common on PCs.
pkazip	.zip	Shareware, mostly used on PCs
arc	.arc	Obsolete, but still used occasionally.
zoo	.zoo	Was popular before LhA
tar	.tar	Mostly used on Unix systems, designed for tape backup, no compression.
compress	.Z	Mostly used on Unix systems, compression only.

LhA is the most commonly used archiver on the Amiga at the time of this writing. Most Amiga files that you encounter will probably be .lha archives.

If you are not on an Amiga-specific system, you are likely to find files with other types of compression. Unless the contents are ASCII or some other format you are familiar with, you aren't likely to be able to use the contents even if you could unarchive them. Downloading programs written for the Mac or PC, for example, isn't likely to do you any good unless you have another machine or an emulator on which to run them.

Some files that aren't Amiga-specific but which you might be able to use include pictures, spreadsheet data files, database data files and word processing files. There are several picture viewers, for-mat converters and 3.0 Datatypes which understand non-Amiga formats. Many Amiga spreadsheets can read Lotus 1-2-3 spread-sheet files, DBase database files and WordPerfect wordprocessing files. Again, you may still have to use a PC or Mac to unarchive some of these files, as there may be no corresponding archive util-ity for many of the other formats.

Accounts

Its nice to be able to customize a system to suit your preferences, and otherwise make it feel like your own. On a system used by only one person, this is easy. You just change the system to suit your preferences. It feels like your own because it is your own. On a system used by many people, this won't work. What will work is providing a virtual system to each user.

Most shared computers are set up to ask who you are. Once they know who you are, they provide an environment unique to you. You get your customized preferences. If the system gives you shell access (i.e., direct access to the operating system), your current directory is your home directory. Such a system might simultaneously provide many different unique environments to many different users. Each user benefits from the illusion that she has the machine to herself. Most users can change most things without affecting anything else in any other user's environment.

When one person asks another "Who are you?" the answer varies depending on context. When a neighbor asks "Who are you?" I might reply "Dale." When I'm asked at a bank, "Who are you?" I answer "Dale L. Larson." At a costume party, my response might be "A Mexican bandito." Computers don't deal well with this kind of ambiguity. Hence, when you set up an account on a computer, one of the things you configure is what your answer to the question "Who are you?" will be. This is your username for that account. A username is sometimes called a login name, a login, a handle, or an account. The system might also keep track of your "real name" or "full name," but it knows you by your username. You might have different usernames on different systems that you use. In some special cases, you might have multiple usernames on a single system.

To keep users from messing with each other's environments and files (whether accidentally or maliciously), shared computers generally have some level of security. Hence, when asking who you are, they typically also ask for a password. If the password you give is the same as the one the system has on record, you are recognized. Otherwise, you are denied access. Once you are granted access, you will have security privileges based on who you are. Generally, you will be able to mess with your own stuff but not that of others.

By the way, many BBSs allow handles which don't look much like real names. Sometimes you are required to use your real name as a username, but may use a handle for chats or to post messages in some areas. If you see messages from "Phred Preak" or "The Orb," you know that they are probably using a handle.

Email

Electronic mail, ("email," or sometimes just "mail"), is a way to use computers to send messages between people. Each person using email has his or her own mailbox and email address. A mailbox is just a file or directory in which the system stores messages. On a simple BBS, the email address will

consist only of the user's login name, and users can send mail only to other users of the same BBS. If you are a user logged into such a BBS, you select a menu item (or enter a command) to send mail to another user. The system prompts you for the other user's name and a subject of the message, then lets you enter your message (usually with a simple editor). When you've finished, the system leaves the message in the other user's mailbox. With a different menu item, you can check your own mailbox. If other users have sent you messages you'll be able to read them one at a time, otherwise you'll be informed that your mailbox is empty.

On more complex BBSs, as well as on most on-line services and network systems, mail can also be sent to users of other systems. In this case, the email address used consists of the user's name and the machine name for the host that the user logs into. Many networks and on-line services have thousands of users. Others are connected to Internet email -- through which any user can send mail to millions of other users throughout the world.

Most email is composed of short messages of simple text. Many BBSs and online services won't work with anything but ASCII text for email. This is because the terminals originally used to access email weren't capable of much more. Some BBSs and online services allow files to be uploaded as attachments to email messages. This lets you send a file privately to another user. Binary files can also be encoded as ASCII (as with uuencode) so that they can be sent as "regular" email. Richer standards allow more sophisticated mail to be sent on some LANs and on the Internet. MIME is one standard for enhanced mail. For more information, see the LAN and Internet sections.

Why Email?
Postal mail tends to be slow. That's why it is often called "snail mail." Telephone calls can be expensive, and it is often difficult to reach a person you are trying to call. If you do reach them, they may be busy. Some email can be slow, but most email offers fast delivery. It does so without the hassles of interruptions. There is no requirement that someone be available at the moment you wish to speak with them, but the message will likely be read at the next convenient time for that person (many people check their email several times a day). Email may also allow you to conveniently send electronic data such as programs and other files, something which is much more expensive and difficult to do most other ways.

Messages (news, SIGs, etc.)

Most BBSs, on-line systems and networks have message areas where public discussions are held. The areas are usually broken up into topical categories (for example, Amiga computers, MIDI, Cars, Movies, etc.). Some systems have literally hundreds or thousands of topics. In the area for a given topic, there may be hundreds of messages. The messages are usually stored at least a week, sometimes much longer. To read messages, one chooses a message area to read from, then begins to read the messages in that area. Most systems have a way to read messages which are new since the user last read messages in that area.

Any user can post a message which can then be read by any other user. As with email, the messages are usually identified with a subject name, as well as who sent the message, when and from where. Many messages are replies to earlier messages, and therefore carry the same subject line. An original message and all of the replies to it are called a thread. Some systems have ways to read all the messages in a thread before moving on to the next thread, rather than forcing the reader to see each message in the order they were entered into the system.

People use message bases to carry on conversations about politics or philosophy, to share information about their hobbies, to rate and review products, to buy and sell almost everything, and to find help or other information.

Many different names are used for areas where public messages are posted: message areas, echos, message bases, SIGs (Special Interest Groups), notes, news groups, etc. Despite the different names, they all work in more or less the same way.

As with email, some systems have only local message areas. That is, the only people who can read or post messages on the system are users of that system. Other systems are connected to networks which distribute messages to many systems. Messages posted in these areas are read by people across the country or around the world. Many of the same networks that carry email also carry messages.

Internet/UseNet is the largest network that carries messages. UseNet news, or just news, is carried on the Internet and via UUCP (defined later) to hundreds of thousands of computers across the globe. Many BBSs and on-line services are connected. At the time of this writing, there are more than 4000 UseNet message areas, or newsgroups. These newsgroups carry dozens of megabytes of messages per day. More than 10 million people read UseNet news. Newsgroups are arranged hierarchically to make finding an interesting newsgroup easier. The names used are (hopefully) descriptive, if abbreviated. Top level hierarchies include comp (computers), rec (recreational), misc (other stuff), us (in the United States), alt (alternative) and others. Dots (periods) separate each level of the hierarchies. Amiga users will be interested in the many comp.sys.amiga.* groups, including the one about networking and communications, comp.sys.amiga.datacomm. Two of my personal favorite newsgroups are comp.risks and rec.humor.funny.

FidoNet is another popular network. In general, only BBSs are part of it. There are actually many Fido-style networks. The message areas in Fido networks are called Echos. Fido traffic is still carried entirely on store-and-forware networks, so users in different parts of the country (or world) will read different messages at different times as the messages slowly propagate from their systems of origin. For more details about BBS networks, see the section BBS Networks, below.

The advantages of networked message areas are obvious -- the larger the scale, the more likely you are to find others who share your interests or can give you information you need. The disadvantage is in overload and in signal-to-noise ratio. Some groups have hundreds of messages posted to them each day. That's way too many to read them all. Worse, most of them aren't interesting anyway -- many are redundant or clueless ("me too!" or "can someone please tell me how to open a book?"). Fortunately, many newsreaders (that's the software you use to read news) make it easy to filter out some messages and to scan headers of the rest, so that you read only the messages you are interested in.

Chatting

Mail and news are asynchronous forms of communication. People check in to look at their messages when they get around to it. The messages will wait for them until they do. If you call someone on the telephone and reach their answering machine, you are engaged in asynchronous communication. If you talk to them, your communication is synchronous. Many computer BBSs, online services and networks offer synchronous communications along with asynchronous.

Even on single-line BBSs, there is frequently an option to 'chat with Sysop.' (The Sysop is the person who runs the BBS, and may therefore be able to use the BBS from her computer even while someone else uses it over the phone.) It works like this: The user requests a chat. The Sysop is paged (his or her computer beeps). If the Sysop is around, she looks at the screen and decides whether to chat with the user. If yes, the Sysop enters a chat. In a chat, what either the user or Sysop types is instantly displayed on both of their screens. This allows a typed conversation to take place. Usually, etiquette provides that either the user or Sysop type while the other reads until the typist hits an extra return or otherwise indicates completion of a thought. (Online or network etiquette is often referred to as "netiquette.")

Some terminal programs have the capability to provide a split window where what the user types is displayed on one part of the screen and what comes from the remote computer (i.e., what other users type) is displayed on another part of the screen. This makes most chat services much easier to use.

On multi-line BBSs, online services and networks, chat features work in similar ways, though one may choose to chat with any other logged in user rather than just the Sysop. Some chat features are limited to just two users, others allow chat sessions with many more. The multi-user chat sessions may have areas similar to message areas in order to separate different topics of discussion.

Multi-user chat sessions are usually line-oriented. What a particular user types is displayed only on his or her own screen until she hits Return. At that time, it is displayed on the screens of all other participants in the chat. Many systems and networks with multi-user chats schedule special sessions to discuss a particular topic or to interview a special guest.

Chat systems go by many other names. "CB simulators," "conferencing," "IRC." and "talk" are a few of the more common names. "Talk" is the two-user chat facility provided on many Unix and other Internet systems. It can be used to chat between two users logged on the same machine or different machines (over a network). IRC or Internet Relay Chat is an Internet facility for multi-user chat.

Navigating BBSs and Online Services

Most systems are menu-based. This means that once you log in (entering your name and password), you'll be presented with a menu of options. You choose from that menu what to do. Sometimes the menus will be simple, taking you directly to some activity. More often, the menus are layered, and you may have to go through a few different menus to get to what you want.

Some BBSs may offer a command based system. Like the Amiga shell, you can type various commands in order to perform various actions. The command system may just be an operating system shell, or it may be a special system for the BBS.

You'll have to learn how to use each different BBS you log in to. Don't worry. Though they are each different, they have many things in common, and they are all set up for first-time users to be able to find their way around enough that they can do everything without help or can at least get to help or documentation files.

Transcript: A Typical BBS Session

This is a capture of a real BBS session with the author's real account on a friend's BBS -- the Freeland Mainfame. This transcript may serve to further illuminate the features discussed in the previous sections. Really, the session is, perhaps, a little atypical. I don't log into the BBS often, since it is located 3000 miles away. I've tried to show as many features as possible in a small amount of space. I did read a few messages to give you some idea of what kinds of things you might find discussed, and entered in to a chat (multitalk) session to show you what that is like, as well as a few other things to give you a glimpse into what is there (though I only scratched the surface). If you haven't used a BBS before, this should give you a good idea of what it is like. Even if you have, it might show you what a top-quality non-commercial BBS is like. The Freeland Mainframe is an Amiga with four incoming lines and a wide variety of services. For various reasons, the formatting of this capture may be a little difficult to read and does not reflect exactly how it would appear on the screen of your computer. The output from the BBS and my input are mixed together, but I have highlighted my input so that you can distinguish it from the rest. You should be able to get the idea, though, and perhaps later you'll want to connect to the Freeland Mainframe and look around for yourself.

```
[NComm dials BBS, modem connects...]

DLG Pro BB/OS v1.0 - Copyright (c) 1989-1993 by TelePro Technologies
Serial #RE0105

New Shell process 10
You have reached port TR2 of the *(Freeland Mainframe)*
```

```
Please enter your FIRST & LAST name => Dale Larson

Please enter your password => ####
```

Note that my password is not displayed as I type it. This is standard, and it makes it more difficult to discover passwords by "shoulder surfing."

```
Welcome to the *(Freeland Mainframe)*
======================================

You are back, Dale Larson, on your Amiga!!  You have called the system 5 times.
You have read 0 messages, and written 0. You have downloaded 0 bytes in 0
files and uploaded 1928234 bytes in 1 files. You last logged in at: Mon 13 Dec
93 11:30. You have 59 minutes for this call...

Checking for new public messages addressed to you...none found
```

At this point, various announcements were displayed (there were several old ones since I hadn't been on the system in months).

```
Main Menu
----------------------------------------------------------------------------
[M] Message SIGS[F] File SIGS[P] MultiTalk
[E] Off-line Events[U] Utility Sub-Section   [O] User Options
[C] Chat With Sysop[D] Direct Mail to Sysop  [B] Message Bundler
[Q] QWK Msg Bundler[K] Online Games![L] List of BBSs-Add one
[R] Read Bulletins[Z] TimeBank[G] Goodbye - Log Out
[?] Display menu[H] Help
----------------------------------------------------------------------------

Time left: 58 - Main => M
```

The main menu is the core of most BBSs. Here, I choose 'M' to go to the message area (SIG) submenu.

```
Message SIGS
----------------------------------------------------------------------------
[Y] Your private mail... [A] Amiga Message Areas   [I] IBM Message Areas
[N] MAC Message Area[E] General Message Area  [M] Back to Main Menu
[G] Goodbye - Log Out    [?] Display menu[H] Help
----------------------------------------------------------------------------

Time left: 58 - Messages => A
```

Most BBS systems have several message areas. Here, they are divided into categories. I choose to go to the the Amiga messages.

```
Now entering message area [1]: General Amiga Messages


Time Left: 58 minutes...

Total messages -> [500]
 Msgs numbered -> [229 to 728]
  New messages -> [728]

[E] Enter Msg[O] Edit Signature  [A] Change Area     [S] Change SIG
[P] Private Mail   [N] Next Area[<] Reverse Read    [=] Cont Read
[I] Message Filter [J] Thread Toggle  [.] Header Scan    [U] List Readers
[^] To file area   [M] Msg SIG Menu   [G] Goodbye[H] Help
[?] Display Menu   [RET] Next Msg[*] Tag/UnTag Area

Press 'Enter' or (cr) to see next new message.
58 mins - Area: [1] [General Amiga Messages] [228/229-728] => A
```

```
New message area [RETURN = List] =>

Area list: [Amiga Message Areas] SIG
---------------------------------------------------------------------------
1     - General Amiga Messages2     - Graphics-Art Room
5     - Technical Info Area8      - CLI/Shell Hints&Tips
103   - Alt.Sys.Amiga.Demos104   - Alt.Sys.Amiga.UUCP
105   - Alt.Sys.Amiga.UUCP.Patches106   - Comp.Sys.Amiga.Advocacy
107   - Comp.Sys.Amiga.Announce108   - Comp.Sys.Amiga.Applicatns
109   - Comp.Sys.Amiga.Audio110   - Comp.Sys.Amiga.DataComm
111   - Comp.Sys.Amiga.Emulations112   - Comp.Sys.Amiga.Games
113   - Comp.Sys.Amiga.Graphics114   - Comp.Sys.Amiga.Hardware
115   - Comp.Sys.Amiga.Intro116   - Comp.Sys.Amiga.Marketplace
117   - Comp.Sys.Amiga.Misc118   - Comp.Sys.Amiga.MultiMedia
119   - Comp.Sys.Amiga.Programmer120   - Comp.Sys.Amiga.Reviews
121   - Comp.Sys.CBM122   - Comp.Sys.Amiga.CD32
123   - Comp.Sys.Amiga.Networking
---------------------------------------------------------------------------
New message area => 1
```

This BBS has local message areas (1 and 5) and carries several UseNet news groups (in the 100s). The local message areas can only be read and written to by callers to this BBS, but the news-groups are carried on systems across the globe. From here, I'll read the messages new in group 1 since I last logged on.

```
Time Left: 57 minutes...
Now entering message area [1]: General Amiga Messages

Total messages -> [500]
 Msgs numbered -> [229 to 728]
  New messages -> [728]

[E] Enter Msg[O] Edit Signature  [A] Change Area    [S] Change SIG
[P] Private Mail    [N] Next Area[<] Reverse Read    [=] Cont Read
[J] Thread Toggle   [.] Header Scan    [^] To file area    [M] Msg SIG Menu
[G] Goodbye[H] Help[?] Display Menu    [RET] Next Msg
[*] Tag/UnTag Area

Press 'Enter' or (cr) to see next new message.
57 mins - Area: [1] [General Amiga Messages] [229/229-728] =>

[From    ] Uncle Buck[MSG 230 OF 728]
[To] All[Has Reply 232]
[Date    ] Sat 16 Oct 93 21:17
[Subject ] HELP!

I'm fairly new to the Amiga world and just got a printer for my Amiga 600. I
would like to know if there are keypresses or something to where I can do a
screen dump without going to and clicking on the screen dump icon. I have a
few pictures that I would like to print but I need to be able to hit return or
something cause a mouse click clears the picture...

Any help would be greatly appreciated...

  (E,R,O,A,S,P,N,L,<,=,!,J,.,+,^,M,G,H,?,RET,*)

Press 'Enter' or (cr) to see next new message.
57 mins - Area: [1] [General Amiga Messages] [230/229-728] =>
```

I went on to read several more messages, but I'll spare you the details. Note that I am given a number of choices of what to do at the end of each message. By hitting '?' I could get an explanation of what all the options are. Typical options include things like going to the next message, responding to the message, and seeing the parent of the message (if it was a reply to an earlier message).

I went back to the main menu and selected the 'F'ile option.

```
Time left: 54 - Main => F

File SIGS
----------------------------------------------------------------------
[.] Your private files    [F] Amiga File Areas[W] IBM File Areas
[V] MAC File Areas[T] General File Areas    [M] Back to Main menu
[G] Goodbye - Log Out      [?] Display menu[H] Help
----------------------------------------------------------------------

Time left: 54 - Files => F

Now entering file area [1]: AMIGA Archive.

Total files -> [349]
  New files -> [346]

[U] Upload file      [D] Download[F] File list[A] Change areas
[S] Change Sig[=] Global list     [P] Private area     [T] Transfer file
[O] Edit signature   [R] Read file[I] View archive    [^] Goto msg area
[@] Send message     [M] File SIG Menu   [G] Goodbye[H] Help
[?] Display menu     [RET] Next file      [*] Tag/Untag Area

Press 'Return' or (cr) to see next new file.
53 mins - Area: [1] [AMIGA Archive] [3/1-349] => F

[F] Natural Order    [B] Inverse Order    [A] Alpha Forward    [R] Alpha Reverse

Select order [|] => F

[A] All files[N] New files[S] Last Call[#] Num Days
[C] Since Date[R] Date Range[F] Filename[D] Filename/Desc

Select filter [] => C

Enter date [eg: 01 Jan 90] => 01 June 9 94

Files in area [1] - [AMIGA Archive]

24   JRC102A.LZH     240k    Well folks, I've decided to re-post JRComm, bec...
324  SPIRODR4.LHA     56k    SpiroGraph (tm?) child's toy simulator
325  INFRARX1.LHA     71k    Infrared remote - ARexx interface, makes the Amig...
326  DELUXEGAL.LHA   149k    This is Galaga Deluxe. An excellent game if you l...
327  VCHCK641.LHA     74k    The latest version of Virus Checker.. Compliments...
328  CANNONFODDER.L    7k    some users comments of the game Cannon Fodder.. M...
329  ENIGMA.LHA        1k    Supposed to be a real hard puzzle. Taken off of G...
330  GENERALGFX.LHA    9k    50 more boards for the REGISTERED version of Mega...
331  GOURMET.LHA       9k    50 more boards (food type) of the game Megaball, ...
332  BANSHEE.LHA     454k    An AGA 1942-like shootem-up. This a demo. The f...
333  A4DPEG.LHA       30k    Framescript for use with Aladdin4D. Automatic JPE...
334  ASSIGNPREFS1_0    9k    Prefs drawer utility for adding and managing star...
335  AMIGARIP.LHA    278k    Rather primitive terminal, but supports RIP Graph...
336  FDP21_01LM.LHA  244k    FighterDuelPro2 Low Memory version. This is an o...
337  FDP21_02FULL.L  278k    T> FighterDuelPro2 Update. This is an officiaae...
338  FDUELCHART.LHA    7k    AGA chart showing availability of FDP2 fighter cr...
339  FDUELCHARTNONA    7k    A non-aga version of FDUELCHART.LHA.
340  FLIGHTTOOLS.LH  191k    A set of tools for use with the movement path inf...
341  FDPERFPIC.LHA    18k    FighterDuelPro 2 performance chart shows the rela...
343  PRTMAN20.LHA     24k    Great printer spooler works w/ all programs (even...
344  DICE207_37.LZH  612k    Dice C compiler evaluation version. Lacks only A...
More [Y/n/=]:
345  DISKSALV11_28.  104k    DiskSalv v.11.28 Latest version of premier Harddi...
346  CONTACT2.LHA     54k    Demo version of nice Address/Phonebook.
347  DISTANTSUNSDEM  413k    Distant Suns 4.1 demo. Although DS is up to v.5....
348  DOCDUMPV36.LHA   64k    Tool for printing program documentation in pamphl...
349  UPCHUG6-94.DMS  392k    The June 94 Disk of the Month from the University...
```

I decided to list the Amiga files uploaded in the previous few weeks. From here, I could have downloaded a few that looked interesting, uploaded my own file, or performed various other tasks with the file libraries.

From the main menu again, I selected the 'U'tility submenu so that I could find out who else was logged in to the system.

```
Time left: 52 - Main => U

Utilities Menu
-------------------------------------------------------------------------------
[R] Read Online Manual[Y] Your Statistics
[U] User Listing[D] Drop To Amigados
[W] Who Is Online[X] Today In History
[T] Todays Events[Z] Quotation
[Q] Show BossHog...[J] Alternate philosophies...
[N] BBS Activity charts[B] Broadcast Msg to Other Ports
[L] Last 5 callers & BBS Statistics     [C] Lotto Number Generator
[K] ASCII 'Digital' clock...[P] Please tell me the Temp...
[M] Main Menu[G] Goodbye - Log Out
[?] Display menu[H] Help
-------------------------------------------------------------------------------

Time left: 51 - Utility => W


Generated on Saturday, 02-Jul-94,  5:44:05pm with DiaWho v0.5...

Line Name                    Baud Action
-------------------------------------------------------------
  0  The Undertaker          2400 MTalking...
  1  User Logging In         1200
  2  Dale Larson            14400 Peeping at others...
  3  (Awaiting next caller)
  4  Scotty                 19200 MTalking...
  5  (Awaiting next caller)
  L  (Awaiting next caller)
  L  (Awaiting next caller)
-------------------------------------------------------------
 Line status:  4 used; 4 free; 8 total

[PRESS RETURN]
```

For kicks, I thought I'd see what the environment was in John's computer room, too.

```
Time left: 51 - Utility => P

 ___   ___
|___ ||___ |
  / /    / /
 / /    / /
 | |    | |
 |_|    |_|
 degrees farenheit
    and

 ___   ___     _   _ _
|___  |___ |  | |   ||_| / /
  _) ) __) )  | |_| |  / /
 (__ ( | __/  |___   | / / _
  __) )| |__    _   | | /_/ |_|
 (___/ |___||_|  |_|    |_|
  relative humidity
  in the *(Freeland Mainframe)*
  computer room...

[PRESS RETURN]
```

I move back to the main menu and select the option to enter a

chat (the MultiTalk area). Several other people are in the chat area
and are having a conversation as I enter. I've highlighted what I
typed to make it a little easier to piece together. Note that the chat
is line-oriented. You see what other people type only when they hit
return. You see what you type as you type it, but no one else sees
it until you press return.

```
Multi-Talk 1.00 -- Multi-User Teleconference System
Copyright (c) 1991-1994 by Sam Yee.
All Rights Reserved.
MT016B -- Registered to John Freeland

Type /help for help; /setenv to set environment; /quit to quit

Entering channel pub...
Channel/User          Flags  Idle  Used Topic/Comment
----------------------------------------------------
pub                   crw--        5:07 this 'n that
  Scotty              urwt-  0:00  0:06
  The Undertaker      urw--  0:00  0:06
  Pandora             urw--  0:00  0:00
  Dale Larson         urw--  0:00  0:00
Message Sent
[pub|5:45P]> <Scotty> The virus deal, TU..
--
[pub|5:45P]> <The Undertaker> oh.
--
[pub|5:45P]> <Scotty> Hi Dale - 'Muffin
--
[pub|5:45P]> Hello all!  I just want to let you know I'm capturing this...
<Scotty> Hi Dale - 'Muffin' is on her way..
--
[pub|5:45P]> <- inserted
[pub|5:46P]> session and am going to be publishing it in a book about Amiga
<The Undertaker> You know scotty that file could of been virus free then could
            of got it over time.
--
[pub|5:46P]> <- inserted
[pub|5:46P]> networking. So don't say anything you don't want in print :-)
<- inserted
[pub|5:46P]> <Scotty> sorry - the youngest took over the keyboard for a sec.. Hi Pandora!
--
[pub|5:46P]> <Pandora> HI!
--
[pub|5:46P]> Greetings   , Pandora.
<The Undertaker> HI AMIGA NETWORKING BOOK READERS!
--
[pub|5:47P]> <- inserted
[pub|5:47P]> Hey, Undertaker, you don't have to shout. And the title is...
<Pandora> Hiya, Dale!
--
[pub|5:47P]> *** The Undertaker is away from keyboard with message `EATING HIS HOOD'.
[pub|5:47P]> *** The Undertaker is back on keyboard.
[pub|5:47P]> <- inserted
[pub|5:47P]> "Connect Your Amiga! A Guide to the Internet, LANs, BBSs and Online Services"
*** The Undertaker is away from keyboard with message `EATING HIS DINNER!'.
[pub|5:47P]> <- inserted
[pub|5:48P]> <Pandora> Better... teehee
--
[pub|5:48P]> Why was the Undertaker eating his hood?
<- inserted
[pub|5:48P]> <Pandora> Hungry?
--
[pub|5:48P]> Hopefully it was an edible hood.
<- inserted
[pub|5:48P]> Out here in the east it is almost 9. Well past hood eating time.
<Pandora> teeheee... yeah... he'll proubly Still get heartburn from it!
--
[pub|5:49P]> *** The Undertaker is back on keyboard.
[pub|5:49P]> *** The Undertaker exits channel pub
[pub|5:49P]> <- inserted
[pub|5:49P]> *** Muffin enters channel pub
```

```
<Pandora> Hi Muffin!
<Muffin> Hey there, hi there, ho there Dale!
[pub|5:49P]> <Muffin> Hi ya Pandora! Good to see ya, as always. :)
[pub|5:49P]> Hello Muffin!
<- inserted
[pub|5:50P]> BTW, your secret identity is safe with my readers.
[pub|5:50P]> <Muffin> Hi ya sysop!
--
[pub|5:50P]> <Muffin> Thank you Dale...names have been changed to protect the innocent!
--
[pub|5:50P]> <Muffin> Pandora, Dale is my buddy who is in Pennsylvania. :)
--
[pub|5:51P]> <Pandora> Cool... Right now?? Cool!
[pub|5:51P]> <Muffin> Yep, Pandora, right this minute he is in Pennsylvania. Sorry if I
             ignore you, but I am excited to see him!
--
[pub|5:51P]> <Scotty> Dale, type /? to get a list of commands, then, /? command for detail
             on each command..
--
<Pandora> NO Problem... ENJOY!
--
<Scotty> type /? channel  for an example..
--
[pub|5:51P]> <- inserted
[pub|5:51P]> /?

Type "/" before the command or door; /help <command> for help

Commands:

alias      asay      away      comment   echo      enter     exec      exit
forget     help      history   if        in        invite    kick      list
lockcmd    lusers    mode      msg       names     noread    pipe      queue
quit       read      say       scan      set       setenv    stats     submit
unalias    unforget  uninvite  unkick    unscan    unset     unsetenv  wall
win


Doors/Information:

banner     broadcast clock     eval      info      motd      last5     temp
time       version   whoson    _about    _codes    _editing  _flags    _intro
_vars

[pub|5:52P]> <Pandora> I got to run... BYE!
--
[pub|5:52P]> Bye Pandora, nice meeting you!'
<Muffin> Pandor, don't go. I won't ignore you I promise!
--
[pub|5:52P]> <- inserted
[pub|5:52P]> <Muffin> Pandora, you go to sysop's today?
--
[pub|5:52P]> <Pandora> Nice meeting you too!
--
[pub|5:53P]> -+- Muffin extends a warm embrace to Dale, her long-distance friend! -+-
<Muffin>
            Cool. Sorry I missed ya, but hubby had my day filled with chores.
            Uggggg!
--
<Muffin> Ha! Dale has no response to my warm embrace. :)
[pub|5:54P]> <Pandora> As did I. You guys are really great people!
--
[pub|5:54P]> <Muffin> They sure are!
--
<Pandora> bye.
--
[pub|5:54P]> <Muffin> Type .smile Muffin and then hit return Dale.
--
[pub|5:54P]> .smile Muffin
<Muffin> bye. :)
--
[pub|5:54P]> -+- Pandora is waving a fond farewell... -+-
[pub|5:54P]> -+- Nice teeth! -+-
```

As you can see, there are several things you can do from chat
other than just type messages. The action commands (like .hug or

.smile, on this BBS) let you "do" something. Muffin used an action command to create the line about extending a warm embrace. When I .smiled back at Muffin, the computer displayed the action to the other participants in the chat, and told me that I have nice teeth. The Undertaker used a similar feature to indicate he was grabbing his dinner, but he managed to misspell "food."

The conversations went on for a while, then I looked at several more features of the BBS. When I was done, I left from (where else?) the main menu.

```
Time left: 61 - Main => G

Goodbye - Log Out - Are you sure? [y/N] => Yes


Connect time: [59] minutes


Thanks for calling, Dale!  Call back soon.

DLG Professional    Copyright 1990,1991 TelePro Technologies


NO CARRIER
```

Static descriptions really don't do a BBS justice. If you don't have a modem, find a friend who has one and ask for a tour.

Fax and Voice

Facsimile machines deliver pages practically at the touch of a button. Computers and fax are a natural blend, and are increasingly intermixed. Understanding computer faxing will help you get even faster results with less effort and waste. It might also save you a buck or two.

Most businesses have a fax, and there are public faxes available in places like corner drug stores (you pay by the page, just as you pay at a public copy machine). It works something like a photocopier. The copy, however, doesn't come out of the same machine as the original went in. It comes out of a different machine, perhaps as far away as the other side of the world. The two machines connect by way of a phone call. The page that comes out isn't called a copy, it's called a fax. (You have to figure out from context whether 'fax' refers to the machines, to the pages, or to the act of sending the pages.)

Faxing is obviously much faster than snail mail, and it doesn't impose an interruption the way a phone call does. Since faxes are transmitted quickly, it is usually less expensive to send a fax than to place a voice phone call, especially for International calls.

Unlike that of photocopiers, the quality of fax output varies only from poor to barely acceptable. Only the speed, low cost and ease of use keep people using fax. Most of the machines use rolls of thermal paper that you have to cut into pages with scissors. The pages feel funny, tend to curl up, and yellow or fade quickly. The printing on the pages isn't much better. It is low-resolution and jaggy. The best machines output to plain paper using ink-jet or laser technology, and are capable of higher-resolutions. If you use your Amiga as a fax, you'll have one of the better machines.

Note that electronic mail has all the advantages of faxes with fewer disadvantages, except that many more people have fax numbers than have email addresses. The more people who read this book, the less need for fax there may be!

How Faxing Works
To understand computer faxing, you have to understand some of the details about how faxing works in general.

What really happens when you send a fax between two fax machines goes like this: You enter the fax number of the remote machine into your local fax machine and feed page(s) into the local machine. The local machine dials the remote machine. The two connect in the same way that two modems do. The local machine scans the pages slowly, creating a digitized version and sending the digitized version over the phone line. The remote machine prints the digitized version as it receives the data. When all pages are sent, both machines hang up.

Obviously, with dozens of manufacturers of fax machines, a stan-dard was needed so that they could all communicate with each other. Almost all modern (from the 80's on) fax machines through-out the world follow what is known as the Group 3 standard. There were earlier Group 1 and Group 2 standards, and if you really have to, you can use most Group 3 fax devices to (slowly) send or receive from one of the obsolete machines. There is a Group 4 standard, but it requires digital phone lines (ISDN) and is not in wide use.

Group 3 faxes are scanned at a resolution of 203x98dpi (dots per inch) in normal mode or 203x196dpi for "fine" mode. They images are compressed and transmitted at 9600 bps (bits per second).

Hence, an 8.5x11" page filled primarily with text is typically trans-mitted in normal mode in about 30 seconds. A page can take from a few seconds (if mostly empty) to about a minute (if there are a lot of graphics and other dense areas). Fine mode can double the transmission time.

An extension to the Group 3 standard, Group 3 bis, provides for transmission at 14.4kbps (thousand bits per second) and a reso-lution of up to 406x196dpi. The higher resolution mode is not in common use, but the 14.4 transmission mode is becoming com-mon. Obviously, the faster speed quickly saves in phone bills more than it may cost in the expense of the faster modem. If you have a device capable of 14.4, you can still send faxes at the lower 9.6 speed.

Other than when purchasing and setting up a fax device, you don't really have to worry about the details of all of these stan-dards. Fax machines automatically negotiate the highest speed at which they can connect. You need to know that fine mode means you'll spend more time on the phone, but otherwise, the standard doesn't matter. If you choose to send a fax in fine mode and the machine on the other end doesn't support it, your machine will automatically fall back to normal mode.

How Computer Faxing Works

Since fax machines send digital data over phone lines, it's a natu-ral for computers to be able to get in on the act. Most new com-puter modems include fax capability. If you have such a modem, you can take advantage of the fax part just by adding fax software (in the same way you use terminal software to take advantage of the data part of your modem). You can display received faxes on screen or you can print them out on your computer's printer. You can send faxes directly from an application rather than printing them out first. You could even scan a document to send it out with your fax modem. Or you could load a received fax into a paint pro-gram, add doodles of your own, and fax the result back out!

All current modems that support faxing support the Group 3 stan-dard. Some only support 9600bps, while others support 14.4kbps. What really separates them is whether they have a Class 1, Class 2 or CAS interface. You can think of Group as a hardware conven-tion, and Class as a software convention.

Just as terminal software uses the 'AT' (Attention) command set for data modems to dial the modem and to set options, fax software needs an interface for fax modems. Class 1 and Class 2 are international standards for fax-specific 'AT' commands. Class 1 uses a small command set and forces the computer to do quite a bit of work in real time during faxing. Most fax modems that don't indicate what type they are use the Class 1 standard. Class 2 uses a much larger command set, allowing the modem's intelligence to free up the computer more. On Amigas, this can be an important consideration. Since serial overrun is a classic problem on the Amiga, something that makes response to the serial port less critical is a Good Thing. Intel modems (and a few others) use the CAS "standard," developed by Intel and DCA, which is incompatible with Amiga fax software.

Besides modems with fax capabilities, there are also internal computer fax cards which only use included software.

While the cheapest fax machines cost more than $200, with good ones going for much more, a good fax/data modem can be had for under $150 (more for 28.8) and is useful for a lot more than faxing. Hence, economics strongly favor computer faxing.

Voicemail
Many of the modems available today offer more than just data and fax. They are also capable of handling voice. Just as an audio digitizer (also known as a sound sampler) lets you save sounds to your computer and play them back from a harddrive, these fancy modems can convert a voice over the telephone into a digital data stream your computer can record and play back. With a little software and some harddrive space, your computer can become a simple answering machine or a sophisticated voicemail system. As well as the voice-capable modems, there are also computer cards designed for voicemail systems.

A modem or voicemail card makes a lousy general-purpose audio digitizer. They are only capable of telephone quality -- much too poor for musical applications, for example.

A voice modem works by digitizing and then compressing audio input in real time. The resultant data-stream (usually at 19.2 or 9.6kbps) is sent over the serial cable to the computer, which can easily save the stream to disk in the same way it would a downloaded file. The stream can be uncompressed and converted to Amiga audio on the computer, or can be sent back to the modem which will decompress it and play it over the modem speaker.

Sending Faxes

Computers excel at sending faxes. Attach a fax modem, plug it into the phone line, install your fax software and go. Most fax software is capable of redirecting printer output so that when you print from your favorite application, the output can go out as a fax rather than to the printer. This saves time, saves paper, and produces higher-quality faxes. By eliminating the scanning done by a fax machine, you eliminate smudges, smears and other marks or errors.

The exact way to send faxes from external applications differs slightly between each fax software package, but the basic idea is the same. You start the fax software and indicate that you want printer output sent to the fax instead. Once you've done so, everything sent to the Preferences printer by any application goes to the fax software instead of the printer. Whatever application you want to fax from (your word processor or paint program, for example), you just print from. Exactly as you'd print to your printer. Unless you have a PostScript printer, in which case you have to make sure to print in "graphics mode" or to the "Preferences printer" rather than to the serial or parallel port. The fax software either creates a file in fax format or prompts you for the number to send the fax to. Once done faxing, you turn off the printer option in the fax software so that your applications can again use the real printer.

Unfortunately, the Amiga's current standard operating system printer support doesn't allow you to choose from multiple printers (or from fax or printer) at the time of printing. The way you configure Preferences and your fax software before you print defines where your printout will go, and you won't be asked. If you forget to activate your fax software when you want to send a fax, your printer will be wasting paper before you realize your error. If you forget to turn off your fax software before trying to print, you'll be dialing instead. One Amiga developer is trying to change this, with his "v42 printer.device" (available for download from may BBSs and online services). It allows you to have multiple printer devices, one of which could be a printer on the parallel port, while another is a printer on a network and a third is connected to fax software. Most software is not compatible with this new printer device, but it might be someday.

Some fax software can also schedule the sending of a fax, delaying until a time when phone rates are lower. As well, it can easily keep a large database of phone numbers, and automatically send a single fax to many numbers. Finally, your software may keep extensive logs of when you sent faxes, where you sent them and what they were. Some software can even estimate the phone bill for sending your faxes!

A fairly minimal Amiga can send faxes. Some software can send straight ASCII or IFF files from floppies on a 512k Amiga. A harddrive is better, though, and expanded memory to hold both the fax software and the application is necessary for faxing from an application.

If you use your computer to send faxes, you may want to have a scanner attached to your computer. That way, you can even fax hand-written notes or other documents not already in your computer.

Receiving Faxes
Once you receive a fax on your computer, you can leave it stored on your harddrive (perhaps in compressed form), display it on your screen, convert it to IFF or dump it to your printer. What to do with it once you have it is easy, getting it on to your Amiga in the first place is the hard part.

If you are going to set up your home or office to receive faxes, you have many decisions to make. Do you need a 24-hour automatic fax line? Do you mind picking up the ringing phone to discover that the call is for your fax machine? Can you justify and afford a larger monthly phone bill for a new phone line or distinctive ringing service? Do you want to leave a computer running 24-hours a day?

The simplest (and most expensive) thing to do is to have an additional phone line installed. Leave your computer with fax software and a fax modem on and attached to that line. This way, you can receive faxes automatically, 24-hours a day. You'll have to remember to kill the fax software before using your modem to dial out to BBSs, and to start the fax software again when you're done.

It is also easy to have a single line that shares fax and data. If you have a BBS, for example, it is easy to set up most modems and software to detect whether a call is fax or data and to respond appropriately.

If you don't receive many faxes, you probably don't want to spend money for a dedicated phone line. If you are willing to give up

automatic incoming faxes, this is still pretty simple. You just tell
people to send faxes to you manually. They call your voice number
(which you've attached a modem to) from their fax machine. You
answer the phone. The caller tells you that they want to send you
a fax. You start your fax software, tell the other person to go
ahead, and tell your software to receive a fax. The caller tells his
fax to start sending.

You can also set up a voice line to receive faxes 24-hours a day,
automatically. When you want something for nothing, though,
receiving faxes is complicated. There are a couple of options.

When most sending fax machines finish dialing, they start sounding a tone on the phone line every few seconds. This is a CNG
tone, also called an Auto Fax Tone or Calling Tone. It alerts any
person or machine picking up the incoming call that a fax is on
the other end. To take advantage of this, you must have special
hardware. Some Supra fax modems have a "Silent Answer" feature. When a call comes in, it is answered by a person or an
answering machine (which you attach to the modem rather than
another jack). If the Supra detects CNG tones, it picks up the line
(and cuts off the answering machine), otherwise, it ignores the
call. A person who hears an incoming fax call just hangs up. Computer and office supply stores also sell fax switches which detect
CNG tones. Unfortunately, not all machines generate a CNG tone.
Some old machines don't generate it at all, and many new
machines only generate it on a call from memory or when the
operator presses 'start' (which they often don't do until they hear
the receiving fax machine). Hence, if you depend on CNG, not
everyone will be able to send you faxes.

The GVP PhonePak works well for sharing a line, since the
answering machine is built-in.

Finally, you may be able to buy from the phone company a service
called Distinctive Ringing (it goes by other names in some areas).
It gives a single line two (or more) incoming phone numbers. When
a call comes in, a distinctive ringing pattern indicates which number was called. Some modems can decipher these rings and
respond only to certain ones. Distinctive ring decoder boxes can
be purchased from many computer and office supply stores. These
connect to the line and have several outputs -- one for each distinctive ring pattern. By plugging your fax into such a box, it will
answer only fax calls.

Faxing is convenient and becoming more widespread all the time. Data/Fax modems are coming down in price and going up in speed (28.8kbps is now affordable for data modems). The software is also getting more sophisticated and easier to use. With it, your Amiga is a great way to send high-quality faxes easily and inexpensively, and it can be a good way to receive faxes, too.

Rules of the Road

Depending on where you were in the world, you probably wouldn't belch loudly at the dinner table. Nor would you likely tell someone you just met that you thought their tie looked funny. Just as in the real world, certain manners should be followed while you're online.

About asking questions: the people on the net aren't paid to make sure your problems disappear. They have lives of their own, with things they'd like to do and places they'd like to be. They'll be happy to try to help you if you have tried to help yourself. Make sure you've read the manual (if there is one for the thing you are interested in). Make sure you've tried looking at any sources of information available (like a list of frequently asked questions -- see the part on FAQs later). Then be polite about how you ask, and thank anyone who answers. If you do get good answers in private mail, post a summary of them to the public place where you asked (for the benefit of others).

It's easy to forget that there is a human being on the other end of your communication if all you can see is text. Be considerate. There really is a person on the other side. Remember that humor which would be obvious with the cues of body language and facial expression may fall flat over a wire. Use smiley faces -- colon minus right-parens intended to be viewed sideways, like this: :-) -- or some other mechanism to indicate your intended tone. If you're ticked off by someone else's apparent insensitivity, remember that it may not be intentional. Take a deep breath or do something else before responding. Even if they meant it, you don't have to respond in kind (that would be engaging in an activity called 'flaming'). If they didn't, it'll be nice for you not to escalate the misunderstanding.

BBS Networks

Just as there are file transfer protocols (for uploads and downloads), there are network protocols. A network protocol specifies how information gets between machines. To use a network, you usually have to understand something about the protocols used. The next several chapters examine different kinds of network protocols.

FidoNet and UUCP are two of the most popular BBS network protocols. Networks using these protocols may contain many machines which aren't BBSs. In fact, UUCP is not at all specific to BBSs. Hence, it may not be entirely accurate to call these BBS network protocols. If you want to be more precise, you can call them by a more general term -- "store-and-forward" network protocols.

By the way, the protocol and the network are often confused. The protocols may be used to connect just a few machines in isolation. There are many small UUCP networks, for example. There is also a huge world-wide UUCP network (called UseNet). Because UseNet is so large, the assumption is often made that there is only one UUCP network, while in fact, any network using UUCP protocols is a UUCP network, whether or not it is part of UseNet.

Most email and news was carried on UseNet until recently. If you got mail and news, you were part of the UseNet, by definition. Now, most mail and news traffic is carried over the Internet. Just because you get mail and news, however, does not mean you are part of the Internet. The Internet is much more than just mail and news. Many systems still haven't connected directly to the Internet, but still use UUCP for UseNet mail and news. (The proliferation of Internet sites has drastically sped up the availability of news and mail to even these sites, because most UUCP systems are polling a site which is directly Internet connected). Many people seem confused on this point, and you might here someone say Internet when they really mean just Internet mail (and/or UseNet news).

Some people refer to mail and news access as Internet access, regardless of the transport mechanism and availability of other Internet applications. At best, that interpretation is quite liberal. It is less confusing to specifically say Internet mail or news when referring to just mail or news.

Even if you don't run a BBS or use one, knowing the principles involved with BBS networks makes it easier to use and understand other networks. We will use UUCP as an example throughout this chapter. The details may be different for other BBS networks, but the principles are the same.

Connections

BBS networks generally use telephone lines and modems to communicate between systems. In this case, the physical connections work just like a user calling a BBS, except that one BBS initiates the call to another BBS, without human intervention required.

A store-and-forward network works in much the same way as uploads and downloads between a user and a BBS. A BBS with data to send over the network to another BBS may dial the remote BBS and upload the data. The protocols used may be different, and the interfaces are different than those presented to human users logging in. How does a BBS on a network know whether to present a human interface or a network interface to a user logging in? The account's username. Special accounts are set up for logins from other BBSs.

Each machine on a UUCP network contains a file with the names and phone numbers and other information for some other UUCP systems. (Actually, the phone numbers may be replaced by other means to communicate with the system, but that is beyond the scope of this explanation.) Using this file, a system can call and log into a special account on another UUCP system.

On some systems, calls are made all day long, on demand. Other systems are programmed to call only at scheduled times. Still others never call out, only accepting calls from others. Data to be sent to another system is stored in a special directory until another system is connected. When a user sends email to a remote system, for example, the email is stored as a file in the special directory (often called a 'spool' directory). When a user requests a file from a remote system, the request is stored as a file in the special directory (spooled). The names of the files, their contents and the directories in which they are located indicate the type of data (email to be sent, file requested, etc.) and where it is headed.

When two systems connect on a BBS network, one says "I have something for you." "Here, take it." It uploads the spooled data. Then it adds "Do you have anything for me?" If the other system does, it then downloads the data from that other system.

Hostnames and Addresses

In most network protocols, each machine Papaya has a hostname. (A host is just another name for a computer or system.) These names are like usernames. Users refer to systems by their human-language names. Instead of calling a machine "Joe's computer," or "that A4000," or whatever, the machine is called by name. UUCP networked computers have hostnames. Hostnames are usually required to be unique -- no two machines on the same network should have the same name.

In most networks, each machine has an address. These are used by computers to identify each other. Humans don't usually have to use network addresses to identify systems. The form of the address is specific to the protocol, but usually is some kind of number. BBS networks don't follow these general rules as well as most other types of networks. In Fido networks, the address is used by humans to identify systems. In UUCP networks, there aren't addresses, or at least addresses aren't numbers -- they are routes.

Routing

In a small BBS network, each system might directly contact any other. In a network with dozens (or thousands) of systems, this is impractical. Instead, data is passed through intermediary systems. In such a network, many systems might connect directly to only one or two other systems, but still be able to communicate with thousands of remote systems.

Let's take an imaginary network as an example. Our network will be small, such that it would be relatively easy to set it up so that each computer could directly call every other computer. Large networks aren't set up this way because it is prohibitively expensive to call every other computer directly, and because it would be impossible to configure thousands of computers with phone numbers, accounts and passwords for each other. There are seven machines on our network. The illustration shows a diagram of the machines and how they connect.

Peach and Grape can only call (or be called by) Apple. If they need to communicate with any other systems, they must do it through Apple. Plum, Kiwi and Orange have similar relations. Papaya only connects to one system -- it does all of its communication through Kiwi.

The path that data takes in moving between systems is called a route (and the data moving between systems is often referred to as traffic). Most users of most networks don't ever have to worry about routing. It is done automatically by the computers based on the address provided by the user.

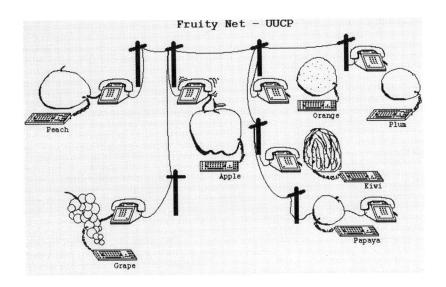

Fruity Net — UUCP

Each of these systems might know about all of the others. But they don't have to. In this example, Orange should know about Papaya, but, other than that, it is only necessary that each system know about the systems it is directly connected to. If Peach tried to send mail (or other traffic) to Papaya, it would route it through Apple. It would be set up to do this simply because Apple is the only other system it communicates with. Apple would know to route all traffic with an unknown destination to Orange. Orange would know about Papaya, so it would know to send the traffic through Kiwi.

In practice, many UseNet sites attempt to keep complete maps of the region or the entire network. Systems which don't contain extensive maps just route all their traffic through systems which do.

In UUCP networks, addresses and routes are synonymous. Addresses are composed of parts separated by explanation points ('!', pronounced "bang"). The address is sometimes called a "bang path." From Peach, the user Joe (with username "joe") on Papaya is addressed as "apple!orange!kiwi!papaya!joe." He could also be addressed as "papaya!joe." If this address is used, Papaya has to contain routing information for Papaya or have been set up to forward mail to somewhere which does. Most UseNet systems are already configured so that most users can mail most other users with the simpler form of address, omitting an explicit path. In fact, most can use Internet addressing (explained in the Internet chapter).

When a user on Peach sends email to a user on Papaya, the email is spooled to a file on Peach. When Peach next calls (or is called by) Apple, the email is transferred to Apple. Apple stores it until the next time Orange speaks with Apple, and so on to Papaya. Each step of the way, the email is stored until it can be forwarded, hence the term "store-and-forward."

Applications

On a UUCP network, a user can transfer files or request execution of a program from remote. It works the same way. If a file is to be sent, it is sent just like email. If a file is to be retrieved, a message goes out requesting the file, then the file comes back. If a command is to be executed, the command line goes out and the resulting output comes back. Of course, all of these actions are subject to limitations imposed by security and system configuration. For more details, see the chapter on UUCP.

Obviously, a store-and-forward network is limited in that it cannot provide interactive applications -- remote logins, real-time games, etc. Store-and-forward networks can also be very slow. Some systems only make calls late at night. If a file has to go through more than one such system, it can take days to arrive at its destination.

Public Data Networks

Something you won't be running on your machine, but which you should know about, are the public data networks. Tymnet and Sprintnet two are examples of PDNs. These are packet-switched (see below) networks spanning large geographic distances. They have pools of modems set up in cities all over the place. Most BBSs aren't connected to a PDN, but most online services are. By calling the local access number for a PDN to connect to the online service, you pay the phone company only for a local call -- not a long distance one -- to connect with the service. The service will charge you for the use of the network, but that will cost much less than a long-distance phone call would. You might be able to access several different online services through a call to one number connected to a PDN.

A packet-switched network is one in which the data sent over the network is subdivided into small parts, each of which has a unique id and the address of the destination for the data. A circuit-switched network is one in which a real circuit is created between the sender and receiver in order to send any data. The telephone network is a circuit-switched network. Packet-switched networks let you have a lot more connections with a lot less wire, so they are much more efficient. That's why the PDNs are less expensive than the phone company.

If you don't understand the idea of packet-switching, don't worry. You don't have to understand it to use it. As far as you have to know, its the same as if the online service were a local BBS which just happens to have the number of the local PDN. By the way, packet-switching is how LANs and the Internet work, and you'll get more explanation of the idea in those chapters.

LANs

A Local Area Network is made up of computers which are physically connected together in a limited area (usually within a single building). Perhaps the most common use of the word "network" has been in reference to LANs. These computers are typically used by groups of people working together, though sometimes one person might use a LAN with several computers. LANs are typically configured so that many computers share space on one or more large harddrives, and so that several computers share a single printer. While many LANs were originally installed primarily for data or resource sharing, many are being used for communications (i.e., email). For simplicity's sake, we are using the word LAN to mean a single physical network, though some LANs are, in fact, internetworked. We discuss internetworking in a later section.

True LANs use special-purpose networking hardware which is capable of connecting many computers on a single cable. LAN hardware is typically an order of magnitude faster than most serial ports. Standards for LAN hardware allow many types of machines to communicate on the same LAN. Ethernet is currently the most popular LAN hardware. It is used by Amigas, PCs, Macs, Unix workstations and many other computers (and even some printers and other peripherals).

LANs also require special software. LAN protocols are somewhat analogous to upload and download protocols -- they direct data, and ensure that it moves along quickly without loss or corruption. LAN applications provide a user interface to the power of the network. Typical applications include network filesystems and networking printing devices, but might also include games or an email system.

Even if you have only a single computer, the information in this chapter will be valuable to you. Having a knowledge of LANs to build on will make it easier to understand other kinds of networks -- especially if you want to understand the Internet.

The Physical Connection

Computers can't read each other's minds, so they must be provided a means to communicate. Depending on the requirements and budget for a network, connections range from the cutting edge of modern electronics to primitive kludges. You need to know about the kinds of cabling used and about the hardware protocols run over those cables. Some of the technology used includes:

·   Fiberoptic cables (glass) and lasers can transmit data at the speed of light for long distances. "It doesn't get much better than this." Glass is rarely used for any but the largest LANs (those with thousands of computers), rather, it is usually used to link expensive computing centers or to serve as a backbone in an internetwork. FDDI is a standard hardware protocol for networking with glass.

·   Coaxial or twisted-pair cables can also send signals between machine. This tends to be slower and have a more limited range than glass, but it is easier and less expensive to work with. Most LANs use this type of hardware and are available for the Amiga. Ethernet and ARCNet are hardware protocols with a coax and a twisted pair version, but the exact specifications of the cables are different for Ethernet and ARCNet.

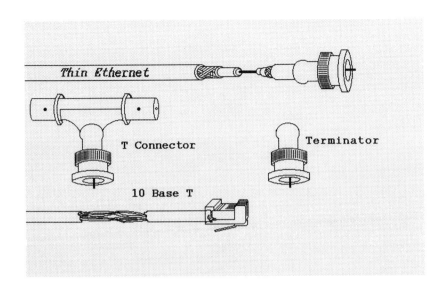

·   Wireless (radio or infrared) LANs exist for PC networks, but have not been brought to the Amiga. These networks are generally very expensive and some of them are relatively slow.

·   Digital phone lines running on copper cable (ISDN, for example) can connect computers at LAN speeds but over long distances as well as short. This is an emerging technology that will become more popular.

·   Most people at least have access to conventional phone lines with high-speed modems. LANs aren't built with modems, but you might use a modem to connect to a LAN.

·   Serial or Parallel ports with null-modems or ParNet cables can connect two computers at relatively slow speeds. As real networking hardware becomes less expensive, the temptation to use such cheap but limited hardware decreases.

·   Finally, when there is no better way, moving floppy-disks manually from one machine to another (SneakerNet) is a proven, if inconvenient, technology.

Regardless of the technology and cabling used, standards come into play. In the same way that a cable with RCA-jacks on each end can be used to connect the video from your TV to your VCR or the audio from your stereo to your speakers, network cables can be used in many ways. It isn't useful to run your stereo's audio outputs to your VCR's video inputs, and you can't run different physical networks over the same wire, even if both standards use the same type of wire (Ethernet and AmigaLink, for example). Network hardware protocols specify what signals are sent over the wires (or fibers or airwaves).

Hardware protocols specify at the lowest level how to electrically encode data into a signal, how to address a particular machine on a network (or how to address many machines), etc. Users and programmers (other than driver writers) don't have to concern themselves with the details of these protocols. They have higher level software interfaces, starting with the SANA-II Network Device Driver Standard, explained later.

Topology

Different network hardware uses different cabling configurations. Whether a single cable runs from one computer to another to another or a separate cable connects each computer to a central hub or a different configuration is used is the network's topology. This is explained more simply with pictures than with words.

While we're at it, we'll also show pictures of some of the connectors and cables used.

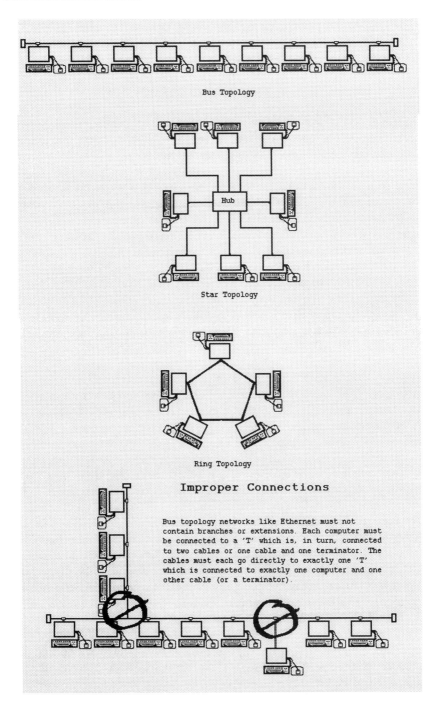

Bus Topology

Star Topology

Ring Topology

Improper Connections

Bus topology networks like Ethernet must not
contain branches or extensions. Each computer must
be connected to a 'T' which is, in turn, connected
to two cables or one cable and one terminator. The
cables must each go directly to exactly one 'T'
which is connected to exactly one computer and one
other cable (or a terminator).

Near or Far (LAN/WAN)

We've already explained the acronym LAN. It stands for Local-Area Network. Network hardware which is used for computers in the same building (or perhaps on the same campus) is LAN hardware. Thick Ethernet has a cable length limit of about 500 meters (without special additional hardware which can extend that a few times). Most other LANs have even less range. You can't use one of these to connect across town (or across continents).

A Wide Area Network (WAN) is used to connect distant computers. WANs frequently use dial-up or leased (dedicated) telephone lines. They can also use satellites or other technology.

LANs tend to be faster than WANs (more about what "fast" means later) and less expensive to set up and to operate. LANs and WANs are frequently used differently because of their respective limitations. LANs are commonly used as an extension of the local computer, sometimes without the user even realizing that network resources are being utilized. WANs are usually used with some conscious effort to go out and get something from a remote site. Sometimes they are set up to be available on demand rather than continuously (as with a normal phone line and modem), saving on cost without causing too much inconvenience (since they are used with conscious effort anyway).

Technology like ISDN and FDDI blurs the distinction between LANs and WANs. ISDN can be economically used to connect computers both near and far at speeds which rival those of slower LANs. FDDI can connect computers spread up to 200km at speeds faster than other LANs.

With the exception of ISDN and standard modems, there are no implementations of WAN-specific hardware for the Amiga.

How Fast (Bandwidth and Latency)

With computers, it doesn't really make sense to ask "how fast?" The only people who look at a simple measure and call it "how fast" are advertising/marketing types and those who are duped by advertising/marketing types. Your choices are probably too limited for the distinctions to matter, so feel free to skip this section if you aren't the curious type.

Depending on what you need your computer or network to do, there are different kinds of fast. On a network, they are called bandwidth and latency.

Bandwidth is how much data can be moved between point A and point B in a given unit of time. It is typically measured in bits per second (bps) or millions of bits per second (Mbps). This measurement is usually a raw theoretical maximum which is not attainable in practice. Ethernet has a speed of 10 Mbps, meaning that in a frictionless universe with lots of favorable coincidences, machine A could transmit ten million bits of data (about 1.2 megabytes) to machine B in one second. In practice, many different factors (collisions, errors, controller speed, computer speed, protocol overhead) will dramatically reduce this number. Some network hardware has fewer things that can reduce this raw number. For example, ARCNet at 2.5 Mbps theoretical, typically has more bandwidth in practice than just one-fourth that of Ethernet.

Latency is how fast a given bit (or a small number of bytes) gets from point A to point B. Latency is typically measured in milliseconds (ms) for a round trip. It's usually more of a practical number than a theoretical one. A lower latency means that a bit takes less time to get there, a higher latency means it takes more time to get there. Read this again, because it seems backwards -- we're used to thing of bigger as better. (Though you may not understand this now, the statistics printed by "ping -l hostname" are mostly about latency.)

Examples from outside the computer world: A barge has high bandwidth but high latency. A Porsche has low bandwidth but low latency.

For most use on most LANs, if the bandwidth is good, the latency is usually adequate. In WANs, latency tends to be much higher, so there may not be enough even when bandwidth is more than adequate. You'll notice this when making voice telephone international calls. There is plenty of bandwidth in that you can both talk in a steady stream and all of your words will still be heard on the other side. There might be a delay, though, that causes a long pause between the time you finish asking a question and the time that you start to hear the answer. On a network, the result of high-latency can be seen in real-time data (i.e., video or audio), user-interface performance (i.e., the length of time before a prompt is returned after a command is executed or how long it takes for a mouse-click to change a GUI), etc.

Note that even in a LAN, latency can dramatically increase with distance and intervening routers/bridges/etc. Each hop across a large internetworked Ethernet adds a little latency without necessarily reducing bandwidth.

In a network used to move large files overnight, bandwidth is typically more important than latency. In a network used for multiplayer interactive video games or remote login, latency is frequently more important than bandwidth.

As a side note, bandwidth and latency are important concepts to have in understanding other parts of a computer. Memory latency, for example, is a measurement of how fast bytes can be read from and written to a memory chip. Two systems with identical clock speeds (MHz) and bus widths (8-, 16-, 32-, or 64-bits) may have different memory systems with different latencies, giving one much better typical performance than the other. Users hear about memory system latencies in terms of wait-states imposed (the more wait-states, the higher the latency). The bus width and latency used in the memory system should really be examined when comparing computer "speeds," rather than relying solely on the clock speed (MHz).

Physical Addresses

On a network with several computers using the same wire to communicate, there must be a way to send data from one computer to a particular other computer. Network hardware uses addresses to distinguish one computer from another and to label data as destined for a particular machine.

Hardware addresses are generally numbers. On some networks, the numbers are set at the factory, and every board ever produced has a different number. Ethernet works this way. Each standard Ethernet card ever made for any computer has a unique 48-bit address in the ROM of the card. Users don't usually ever have to concern themselves with hardware addressing on an Ethernet network.

Other networks may use DIP switches or software to select a much smaller number as a network address. ARCNet, for example, uses an 8-bit address. Since there are only 256 possible addresses (usually many fewer are used), whoever sets up the network must make sure that each card on the network is configured to use a different address. Of course, some networks have a lot more than 256 machines, but those are internetworks rather than one large single physical network. More about that later.

Physical Packets

LAN network hardware sends data in small parts called packets. Typically, packets contain less than 1k of data. The amount of data which fits into a given network's largest packet is that network's MTU -- Maximum Transmission Unit. Software protocols break up large amounts of data into individual packets for use by the hardware (see Software Protocols).

Sending small packets allows garbled data to be resent economically. Some network hardware (such as Ethernet), uses checksums and acks to ensure that if a packet gets there, it gets there error-free. An "ack" is an acknowledgement -- it indicates to the sender that something was received intact.

Besides data, packets typically contain information like destination address (where the packet is going), source address (where the packet came from) and packet type. The packet type indicates what kind of protocol software the packet is for. This allows multiple protocols to simultaneously use the same hardware.

Broadcast and Multicast

Another valuable feature of some LAN hardware is broadcast and multicast. A packet which is broadcast is sent to every machine on the LAN at once. This allows data to be sent to many machines as a single packet rather than as many packets (one to each machine). Multicast allows data to be sent as a single packet to a set of machines.

While some network protocols depend on broadcast for some features (TCP/IP on Ethernet, for example, uses broadcast for address resolution), most network applications don't take advantage of broadcast or multicast. Clearly, however, some applications might benefit greatly from these features.

Device Drivers -- SANA-II

We've discussed a few of the many details of how networking hardware works. If every software developer and every user had to be intimately familiar with all of these details, I'd have to write another whole book. Instead, an abstraction is used to isolate these details. The SANA-II standard is therefore critical to Amiga networking. A SANA-II device is to using a network as serial.device is to using your modem.

SANA-II is a detailed, low-level specification. While some network developers need to understand it in detail, users don't. If you are confused during this explanation, bear with me. Read on through the rest of this Part, and come back to this section again later, if necessary.

As I wrote in the SANA-II Network Device Driver Specification:

"The SANA-II Network Device Driver Specification is a standard for an Amiga software interface between networking hardware and network protocol stacks (or for software tools such as network monitors).

A network protocol stack is a layer of software that network applications use to address particular processes on remote machines and to send data reliably in spite of hardware errors. There are several common network protocol stacks, including: TCP/IP, OSI, AppleTalk, DECNet and Novell.

SANA-II device drivers are intended to allow multiple network protocol stacks running on the same machine to share one network device. For example, the TCP/IP and AppleTalk protocol stacks could both run on the same machine over one Ethernet board. The device drivers are also intended to allow network protocol stacks to be written in a hardware-independent fashion so that a different version of each protocol stack doesn't have to be written for each networking hardware device.

The standard does not address the writing of network applications. Application writers must not use SANA-II Device Drivers directly.

Network applications must use the API provided by the network protocol software the application supports. There is not an Amiga standard network API at the time of this writing, though there is the AS225 TCP/IP package and its socket.library as well as other (third-party) packages."

Since that writing, an Amiga standard networking API (Application Program Interface) has been released by Commodore. It is contained in Envoy (see the chapter on Envoy for more details).

All current Amiga networking hardware comes with a corresponding SANA-II driver, and drivers have been made available for older hardware, as well. All current Amiga network software uses SANA-II device drivers to access the hardware. Unfortunately, not all protocols have been updated in the last few years.

Especially unfortunate is Oxxi's choice not to use the SANA-II standard in their ACS (Netware client software) package. Oxxi has created a version of ACS which uses SANA-II, but, as of this writing, they won't release it because they believe that using standards would encourage people to buy fewer high-priced copies of ACS (this according to public postings made by Oxxi employees).

SANA-II drivers have been written for serial ports, parallel ports, Ethernet, ARCNet, a PCMCIA Ethernet card, a floppy-port networking device, and other hardware. Whatever LAN you are going to set up, you probably need to know about and use SANA-II.

SANA-II drivers belong in a drawer called devs:networks. Most networking software automatically creates this drawer during installation. The driver for the A2065 Ethernet card is devs:networks/a2065.device, and other devices are named similarly. Some drivers require configuration files which must be created with a text editor or a preferences editor. The SLIP (serial port) driver, for example, requires that you hand-edit a file called "envarc:slip0.config." The details for configuring specific drivers are included with the drivers.

Most protocol software (see below) contains, as part of its documentation, everything that most users need to know about SANA-II as it relates to that protocol software. Hence, don't worry if you don't yet understand all the details. For the most part, it is sufficient to know that you want networking hardware with a SANA-II driver and networking software which uses SANA-II.

The standard documents themselves are written for developers, and most users don't really need to be familiar with it. There is a freely redistributable SANA-II archive. Besides the standards documents, the archive contains a driver for the A2060, A2065 and SLIP (with source for SLIP), so you may want it. Both the Fish Disks and the AmiNet FTP sites have the SANA-II specification. The latest version as of this writing comes in an archive called "sana2_v2.lha" from early 1994.

The earlier approved version of the standard was sana2.lha. The difference between the two standards is simple to users. It means that AmiTCP and Envoy can be used together on the same machine at the same time. If you need these two protocol stacks to run at the same time on your machines, you'll need to use SANA-II drivers compatible with the new standard.

Protocol Software

Hardware and a SANA-II driver does not a network make. Network applications provide functionality and interfaces to users. Network protocol software provides the interface applications needed to take advantage of the hardware. SANA-II drivers provide only a raw interface to the hardware, without the important niceties that make a network usable. Hence, LANs use network hardware, a SANA-II driver, protocol software and application software.

In most environments, no single network protocol is used. A complementary and compatible suite of protocols handles a wide range of needs. Higher-level protocols providing more sophisticated services are built on the simplest of protocols. TCP/IP, for example, is a suite named for one of its high-level protocols (TCP) and one of its lowest-level protocols (IP). IP is so low-level that applications do not use it directly -- it is only used by higher-level protocols. An implementation of some part of a protocol suite is called a protocol stack because of the way protocols build on each other. In practice, many uses can talk about a whole suite of protocols as if it were one protocol because the differences aren't usually made apparent to users of applications.

Among the features that protocol software provide to network applications are:

· identification of ultimate destination
· fragmentation and reassembly of packets
· reliable delivery

The ultimate destination of network data is the particular application on a particular machine that data is destined for. Since many network applications may be running simultaneously on each of many machines all on a single LAN, and multiple applications might be running on each of those, mere hardware addressing is not adequate to this task.

Data to be sent over the network is usually larger than the maximum single packet allowed by the hardware. Protocol software breaks up data to be sent over the network into MTU-sized packets for transmission over the network hardware, then reassembles them at the destination machine.

Networking hardware doesn't ensure that data arrives. Sometimes packets of data are lost due to poor connections, overloaded processors, or for other reasons. For packets which aren't lost, some networking hardware checks to ensure that received packets are not corrupted, but not all networking hardware does. Protocol software makes sure that the data gets there if at all possible (resending packets which aren't somehow acknowledged or don't pass a data integrity check), or informs the application that it cannot (as when a destination computer is off or a cable is broken).

Note that different network protocols may provide different services. Some services will not have all of these characteristics, other services will have all these and additional features. The details are left to the documentation for the specific APIs and protocols in question. What is important to recognize is that applications developers must write to a network protocol (not to a SANA-II driver) and that users must have applications in addition to a SANA-II driver and a protocol stack. Most networking software packages come with all three.

Understanding the details of a particular protocol makes understanding other protocols easier, and can help to make more general issues in networking clearer. TCP/IP is probably the best documented complex protocol, and will be used for some examples here. This is, however, a very incomplete look at TCP/IP and networking protocols in general. If you are interested in the workings of TCP/IP out of curiosity, or because you will maintain a complex network, or if you need to understand more details about networking protocols, you should also pursue other readings from the Recommended Reading section.

Network Host Addresses

As mentioned earlier, there are really two kinds of host addresses. Humans call machines on most networks by host names. The host names are convenient, human-language names. Not all networks use host names. The real network addresses (sometimes called network numbers) are usually some kind of number. Neither of these should be confused with the physical address of a machine, which is how the hardware itself distinguishes between different hosts.

The networking protocols use network addresses to direct data to the correct machine. They use special information included by the protocol with the data to direct the rest of the data to the appropriate application.

On a simple LAN, network addresses could be identical to hardware addresses. On a network which joined several LANs (an internetwork), there would have to be a way to identify the LAN and the machine. Most modern networking protocols are capable of internetworking, and their network addressing reflects this.

IP, for example, uses a 32-bit address. Each host on a IP network has a unique address. Different ranges of addresses divide the network ID and the host ID differently. For the range of addresses known as Class C, for example, the host ID is the last eight bits of the address, while the rest of the address identifies the network. IP addressing allows the specification of a network rather than a specific machine (by making all bits of the host ID 0) and broadcast (by making all bits of the host ID 1).

The way that IP addresses are usually written and used by humans is in dotted-decimal format. Four eight-bit quantities are separated by periods like this: 128.252.135.4. This represents a 32-bit number. It is separated like this because each of the parts may be meaningful. In a Class C address, for example, the first three octets make up the network number and the last octet is the address of the host within that network.

More details about network addressing are provided with some of the later sections on specific protocols and with the documentation for the various network protocols.

Address Resolution
It is simple for LAN networking software to convert a host name to a host network number or network address. It can just keep a simple table. More complex is converting those network addresses into physical addresses. We'll use Ethernet hardware as an example.

Every standard Ethernet card has a unique hardware address. Ethernet packets are sent to a card with a particular address (unless they are broadcasted). So the protocol software must, at the lowest level, know about Ethernet addresses and be able to map network addresses to Ethernet addresses. It could just keep a simple table, as it might with host names. This would lead to several problems, however. Say, for example, that you needed to change Ethernet cards in a machine. You'd then have to update the table in all of your other machines, even though the name and network address of the host haven't changed.

One of the TCP/IP suite of protocols is ARP -- Address Resolution Protocol. It allows TCP/IP to find the physical address without resorting to another table. When a machine needs to send a packet to a machine it doesn't know about, it broadcasts a packet saying "Would host X please reply?" All machines listen for such broadcasts, and when host X gets it, it replies. All machines listen to the reply so that they can remember X for the next time they need to send a packet to X. After a while, they purposely forget X, so that a fresh check of what X's physical address is can be made.

Fragmentation and Reassembly

The typical MTU of standard networking hardware is well under 2k. Ethernet uses a 1500 byte MTU. The hardware is incapable of sending a single chunk of data larger than that. Since a lot of data to be sent over a network is much larger than that, something must be done in software to compensate. The answer is fragmentation and reassembly.

In a TCP/IP protocol stack, IP is responsible for fragmentation and reassembly as well as addressing. When an application gives data to the protocol stack, it is eventually passed down to IP. If it is larger than the hardware MTU, it is split up into MTU-sized packets, each with a unique identifier and sent out. On the receiving side, the packets are stored until they can be put back together (using the unique identifiers) into the original contiguous block of data.

Ports

Applications which don't need reliability (but which do need addressing, fragmentation and reassembly) don't use IP directly. They use UDP (User Datagram Protocol). What UDP adds to IP is ports. This is a mechanism to allow multiple recipients of UDP packets on a single machine. Each recipient "listens" on a specific port. UDP packets are sent not just to a particular host address, but also to a given port at that address. Standard ports are assigned to standard services.

Data sent with UDP may not get there, or may get there twice. With the use of checksumming, UDP data which does arrived can be automatically checked to at least ensure that it is not corrupted.

UDP is connectionless -- an application "listens" for UDP packets and can then receive them from any number of other applications, without any arrangements being made in advance. Contrast this with TCP, below.

Reliable Delivery

Most network hardware is not infallible. As you may have noticed using serial ports and modems, for example, sometimes there is "noise" resulting in dropped characters or randomly added characters (baud barf). Just as you use a file transfer protocol to keep your data intact when up/downloading to a BBS, network protocols include error detecting and correcting routines. Because of the complexity and speed of many networks, the problem of reliability is even larger in a network. One example of the added complexity: unlike in a simple serial link, many networks have the potential to send data such that different parts arrive at different times, and not necessarily in the order sent.

There are many trade-offs to be made in designing reliability, so most protocol suites have several protocols with different degrees and kinds of reliability.

TCP is a stream-oriented reliable protocol. When two applications are connected via TCP, they can each send continuous data, assured that if anything can reach the other side at all, it will get there intact and in order (if you cut all the wires between two machines, though, not even TCP will help you). No extra characters will be inserted, none will be lost, and none will be swapped. Each "write" can be as long or short as desired.

To use TCP, two applications must make a connection. You can't simply send a packet to a specified port on a specified machine (as you can with UDP). It's analogous to making a telephone call with a more perfect telephone system. One application says "I want to connect to the other application X." The "operator" (the network protocol stack) sets up a "call" to the other end. If the party on the other end accepts the call, everything said can be heard clearly as the conversation progresses. Wouldn't it be nice if your local phone company never gave you poor connections? Even with this improved telephone system, however, on rare occasions, calls are sometimes cut off and disconnected (as when wires are cut or computers turned off).

TCP is a complex protocol which is difficult to implement. It might be fair to say that in most TCP/IP protocol stacks, TCP takes up half (or more) of the code space, while all the other protocols combined make up the rest.

Network Applications

Network software automates a lot of work that would otherwise make it inconvenient to share resources and data or to communicate between people. Three kinds of software are needed. A hardware device driver provides an interface to the hardware (like how serial.device provides an interface to the 8520 CIA chips on the Amiga). A network protocol stack provides a way to direct data to a particular machine and to transmit data without error (like using X-modem or Z-modem to up/download files to a BBS). A network application actually does something -- like directing printer output across the network to a remote printer, letting the user read electronic mail, or mounting a network filesystem.

We have already discussed BBS (store-and-forward) networks. In those networks, the hardware is generally a modem, and the protocol software is something like UUCP. In the case of UUCP, there is very little application software and it is not as separate from the protocol software as it would usually be in a LAN environment.

In a LAN or internet, many different applications exist to perform many different tasks. These applications are just as independent of the network protocol software as other applications are independent of the operating system. Just as some word processors are available in versions for several different computers, but they all read the same file formats, so are many networking applications available for several different computers (or even different network protocols) but they can communicate with each other.

Client/Server and Peer-to-Peer

There are two different models for network applications. Under one model, some computers act as servers. All other computers act as clients. A server computer stores files or database information or electronic mail or whatever. Anyone who needs to access that information runs a client program which accesses the server to get it. In general, no one uses the server machine directly. For example, a machine might be set up to do nothing but provide disk space to all other machines. If two users want to share a file, they put it on the fileserver.

In a peer-to-peer application, there may still be client and server programs, but they might run on any machine and both might run on the same machine. For example, each user on a network might share some of her computer's hard disk space and also access that of some other computers. If two users want to share a file, one says to the other "get it off my computer -- it's in directory such-and-so."

A client imports services. A server exports services.

The difference between client/server and peer-to-peer is not always clear, and it is often the topic of religious discussion. In general, it's nice to have the flexibility of peer-to-peer -- you can always choose to configure a peer-to-peer network so that it is used in a client/server manner and move back and forth without needing to change software.

Filesystems

One of the most common uses of LANs is the sharing of filesystems.

Moving floppy disks or dialing modems with a terminal emulator is a highly inconvenient way to get a file from one system to another. If two people want to work on different parts of the same file at one time (as with a database program, for example), it is virtually impossible to do with floppy disks because you have to merge two separate files once you are done.

To the user of a network filesystem, a remote hard disk (or some part of one) looks just like a local hard disk. It can be read to or written from by any application, files can be browsed with the Workbench or any file requester, etc. To the user of a peer-to-peer network exporting a filesystem, the local hard disk continues to work the same, except that it is occasionally also accessed from somewhere else.

The computer which has the hard disk is referred to as a server, even in a peer-to-peer network. The computer which accesses it remotely is called the client. Note that, in a peer-to-peer network, a given computer might be both a client and a server, perhaps several times for each.

Printers

The other thing almost every network does is to allow printer sharing. Usually, a single printer will serve the needs of several users. If only one computer has a printer connected, the owner of that computer is likely to become annoyed very quickly with constant interruptions from those wishing to use the computer. Either they bring a floppy and ask to print a file, or copy a file over the network then ask to print a file.

With network printing services, computers with printers can export them. Clients of the printer services are configured so that applications print as if a printer were attached locally, but the output is automatically sent to the remote printer. It is as if the remote printer were a fax machine to which you faxed your output. The user of the computer with the printer simply notices that other people come by and remove their printouts, but doesn't otherwise have to be bothered.

Email

Just as you can send and receive electronic mail on a BBS, you can also do it on many LANs. Some LAN email systems make each computer a post-office, others have a central mail server which contains all of the mailboxes. Either way, each user gets her own mailbox, and using a LAN to send notes to other computer users can be very convenient. In a large company, it allows you to avoid sending quick notes or computer files through interdepartmental mail, in a house with a LAN, it may let you avoid a refrigerator full of Post-It® notes.

Unlike BBS email, LAN email often has a graphical user-interface, and may provide features such as beeping each time new mail arrives.

Remote Login

Physically moving to another computer in order to execute some command on that computer is sometimes a necessary pain. With a LAN, you may be able to execute remote commands or even to open a remote shell.

Rendering

If two heads are better than one, two CPUs must be better than one, right? Borrowing your friend's head while it is not in use is probably not often possible. Borrowing his CPU might be. Computers connected in a LAN can share spare CPU time to work on intensive calculations. On the Amiga, this usually means rendering computer graphics, though CPU time on the Internet has also been used for things like cracking incredibly complex cryptographic codes. With the right software, a rendering engine can distribute its work across several machines. Usually this is done by having each machine work on a separate frame or scene and saving them all to a single place. Sometimes this is implemented by taking advantage of a network filesystem.

This has been only a representative sampling of some of the applications used on typical LANs. Multi-player games and simulations, chat lines and many other applications are available for LANs.

Homo or Hetero

Computer networks may consist entirely of like machines communicating (all Amigas or all Macs, for example). Such a network is homogeneous. 'Homo' means 'like.' Many networks are made up of completely different types of machines communicating with each other. Heterogenous ('hetero' means 'different') networks are much more complicated than homogenous networks, but give obvious additional benefits.

So far, we've ignored the distinction between homo- and heterogenous networks. Clearly, though, in a world dominated by PCs and Macs, many Amigas are likely to need to join a heterogenous network.

In heterogenous networks, little things we don't usually think of become immediately important. A trivial example is that different CPUs store and use bytes in different orders. Most Intel processors use little-endian order (least-significant byte first), while God intended, and most Motorola processors use, big-endian ordering -- storing the most-significant byte first. To send a 32-bit number between two different machine types, therefore, requires agreeing on a common byte order.

There are many other details like this that make heterogenous networking complex. The obvious benefit, however, is the ability to use different types of machines together in concert. It's nice to be able to execute a command on a different machine running a different operating system without leaving your desk.

Heterogenous networking requires that the various platforms on the network all have implementations of network hardware, protocol software and application software based on the same standards. Platform-independent standards tend to be more powerful, but also more expensive to implement and less efficient to run than proprietary solutions limited to a single platform. This means that a network of all PCs or all Amigas is likely to be less expensive and to perform a little better than a network with many types of machines. By far, the most popular independent standard for heterogenous networking in LANs is TCP/IP on Ethernet, but there are other possibilities.

There are "standards" for networking which are more limited, however. Some network protocols and applications, for example, exist solely for file sharing between an Amiga and a PC. Other protocols began as completely closed, proprietary solutions for a single platform and have become somewhat publicly documented standards with implementations available for several machines. Netware is such an example.

Note that networking software doesn't solve problems like document or picture formats. If you want to share most data between different platforms, you are still going to need to have the ability to read and write multiple file formats or to use standardized formats. For example, if you want to share word processing documents between platforms, make sure your word processors can read and write some format common to each other (like ASCII, or perhaps WordPerfect), or if you want a database of pictures, use a standard format like GIF or JPEG which can be directly read and displayed on multiple machines.

Using SneakerNet

If you want to share a small amount of data between two Amigas that are close together, but you can't afford a "real" network, use SneakerNet. Just format a floppy and call it "network:." Every time you want to read or write a file on the network, refer to the "network:" device. When you access shared data, your machine may bring up a requester saying "Please insert disk Network: into any drive." If so, put the "network:" floppy into a drive on your machine. Simple, cheap and effective.

If you need to use SneakerNet to share a large amount of data, or a resource like a printer, you're out of luck. I almost wrote an example SANA-II driver for SneakerNet which, used with something like Envoy, would have solved this problem. The real reason I wanted to write it was to convince upper management at Commodore that Amigas couldn't do any serious networking without additional hardware (and that we therefore needed such hardware). The driver would have worked something like this: If you had mounted a network filesystem (foo:) on some remote machine and then said "dir foo:", you would have had to insert a scratch disk and then carry that disk to the remote machine. The remote machine would have read the disk to see the packet requesting a directory, then would have replied with a packet containing the directory listing (or part of it). It would literally have worked just like any LAN hardware except that you'd have to walk between machines for each of the dozens of packets involved with even the most simple of requests. Network hardware with an MTU of 880k but lousy latency!

Internets

When two or more simple LANs are connected so that traffic is capable of moving from a machine on one physical network to a machine on another, the resulting network is called an "internetwork." Internetworking requires network protocols capable of routing traffic across simple networks, and on physical connections between simple networks. To the user of a networking application, there appears to be no difference between a LAN and an internet -- machines connected to the local Ethernet are accessed in the same way as machines which may be located in China (assuming that the machines are on the same internet).

Increasingly, the word "network" is used not in reference to a LAN but in reference to the Internet (or at least an internet). In the same way that there is a single very large network including most machines running UUCP (the UseNet), there is a single large network including most machines running TCP/IP. That huge network is the Internet (capital 'I' -- a generic internet is lower-case 'i'), and it is quickly changing the way that most of us communicate through our computers. More than two million computers in more than 60 countries are on the Internet. It is not known exactly how many users the Internet has, but there are at least tens of millions. The number of users and computers, as well as the amount of data accessible, on the Internet appears to be growing exponentially. When governments talk about the National Information Infrastructure (NII) or the Global Information Infrastructure (GII), they are usually referring in large part to the Internet.

Getting Connected

Using the Internet can be as easy as calling a BBS or online service. Many offer some Internet access. Often, they offer UseNet news and mail with an Internet domain address (explained later), but are not really connected.

Some BBSs and online services are a part of the Internet and offer their users access to several Internet applications. This can have drawbacks. Users are limited to the specific applications and interfaces provided by the BBS or online service. That may mean that there are neat new things that can't be used. On the other hand, having a pretty interface may be the difference between something you can use and something you can't make sense of.

For people who are more technically oriented, there is something called a shell account. This works just like a BBS, but instead of connecting you to a menu-oriented system, it dumps you at a (usually) Unix shell prompt. You can enter any standard operating system commands. You have your own directory in which you can create and delete files. You may even be able to compile new programs. With an Internet shell account, the system you log into is connected to the Internet. Hence, you can run standard Internet applications. Unlike with a BBS or online service, it is very easy for the system administrator to add new applications, so you can expect a wide variety of them. If there is an application that uses a text interface that you want but isn't available, you may be able to get it and compile it yourself!

For the lucky few, it is possible to connect your computer directly to the Internet. Actually, this is becoming more possible all the time, as most providers of shell accounts also provide dial-up IP connections. It is even more involved and difficult than using a shell account, but it allows full use of your computer as a network host, rather than piping everything through an ASCII terminal (or other single interface). If your computer is at work or school where there is an Ethernet network connected to the Internet, you can really fly.

There is a lot more to know about getting connected. Besides the information below about how the Internet works and in later chapters about specific software, make sure to look at the recommended reading list.

Internet Applications

Below are listed some of the most important Internet applications, there are, of course, many others. Some additional details are provided in Part IV. Given an Internet connection (which you likely have to pay for), the use of all these services are generally free. Each of the applications has client and server software associated with it, and the software is generally available for free. If you have a shell account, the software is likely to be already installed for you. If you are directly connected to the Internet from your Amiga, various software is available, or you can use Telnet (included with AmiTCP and AS225) as an alternate way to access many kinds of servers.

WWW

Most introductions to the Internet end here. I begin here. Whichever way you approach it from, the World Wide Web is the most quickly growing application on the net, and may soon be the largest. The client application used to access the Web is called a WWW browser. From most browsers, you can use almost any Internet application without leaving the browser. (Some people use Unix the same way -- without ever leaving Emacs.)

The Web is an Internet-wide hypertext system. Imagine an AmigaGuide where the buttons don't all lead to files on the local machine. Some buttons lead to files on other machines. Some buttons lead to pictures, animations, sound files, binary files to download, etc. The size of the documents is no longer limited to the storage of a local machine. Distribution is no longer limited to who you can give your file to, but to who points to your file with one of their buttons. Further, one person doesn't have to integrate several sources in order to produce a document. Authorship becomes a combination of original creation and research. Footnotes aren't just words, they're active documents. Some documents consist almost entirely of pointers to other documents.

The speed with which documents are being added to the Web and the kind of information you can find is astounding. Want to know the local weather report? The map coordinates of St. Louis? The schedule for shuttle launches? The words to a particular Monty Python sketch? Need to look something up in the Qur'an, or the Christian Bible? Wonder what's in the latest White House press releases? Need info about skydiving? Need to know something about dinosaurs (no, not IBM mainframes)? There is all of this and lots more available on the Web.

With all this content, both in text and in pointers, it becomes easy to start looking up one thing and spend hours following pointers to related topics which interest you. Since all the information is just a mouse-click away, you can cover ground much faster that you could in any library. Chasing pointers like that is called "surfing the net" or "net surfing" or "web surfing."

Want to go shopping? There are several Internet malls on the Web. You can look at pictures of flower arrangements you might like, then fill out interactive forms in order to place on order, including a credit card number to pay with.

Other interactive services allow many other neat things. For example, you can get a list of what new freely redistributable files have been added to a site since the last time you were there. Imagine if the library could tell you what books came in since you last looked, or just those new ones which match your interests.

By the way, a Web page is a fairly short document about the size of a large computer screen (though some are much longer). Because of the link capabilities, most of the text on the Web is split into short pages. Sometimes you'll follow a link to a text file which is fairly long (and contains no links). Also, the text in a Web page is rich (containing different sized fonts and bold and italics), and a page may contain graphics as well as text.

Telnet/Rlogin

Telnet is the standard Internet way to log in to a remote machine or service. Rlogin is an alternative method that generally works only with Unix machines and is for login only. Besides standard shell accounts, some of the places you might Telnet to are a Go server (Go is an oriental board game), an information server, etc. If you don't have WWW client software, you can Telnet to a site which does. Sometimes a WWW link will point to a Telnet site.

FTP

File Transfer Protocol. This is the standard way to copy files over the Internet. Many servers around the net keep freely redistributable files and allow anyone to log in with the username "anonymous." Those are called, strangely enough, "anonymous FTP servers" (or just FTP servers). If you thought a BBS or online service with many files was a good find, wait 'til you find that you can grab files from hundreds of huge FTP servers all from one place. A lot of WWW links point to files available for FTP. Many of the larger FTP sites have their own Web pages as a way to locate and "download" files.

Archie

With all those files all over the place, finding the file you want (or finding out if such a file even exists) is a daunting task. Archie makes it much easier. There are many Archie servers, all of which mirror the information on the other servers. There are at least a few thousand servers, and they keep track of literally millions of files. You give Archie a string and ask Archie to match the string to part of a filename or part of a file description. It returns the locations of the matches it finds.

Archie is often accessed via Telnet, though there are other Archie client programs. Some WWW links point to Archie servers.

Gopher

Gopher is a lookup tool. In many ways, it is a lot like the Web. The Web is newer, and more flexible. It can't work two-way communication, nor does it display pictures, text and audio all on one "page." Gopher is still a valuable tool.

Gopher, unlike the Web, only gives you access to resources you could get at some other way. It just provides some organization for those resources, presenting them in an easier to use fashion.

The easiest way to understand Gopher (as with the Web) is to get an Internet shell account in order to try it.

WAIS

Wide Area Information Server. A standard for accessing text based information on the Internet with whole text searches. Given the wide variety of texts available somewhere on the Internet (legal documents, literature, etc.), this is a great way to find lots of information. If you have a string that you'd like to find in a set of documents, this is the way to do it with the Internet.

Talk

With the Talk application, you can type back and forth with someone on another computer anywhere across the Internet. You tell it
who you want to talk with on which computer, and it tries to page
them. If they are logged in, they may answer the page and enter a
session with you. A simple application called "finger" can be used
to at least find out who is logged in to a particular machine or
whether a particular person is logged in.

IRC

If you want to join a conversation on a broad topic with people
using computers across the planet, IRC is the Internet way to do
it. Internet Relay Chat allows virtually unlimited numbers of people to type (and read) lines of text. It is broken up into channels --
there may be any number of channels and any number of people
on each channel.

There is very little organization to IRC, and what organization
there is comes from kind and cooperative humans, not dictators.
You can Telnet to an IRC host in theory, but really, you need an
IRC client to use IRC. Again, if you have a shell account, the client
is probably already available to you, but otherwise you may need
to find the software (see Part IV, Amiga Internet).

More than just people use IRC. Various "'bots" are available to perform functions on IRC. You can stay in IRC and get some kind of
work done with the 'bots. I'm not about to try to explain them
here, though.

IRC is pretty crazy. There might be a thousand channels at one
time and thousands of users. Some people think it is the greatest
thing since sliced bread, and they're not all adolescent hackers. At
least give it an open-minded try to see if it is something for you.

Internet Shell Account Transcript

As with the BBS section, giving some examples will make all of
this a little less abstract and to show you what it looks like to use
Internet applications. While this is mostly from a capture from a
session with a shell account from an Internet service provider,
many of the same commands work identically with an Amiga that
is connected to the Internet using AS225 or AmiTCP. Just as when
logging in to a BBS, I use a terminal emulator to dial in to the service provider with a modem. Once I've connected and entered my
username and password, I get a Unix command prompt. Some

service providers offer a menuing system with common commands and an option to escape to the shell command prompt.

Here I'm going to send a quick mail message to myself. Generally, it is more useful to send mail to someone else.

```
$ mail dale@iam.com
This is just a note to show my readers how simple sending email
can be!
.
$
```

If I want to check on the status of a host, I can use the 'ping' command to see if it is reachable. Following is a little reassurance (at least for now!)...

```
$ping commodore.com
commodore.com is alive!
$
```

Here, I decide to check in on Billy Idol. Did you know he has used several Amigas with Toasters for video effects he uses on monitors during his live performances? It's been a while since I've sent email to him, and I wonder if his finger information says anything about what's up with him recently...

```
$ finger idol@well.sf.ca.us
[well.sf.ca.us]
The following includes information on only those WELL users who have
specifically chosen to make information about themselves publicly
available. For help contact <support@well.sf.ca.us>.

Login: idol                          Name: William Broad
Directory: /home/i/d/idol            Shell: /usr/local/shell/gone
Last login Sun Jul 24 09:14 (PDT) on pts/13 from well.sf.ca.us
Plan:
Mail Address: idol                   Registered: Wed Mar 31 16:24:17 1993
Computers:  PC Clone
Terminal: vt102


Dear Net Surfers:

I'm very sorry if you are in receipt of an automated message from my Well
account, but after almost one year of answering my mail, I've found the task
to be overwhelming. Right now, as I am writing this, my mailbox has over
4000 messages and there is no way I can personally answer all of them without
spending all of my days at the computer.

So, I'm signing off of this account. If you are truly creative, you may be
able to figure out my other account. If not, stay tuned, I am trying to set
up a way to reach all of you in a more general way.

Keep rockin'

lyl libido a.k.a. Billy Idol

April, 1994

$
```

Oops. Well, I guess I won't be sending him email again soon, though I could probably find him if I tried hard. On the other hand, if all I wanted were more general information about him, I might start by nosing around at mtv.com.

Now I'm going to use the local Gopher. The menus are screen-oriented and use the cursor keys to move between selections, but I'll have to just show you snapshots. The first thing I do is use the Gopher to get a local weather forcast...

```
$gopher
Press ?for Help, q to Quit
Receiving Directory...
Connecting...
Retrieving Directory...
Internet Gopher Information Client 2.0 pl11

Root gopher server: gopher.voicenet.com

1. About this server -- look here often/
2. About Voicenet/
3. Computers/
4. Gophers the world over/
5. Government information/
6. Leisure activities/
7. Philadelphia and the Delaware Valley/
8. Programmer's corner/
9. Reference Desk/
10. Wide-area networks (BITNET, Internet, USENET, ...)/
11. Search all menus in Voicenet's server/Press ?for Help, qto QuitPage: 1/1

>1

Philadelphia and the Delaware Valley

1. BBSes in the Phildelphia area, Apr '94
2. Cultural happenings in the Delaware Valley/
3. Events in the Philadelphia area/
4. Gophers in the Philadelphia area (TJU)/
5. Map of Philadelphia <Picture>
6. Music in the Delaware Valley/
7. Sports in the Delaware Valley/
8. Statistics for the Philadelphia area (UPenn)/
9. Transportation alternatives for the Philadelphia area/
10. Weather forecast for the Philadelphia area (TJU)Press ?for Help, qto Quit, uto go up a
menuPage: 1/1

>10

Philadelphia-area weather:

Weather Conditions at 4 AM EDT on 9 AUG 94 for Philadelphia, PA.
Temp(F)   Humidity(%)   Wind(mph)    Pressure(in)    Weather
========================================================================
     6480%SW at 530.13N/A

PHILADELPHIA-
400 AM EDT TUE AUG 9 1994

  TODAY...MOSTLY SUNNY. HIGH IN THE MID 80S. SOUTHWEST WIND 10 MPH.
  TONIGHT AND WEDNESDAY...PARTLY CLOUDY. LOW TONIGHT IN THE MID 60S WITH
A LIGHT WIND. HIGH WEDNESDAY IN THE MID 80S.

  EXTENDED FORECAST...
  THURSDAY...FAIR. LOWS IN THE MID 50S TO MID 60S. HIGHS IN THE
MID 70S TO LOW 80S.
  FRIDAY...PARTLY CLOUDY. LOWS IN THE MID 50S TO MID 60S. HIGHS IN THE
MID 70S TO MID 80S.
  SATURDAY...CHANCE OF SHOWERS OR THUNDERSTORMS. LOWS IN THE UPPER 50S TO    57% 100%

MID 60S. HIGHS IN THE UPPER 70S TO MID 80S.
```

```
THE SIX TO TEN DAY OUTLOOK FOR SUN AUG 14 THROUGH THU AUG 18 CALLS FOR

TEMPERATURES TO AVERAGE NEAR NORMAL NORTH AND ABOVE NORMAL SOUTH WITH
NEAR NORMAL PRECIPITATION. NORMAL HIGHS ARE 75 TO 85. NORMAL LOWS ARE
IN THE 50S AND 60S. NORMAL PRECIPITATION IS 5 TO 7 TENTHS OF AN INCH.

JWH


The National Weather Service information is provided by the University of
Michigan Weather Underground project and the National Science Foundation-funded
Unidata project, from a data feed broadcast by Alden/Zephyr Electronics, Inc.
```

Now that I've gotten my weather report, I might browse around. I'll go back to the main menu for this Gopher, then I'll show you a few menus to give you some idea of the breadth and depth of information available through Gopher. The first is some of the references available.

```
Reference Desk

1.  Assorted historical documents (Univ of Minnesota)/
2.  Copyright info (Library of Congress)/
3.  Dictionaries/
4.  Fact books/
5.  Patent database for 1994 (Town Hall)/
6.  Periodic Table of Elements (Univ of Minnesota)/
7.  Phone books at various institutions (GDB)/
8.  Sacred texts (NCSU)/
9.  Thesauruses/
10. US Census, 1990 (Univ of Michigan)/
11. US Census summaries, 1990 (Univ of Michigan)/
12. US geographic names (Rice)/
13. US postal code abbreviations (Univ of Oregon)
14. US State Dept travel advisories (St Olaf)/
15. US zip codes (Univ of Oregon) <?>
16. Weights & Measures (Univ of Oregon)
17. World telephone area codes (Univ of Oregon)/
```

You can even use Gopher to find other Gopher holes (and to connect to them). Here, I'll go back to the main menu, then look for some of the Gophers which have the arts as their subject matter.

```
Gophers the world over

1.  All gophers (UMinn)/
2.  Gophers by location/
3.  Gophers by subject/
4.  Gopher Jewels (Univ of Southern California)/
5.  Interesting gophers/
6.  New gophers (Washington & Lee)/
7.  Search for gophers by name (WLU) <?>Press ?for Help, qto Quit, uto go up a menuPage: 1/1

>4

Gopher Jewels (Univ of Southern California)

1.  GOPHER JEWELS Information and Help/
2.  Community, Global and Environmental/
3.  Education, Arts & Humanities, Social Sciences/
4.  Economics, Business and Store Fronts/
5.  Engineering and Industrial Applications/
6.  Government/
7.  Health, Medical, and Disability/
8.  Internet and Computer Related Resources/
9.  Law/
10. Library, Reference, and News/
11. Miscellaneous Items/
```

```
12. Personal Development and Recreation/
13. Physical Sciences including Mathematics/
14. Research, Technology Transfer and Grants Opportunities/
15. Search Gopher Jewels Menus by Key Word(s) <?>

>3

1. Anthropology and Archaeology/
2. Arts and Humanities/
3. Education (Includes K-12)/
4. History/
5. Language/
6. Religion and Philosophy/
7. Social Science/
8.  Jump To Gopher Jewels Main Menu/
9. Search Gopher Jewels Menus by Key Word(s) <?>Press ?for Help, qto Quit, uto go up a men-
uPage: 1/1

>2

Arts and Humanities

1. AMANDA gopher server at U-Wisconsin Madison, USA (Art)/
2. Arts & Humanities Resources - Michigan Dept. of Education/
3. Center for Safety in the Arts/
4. Dallas Museum of Art - Via Univ. of N. Texas Gopher/
5. Dartmouth College (Arts and Leisure)/
6. Ejournal - New Republic, The (Magazine)/
7. Ejournal - Yellow Silk, Journal of Erotica (Magazine)/
8. Entertainment & Technology Center - USCgopher/
9. Go M-Link (Music)/
10. Gothenburg University, Faculty of Arts, (SE)/
11. HELLENIC CIVILIZATION - Ariadne Network Gopher/
12. Indiana Univ, School of Music & Music Library Gopher/
13. Institute for Advanced Technology in the Humanities/
14. Internet Wiretap (Music)/
15. Library of Congress (LC MARVEL) (Arts)/
16. Lute Files - Dartmouth College/
17. Master Gopher Server @ Univ. of Minnesota (Music)/
18. Michigan State University (Vincent Voice Library)/
19. Minneapolis College of Art & Design (MCAD)/
20. North Carolina State University Library gopher (Arts)/
21. Norwegian Computing Center for the Humanities, (NO)/
22. RiceInfo (Rice University CWIS) (Music)/
23. Society for Music Theory - Harvard University/
24. Texas A&M (Fine Arts)/
25. Texas A&M (Music)/
26. The Well (Art, Music, Film, Cultural works, etc)/
27. U. of California - Santa Cruz, InfoSlug System (Arts & Humanities)/
28. U. of California-Santa Barbara, Humanities Computing Facility Goph../
29. U. of Manchester UK (Actors/actresses/directors etc. database) <?>
30. Univ of Texas at San Antonio (Music)/
31. University of California - Santa Barbara Library (Music)/
32. University of Michigan Libraries (Arts & Music)/
33. University of Michigan Libraries (Humanities)/
34. University of Nevada (Humanities)/
35. University of Utah Music Gopher/
36. University of Wisconsin - Parkside (Music)/
37. Washington & Lee University (Humanities)/
38. Jump To Gopher Jewels Main Menu/
39. Jump Up A Menu/
40. Search Gopher Jewels Menus by Key Word(s) <?>Press ?for Help, qto Quit, uto go up a
menuPage: 3/3Internet Gopher Information Client 2.0 p111
```

That's enough Gopher. You really have to play with it to fully understand how cool it is.

If someone told me that the game AutoMobiles was really cool and that I could "download" it from AmiNet, here is what I'd do. If I didn't the directory it was located in, I could grab the INDEX file in the AmiNet root directory, or I could use Archie. In this case, I know the directory. I'm connecting direct from my Amiga, but it would be the exact same under Unix (except that the prompt might be '$' instead of '10.DEC:>').

Note that, since I have a .netrc set up with a default username of "anonymous" and password of "dale@iam.com," FTP automatically logged me in. Otherwise, I would have been prompted for a user-name and password, and I would have had to type them in myself.

```
10.DEC:> ftp ftp.wustl.edu
Connected to wuarchive.wustl.edu.
220 wuarchive.wustl.edu FTP server (Version wu-2.4(1) Mon Jul 18 11:53:55 CDT 1994) ready.
331 Guest login ok, send your complete e-mail address as password.
230- If your FTP client crashes or hangs shortly after login please try
230- using a dash (-) as the first character of your password. This will
230- turn off the informational messages that may be confusing your FTP
230- client.
230-
230- This system may be used 24 hours a day, 7 days a week. The local
230- time is Tue Aug  9 05:26:54 1994.
230-
230- You are user number 100 out of a possible 100.
230-
230- All transfers to and from wuarchive are logged. If you don't like
230- this then disconnect now!
230-
230- Wuarchive is currently a DEC Alpha AXP 3000, Model 400. Thanks to
230- Digital Equipment Corporation for their generous support of wuarchive.
230-
230-Please read the file README
230-  it was last modified on Mon May 17 15:02:13 1993 - 449 days ago
230-Please read the file README.NFS
230-  it was last modified on Tue Jun 29 12:12:27 1993 - 406 days ago
230 Guest login ok, access restrictions apply.
ftp> cd /pub/aminet/game/2play
250-game/2play - 2 and more player games
250-
250 CWD command successful.
ftp> bin
200 Type set to I.
ftp> get automobiles.lha
200 PORT command successful.
150 Opening BINARY mode data connection for automobiles.lha (343214 bytes).
226 Transfer complete.
343214 bytes received in 215.14 seconds (1.56 Kbytes/s)
ftp> quit
221 Goodbye.
10.DEC:>
```

Since I was only connected at 14.4kbps in this case, and since the file was large, it took a few minutes for me to get. The "bin" com-mand, by the way, is an important detail to remember for all non-text files. It puts FTP into binary ('I' or image) mode so that no translation is done on your files.

Now, if I wanted to locate freely redistributable files, I might use Archie. By searching for files named 'Envoy' I find several directo-ries which contain files for use with Envoy.

```
$ archie envoy

Host ftp.edvz.uni-linz.ac.at
```

```
     Location: /pub/amiga/aminet/comm
        DIRECTORY drwxr-xr-x        512  Apr 11 04:07   envoy
     Location: /pub/amiga/aminet/info/goph/comm
        DIRECTORY drwxr-xr-x        512  Jan 19 06:00   envoy
     Location: /pub/amiga/netz/AmiTCP
        DIRECTORY drwxrwxrwx        512  Jun 23 07:30   envoy

Host plaza.aarnet.edu.au

     Location: /micros/amiga/aminet/comm
        DIRECTORY drwxrwxr-x       1024  May 27 10:34   envoy

Host ftp.cs.ubc.ca

     Location: /pub/local/cdnnet
        DIRECTORY drwxrwxr-x        512  Jan  3 1991   envoy

Host litamiga.epfl.ch

     Location: /pub/amiga/aminet/comm
        DIRECTORY drwxr-xr-x       4096  Apr 12 13:29   envoy

Host freebsd.cdrom.com

     Location: /pub/aminet/comm
        DIRECTORY drwxrwxr-x       1024  Jun 11 16:04   envoy

Host faui43.informatik.uni-erlangen.de

     Location: /mounts/epix/public/pub/amiga/aminet/comm
        DIRECTORY drwxr-xr-x       1024  Jun 11 19:06   envoy
     Location: /mounts/epix/public/pub/amiga/aminet/info/goph/comm
        DIRECTORY drwxr-xr-x        512  Jan  6 01:16   envoy

Host ftp.uni-kl.de

     Location: /pub3/amiga/aminet/comm
        DIRECTORY drwxrwxr-x        512  Jun 24 15:01   envoy
```

Mosaic

The joy of Internet is Mosaic. You thought AmigaGuide was neat? What if clicking a button could send you to a document stored on another computer? That is Mosaic. To use Mosaic on the Internet, you must have a direct connection, not a shell account. There are, however, text-based WWW browsers like Lynx which may do the same thing for you, if with less style.

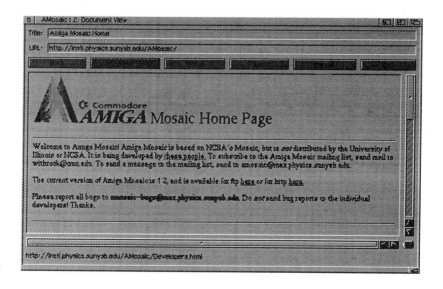

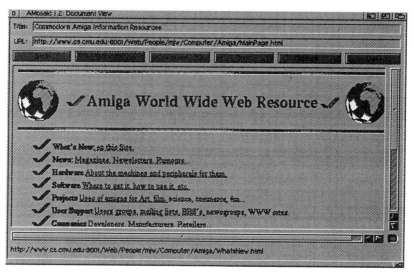

Protocols

Everything we discussed in regards to LAN protocol software applies to internet protocol software. Internet protocol software just has to do a little more work in order to allow packets to seamlessly flow from one physical network to another, as needed. TCP/IP was designed for internetworking, and is again the protocol we'll be using as an example.

We've mentioned IP before. It is the lowest level protocol in the

TCP/IP stack. In a LAN application, we've seen that it is responsible for addressing and for fragmentation and reassembly. In an internet, it is also responsible for routing. TCP and UDP and other higher-level protocols don't know the difference between whether they are running on a LAN or an internet -- IP takes care of the details. Note, however, that TCP and UDP are designed to handle some of the problems unique to a global internet -- varying latency (delays on a local Ethernet are much lower than across several physical networks which may include low-speed serial links), out-of-order packets (changing network conditions may cause one packet to be routed differently than another, resulting in different delays along the way), lost packets (much more common on connections across the country than on those across a room), etc.

Routing

On a simple LAN, protocol software can assume that every packet sent is directed to a machine on the single physical network. Address resolution (ala ARP, for example) is all that is required to get a packet from point 'A' to point 'B.' Once you know the hardware address, you just send the packet out on your local net (the only one) with that address. On an Internet however, determining the path for a packet can be significantly more complicated.

Really, this is quite similar to routing in a UUCP network. There are two differences. First, with UUCP, the address (the bang path) is the route. The software doesn't have to do anything special to find the route. (Actually, this isn't entirely true. Smart UUCP software can do sophisticated routing based on maps of well-known UUCP hosts.) Second, UUCP hosts often have one modem which is used to connect to many hosts, while in an internet, some hosts (or other devices) must be connected to two networks simultaneously.

For two physical networks to be connected in an internet, there must be some hardware which connects the two. We'll discuss this hardware in more detail in the next section. To simplify our discussion for now, we can just assume that the hardware is a computer which is connected to both networks. If the two networks are both Ethernets, for example, the connecting computer would have two Ethernet cards, one connecting it to network 1 and the other connecting it to network 2.

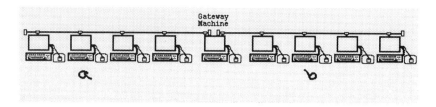

Every host running TCP/IP has a routing table. On a simple LAN, that routing table may contain only one entry -- that for the local network -- making all packets go onto the local network. On our small two Ethernet internet, each host (except the gateway) has a routing table entry for the gateway and a routing table entry for the local network. The gateway has a routing table entry for Ethernet 1 on one interface and Ethernet 2 on the other. By the way, the gateway is called a multi-homed host and has two IP addresses -- one on each network.

Because of the format of IP addresses (and something called a subnet mask), a host can tell from its own IP address whether another IP address belongs to the local network. Hence, each packet sent on our example network will go to the physical address of the destination host on the local net if it is local host. Otherwise, it will go the physical address of the gateway.

While hardware addresses are used at the lowest level, TCP/IP also uses network (IP) addresses. The IP destination address for each packet that comes in on the gateway is examined to determine its ultimate destination. If the ultimate destination is that host, it passes the packet up to the appropriate higher-level protocol. If the ultimate destination is the other network, it sends the packet back out on its other Ethernet interface, with the physical address now set to match the ultimate destination.

On a larger internetwork, packets may have to make several hops through gateways to reach their ultimate destination. Routing is greatly simplified by the format of IP addresses and by intelligent gateways. Most single-homed hosts have only two routing table entries -- the local net and a gateway for all non-local traffic. The gateway, in turn, only has to know how to get to any nets it is local to and to a "higher" gateway.

There are two types of routing tables -- static and dynamic. Static routing tables are set in a configuration file. For hosts on a simple LAN or an internet with only one local gateway, static routing is the way to go. For complex internetworks with multiple gateways, a routing protocol which dynamically creates routing tables may be desirable. Routing protocols are beyond the scope of this work.

Bridges, Gateways, Repeaters and Routers

We've already mentioned one use of the word "gateway." You'll hear that and several other related terms in any internetworking discussion. If you are just connecting a single computer to an internet, you won't need to be concerned with the distinctions. If you are creating your own internet, knowing the differences may be crucial. The fine details are beyond the scope of this work (and, in fact, change based on context), so take a look at the suggested reading list.

A repeater is a hardware device that copies electrical signals from one network to another. They are used to make a single physical network larger. If you have twenty machines which you want to be on a single physical network, but ten are in one building and ten in another, you have a problem if the buildings are too far apart for the physical limits of your networking hardware. A repeater might solve that problem.

A bridge is like a repeater, except that it is intelligent. It stores and forwards complete Ethernet packets rather than electrical signals. This lets it forward only packets which belong on the other net. Further, it doesn't amplify noise, so bridges are usually better (but much more expensive) solutions than repeaters.

A router is any device which makes decisions about which path network traffic takes. A bridge is a kind of router which makes decisions based on hardware addresses. A gateway is a kind of router which makes decisions based on IP addresses. Special purpose stand-alone routers are designed to efficiently handle high volumes of traffic. They usually are faster than using a computer as a gateway and let you keep using the computer for other work.

Addressing: Domains

While a simple table easily suffices for mapping host names to network addresses on a simple LAN, it is woefully inadequate for the global Internet. Further, keeping hundreds of thousands of names unique is no small task! The solution is to break up the name space for the Internet into hierarchical domains, in much the same way as hard drives are broken up into directories and subdirectories.

The domain name system on the Internet breaks up names into levels separated by dots. The address for one of the author's machines is calvin.iam.com. "Calvin" is the host name and iam.com is the domain. There are several other calvins in other domains, but each is unique within its domain, and so is uniquely identified by a fully-qualified domain name. "iam" is the domain for Intangible Assets Manufacturing, within the "com" top-level domain. All the machines at IAM are within the "iam" domain. There might be an "iam" within another top-level domain, but each is uniquely identified within it's fully-qualified domain name. This is analogous to how files are uniquely identified when their full pathname is used.

Top level domains on the Internet include .com (commercial companies), .edu (educational institutions, usually universities), .gov (government), .org (usually not-for-profit organizations), .net (networks), .mil (military), and national (.us, .uk, .de, etc.). The first six domains are mostly used by those based in the USA, while computers in other countries usually have their country code as their top-level domain. There is a .us domain which is coming into wider use. The geographic domains tend to be split to a locality (i.e., state) and city. Geographic domains do have the disadvantage of appearing to limit networks which may span a much wider area. While IAM's network (and hence the iam.com domain) is physically contained within a single building, the networks of many international corporations are not -- they may connect machines in many countries.

For each domain, there is a naming authority (in the form of a person or organization). This authority serves two functions. First, it allocates the names of new domains immediately under it. The naming authority for .com, for example, is the only source of new domains X which will be X.com. Second, it has computers running a protocol called Domain Name Service (DNS) which give the network addresses of the computer responsible for a given domain under it. So, for example, there are .com DNS servers which are consulted whenever someone needs to know the network address of a machine responsible for any domain ending in .com. Because domain names are hierarchical, several servers may be consulted to resolve a single network host name. The lowest level server knows the addresses not of a another server, but of each host in it's domain. Here is an example. DNS servers for the domain .com know the address of the DNS server for the iam.com domain. That server knows the addresses of hosts within that domain. If IAM choose to, it could have multiple domains under iam.com. It might have research.iam.com and marketing.iam.com, for example. If it did, each of those domains would have a DNS server known to the iam.com DNS server.

DNS, by the way, also allows for various other information about domains and hosts to be stored and shared. One of the most common of these features is MX forwarding. With MX forwarding, some Internet host acts as the forwarding agent for mail addressed to anywhere within an entire domain. This allows domains which aren't connected to the Internet directly (or not full-time) to receive domain addressed mail.

SLIP, CSLIP and PPP

TCP/IP was originally designed for networking hardware. Using it over a simple serial port was not a real possibility. As the Internet has grown and high-speed modems have become available, running TCP/IP over a standard serial line became desirable.

If you have a computer which isn't in a large business, government or university setting which you want to connect to the Internet, you'll almost certainly use SLIP, CSLIP or PPP. (Of course, you might choose to use a terminal program to access a shell account rather than actually joining the Internet).

SLIP (Serial Line Internet Protocol) is a specification for the simplest way to do this. SLIP has never been formalized into a standard, but almost all implementations are compatible because it is so simple. CSLIP (Compressed SLIP) adds a twist by removing a little extra information from most IP packets. CSLIP is probably used more often than true SLIP, and CSLIP is often (incorrectly) refered to as just SLIP. It too, is not a formal standard. Both have several shortcomings (which is why they won't become standards) which are beyond the scope of this work. Their one plus is their simplicity.

PPP (Point-to-Point Protocol) is the new standard for serial connections. It is a much more complex protocol (that's its one shortcoming). It has provisions for checksums, multiple protocol stacks, dynamic IP addressing and mapping of control characters (for XON/XOFF handshaking, for example).

Many service providers allow you to use any of the three protocols, some require that you use PPP. If you have a choice, you should probably use PPP.

Part II. Amiga Telecomm

In this section, we examine the software, products and packages available for various aspects of telecommunications using the Amiga. Terminal emulators, utilities, voice mail, fax, remote login and various other subjects are covered. Where available, current pricing and other information are provided. Contact information for many vendors is provided in an appendix. In addition to purely factual information, I've included subjective information about some of the software. Take this with a grain of salt -- you might like something I don't.

Besides the author's own experience, information is provided from manufacturer's advertising, spec sheets or answers to questions. As well, some information was culled from the comp.sys.amiga.datacomm Amiga Networking FAQ (FAQs are explained later), author's descriptions of freely redistributable files and from various other sources.

Where version numbers are given, the most current version at the time of publication is given. Much freely redistributable software is updated frequently, so try to find the latest version, but in no event (if you can avoid it) a version earlier than the one given.

Terminal Emulators

There are many freely redistributable and commercial terminal emulators for the Amiga. This is one area where the shareware is often better than the commercial offerings. Those who have been online for a few months usually develop strong preferences about what they like (and don't) in their terminal software. There are so many features used in so many different ways to do various things, that no one program is likely to suit everyone. A set of features that I might never use might be critical to you, or vice-versa. You should examine at least the four shareware programs below for yourself, perhaps giving one or two another look after you've used one for a while.

While the commercial offerings I've tried haven't suited me personally, this may be about to change. Oregon Research is expected to release a new terminal emulator soon. Since I haven't been able to use it or see it, I don't know whether I'll like it, but maybe you should have a look. Other commercial offerings which I haven't tried include ATalk-III and GP-Term.

VLT
Freeware, Willy Langeveld

The Valiant Little Terminal is widely used by those who love ARexx. It was developed at SLAC (the Stanford Linear Accelerator Center) for internal use, but has been publically released. The flexibility of its ARexx interface makes it very suitable for constructing front ends to online services, and just such a beast exists for BIX.

NComm
Shareware, US$40, Daniel Bloch and Torkel Lodberg

I've probably used NComm on and off for about five years. I've tried most others, but, so far, I've always come back to NComm. The current version is 3.02.

The shareware version of NComm has some save features disabled, but it is mostly functional. When you register, you may receive a new disk or just a key file which enables all features (if you already have the latest version, the key file can be emailed to you in order to save the time of a disk traveling through the snail mail). This registered version is personalized for you and may not be distributed.

Term
Giftware, Olaf Barthel v4.0

This is a very popular terminal program. A new major revision of

Term was released recently, and the various files of its distribution made up most of the top ten downloads from AmiNet for two weeks in a row.

Terminus
Shareware, $40 Jack Radigan

Perhaps the most popular shareware terminal for the Amiga.

Utilities and Other Miscellaneous Files
File Compression
To effectively deal with freely redistributable files, you'll need to have programs to compress and decompress them. Using compression saves time and money by making uploads and downloads happen faster. Compression can also save valuable space used in the storage of files.

There is something of a bootstrapping problem with file compression utilities. If you have an archived terminal emulator but not the program to decompress it, how do you get online to download the decompression utility? The answer is to start out with files obtained through some other means. The Fred Fish disks have all of the popular decompression utilities and many terminal programs. If you ask a friend with an Amiga and a modem, she'll likely be happy to give you a disk with her favorite term and utilities.

LhA
Shareware, US$20 Stefan Boberg

If you're lucky, you can almost get by with LhA as your only file compression/decompression utility. It understands several formats, and is the most popular such utility on the Amiga.

ZOO
Freely Redistributable J. Brian Waters and Rahul Dhesi

Zoo has mostly been superceded on the Amiga by LhA, but it is a pretty reasonable format and you will still find many older files compressed with it.

ARC
It stands for ARChive, and it has been around almost as long as modems. A number of versions exist for the Amiga should you

need one.

RUN

A few utilities create self-extracting archives. If you don't recognize the extension, or if it is something like ".run," try running the file as an executable. See the section on Viruses first.

UUencode

To distribute binary files over ASCII media (like email), it is necessary to convert the binary files. Once standard way of doing this is Unix's uuencode/uudecode. Several ports of these standard programs exist for the Amiga. They are often difficult to use because of the odd syntax of the original program. Another Unix program (shar) exists to join files into one without compressing them. To compress files under Unix, compress creates files with the .Z extention.

For sending Amiga files over mail, the standard operating procedure is to use LhA for joining and compressing files into a single archive, then uuencoding the archive. If it is an option for you, using a MIME mailer which supports sending binary files is easier (see the Internet section).

Scripts

There are several ARexx and other scripts which work with various terminal emulators and other software to perform various functions. Among them are things like estimating your phone bill from a log of your calls, logging into a specific type of bulletin board and performing certain functions (like downloading a QWK packet or uploading a reply packet), etc.

Often when someone needs to write a script such as this, they realize that other people can use it, too. Once they've written the script, they document it, create an archive, and make it publicly available. So while scripts aren't usually stand-alone software, they are useful files to download.

XPR

XPR isn't a utility onto itself. It is a standard for plug-in transfer protocols. A terminal emulator on the Amiga can use XPR calls to access external transfer protocols rather than embedding them. This is a very good thing. It reduces the size and complexity of the terminal emulators, and it allows for work done on an XPR implementation to be taken advantage of by many more people than if it was done on an implementation in a particular terminal emulator. Hence, the XPR protocols tend to be good implementations. It also means that more protocols are available and that new ones can be added easily.

The way it works is this. External protocols are placed into libs:. libs:xprzmodem.library, for example is the XPR Z-Modem implementation. Then, if you use a terminal emulator or other software designed to use XPR, that shared library is loaded and used when you make file transfers.

Many distributions of terminal emulators will come with basic XPR libraries. If you need one you don't have, look on BBSs and at other sources for freely redistributable software. It's probably out there somewhere.

Offline Readers

It is easy to save time and money by collecting all your messages in one compressed file which you download and read locally. The savings are greater if you call long distance or if you call several BBSs. There are many OLRs available to the Amiga. Here are just two of the many freely redistributable ones.

AmiQWK

Shareware, US$15 Jim Dawson

QWKMail is an offline message format. Using QWKMail allows you to call a BBS, collect all waiting messages, transfer them to your computer, and read them after you have logged off of the BBS. You can then read them with a QWK compatible message reader such as `AmiQWK`. New messages can be edited with your favorite text editor. Some of the advantages of using QWKMail include: collecting all waiting messages into a QWKMail packet usually takes only a fraction of the time it takes to read messages online, resulting in lower phone bills; since your replies are edited offline, you can take as much time as you need to enter and reply to messages; you have the advantage of using tools that may not be available when using BBS editors, such as spelling and grammar checkers; you can easily save or print messages for future reference.

The QWK format was created in 1987 by Mark 'Sparky' Herring. It is based on Clark Development Corp.'s `PC-Board` Version 12.0 BBS message base format. The QWKMail format is now supported by most BBS programs either internally or by an external 'door' program.

`AmiQWK II' is a full featured QWKMail offline message reader for the Commodore Amiga computer. Goals for `AmiQWK' are (in no particular order) takes advantage of features found in Release 2 and higher of AmigaOS, is easy to use and highly configurable.

THOR

The Ultima Thule Offline Reader System 1.22
Shareware $40

THOR is an advanced offline reader system developed for saving online time while connected to BBS systems, for building and maintaining a database of the messages from the boards, and for supporting a wide range of terminal programs and BBS systems (and simple implementation of new systems). Includes support for QWK, HIPPO, ABBS and MBBS.

Fax, Voice and OCR

There are several products for faxing to and from your Amiga, and even some to let you use your Amiga as a voice mail system. As well, if you've been using your Amiga to receive faxes, you may want to convert a fax to ASCII with Optical Character Recognition.

GPFax

v2.346, GPSoft, about US$70

GPFax is the most well-established software of the lot. It has undergone continuous revision since 1991, making it a powerful, flexible and reliable package. The latest version works with just about any Class 1 or Class 2 fax modem, and can take advantage of most special features. If you want to take advantage the "Silent Answer" feature of Supra modems, or to use a Class 1 modem, GPFax is your only choice. It used to be distributed in several different versions for different types of modems (including a Supra-specific version), but it now comes as a single disk and uses Installer to install the correct options for your modem.

The user interface is a single program with a point-and-click interface, much like the old version of Art Department Professional. The non-standard nature of the interface bothered me with AdPro, but for some reason, it doesn't with GPFax. It is simple and easy to use, and everything a single mouse-click away. GPFax also has extensive ARexx support.

My one complaint with GPFax is that it uses A4 paper as its standard size. A4 is longer than 8.5x11. Therefore, when GPFax is used to send text output as a fax, the receiving fax may alternate full and very short pages. The way around this is to always use GPFax's printer device and to print from another application in order to send a fax.

Excellent technical support is available directly from the programmers at GPSoft -- phone, fax, email, UseNet. Some support is available from Supra, at least for copies purchased from them or bundled with their modems.

TrapFax
VillageTronic v1.0 (in the US: Expert Services) about $100

Released last Fall, this new-comer is sure to start a healthy rivalry with GPFax. While it doesn't have all of the little features and polish from GPFax's long history, it does have most of the same major features. TrapFax does not have ARexx support, nor does it support Class 1 modems. Manual faxing also seems to be missing from TrapFax. Like GPFax, though, it does allow faxes to be scheduled for sending at a later time, printer capture for faxing from other applications, log files and good support for flexible viewing of faxes on screen.

TrapFax's user-interface is based on a Workbench drawer containing several programs. Each program handles a different task, like viewing faxes, or setting up to receive incoming faxes. I found this interface more difficult to use, but I saw several clear advantages for some advanced applications. For example, handling faxes on a network of Amigas looks much easier with TrapFax than with any other Amiga software.

In addition to a few minor features I wished for, I found a few minor bugs. Hopefully, future versions of TrapFax will expand on the good start they've made with 1.0.

Expert Services provides courteous telephone, mail and fax support in the US, and a mail address is provided for the software's authors in Germany.

AmigaFax
Shareware, $50, C-Born

This shareware package has many of the same major features as the other two commercial programs. Its documentation does not indicate that it supports Class 1 modems, so presumably it only supports Class 2. It has special support for TeX, however, making it especially well-suited for some programmers.

Unlike the other two commercial Amiga fax packages, this one does not use the standard IFF FAXX form for its data files. Also unfortunate is the lack of a 2.0-style user-interface.

For those on a budget or using TeX, AmigaFax might be a good alternative.

El Cheapo Fax
Freely Redistributable

Just like the name says. The bare minimum to send and receive faxes with your Amiga and a Class 2 fax modem. Nothing is automatic. No phone book, no scheduling, nothing. You can use a special preferences printer driver to create fax files as output from other applications, but you must then send that file on your own. You cannot directly view faxes, but must convert them to IFF for display.

The interface is CLI-only, but there is a shareware add-on package called ECFax Enhancer which provides a GUI. The English documentation for ECFax Enhancer is difficult to read, though I'm sure the French is much better.

If you're only going to send a couple of faxes during the decade, or your budget has you choosing between dinner and software, you might get by with El Cheapo Fax. Otherwise, the luxuries afforded by the commercial programs are well-worth the price.

GVP PhonePak
street price $300

The PhonePak is a Zorro-II voice mail and fax solution, but does not include a data modem. It is only compatible with its own (included) software. I haven't had the opportunity to play with one.

MicroBotics Modem 19

This fast internal (Zorro-II) fax/data modem was advertised for a few months by some mail-order houses. Unfortunately, it was canceled before it came to market. Incidentally, MicroBotics is now Paravision, Inc. (500 E. Arapaho, Suite 104, Richardson, TX 75081, +1 214 644 0043, microbotics1@bix.com).

Black Belt Systems ClickFax

This Amiga fax/data modem (9600bps fax, 2400bps data) with Amiga software is no longer on the market. Since the modem used a custom interface (from before even Class I was standardized), it requires Black Belt's software. Anyone with a 1.0 release version of the software should contact Black Belt, as considerable improvements to the software were made before the product was taken off the market.

Teledisk Systems FaxPak

street price $249

While not an Amiga-specific solution, this is a valuable yet little-known piece of hardware. It turns your computer's printer into a plain paper fax (receive only). It has a small, attractive case which houses fax receiving hardware, phone in and out, parallel in and out and serial in and out. It also functions as a printer switch (you can hook one computer to the serial in, one to the parallel in and they both print to the printer connected to the parallel or serial out). It stores up to 40 pages of faxes received while the printer is off or offline (i.e., out of paper). The interface is a bit trying (you must call the box from a touch-tone phone to program it), but most people just need to set it once and then forget it, so that is tolerable. If you want printouts of all your incoming faxes, and you've decided that your computer is the best way to send faxes, the FaxPak is a great way to receive faxes.

avmNfax

v1.33, Shareware, $20-$50, Al Villarica (rvillari@cat.syr.edu)
Use your ZyXEL, LineLink, Dolphin or Rockwell based voice modem (Supras are not yet supported) for voicemail or as a simple answering machine with fax capabilities. This version includes EFax, which handles Calls 1 and Class 2 modems. This fax capability can be used even if you don't have a voice-capable modem (e.g., Supra LC). Of course, if you do have a voice capable modem, then you get faxing and voicemail capabilities. You can use GPFax or TrapFax with avmNfax in lieu of EFax.

OCR: What to do with Fax

The main reason that email is better than fax is because email contains structured data -- it could be ASCII text or IFF pictures. Faxes are always images. Text is better than a picture of text. If someone can't send you email but can send you a fax, and you need ASCII text, there is a solution. No, I'm not talking about a secretary, I mean OCR.

OCR stands for Optical Character Recognition. OCR software attempts to convert bit mapped images of typed text into ASCII text. At best, it gets 99% of the characters right. At worst, it's a lot worse. It is most successful when images are: high-resolution (200dpi or better), clean (no extra marks), monospace fonts (like courier). Hence, computer faxes sent in fine mode work best.

None of the Amiga fax software packages include OCR at this time. Migraph has two OCR software packages for the Amiga -- Migraph OCR and Migraph OCR Jr. The Jr. version only works with hand scanners, but the Sr. version handles IFF files which you could output from your fax software. Migraph's standard package goes for around US$150 (unfortunately, that is more than some PC fax packages that include good OCR).

Special Applications

For most online services, someone has written a special OLR (OffLine Reader). CIS and Portal have well-publicized and well-supported ones. BIX has a few half-way solutions floating around, but not a well-supported one. There are probably Amiga OLRs for other services that I am not aware of because I don't use those services. The Amiga file areas on each service is where you can find these programs

AutoPilot

Shareware, $69.95, Steve Ahlstrom (AForums Ltd.)

This is the way to use CompuServe (CIS) from an Amiga, if your Amiga is up to the task (requires 1MB chip, 2MB fast and 5MB HD). AutoPilot is an OLR for CIS written by the WizOp of CIS's AmigaUser forum. It not only makes downloading files and reading mail and forums easier, it saves you money by keeping you online less. A description of AutoPilot, and the program itself, are available for download in CompuServe's AmigaVendor forum in the AutoPilot section. It is shareware, and you pay for it by registering online.

I've been a regular user of CIS for a while, and CIS is a pretty good service, but I probably wouldn't use CIS at all if it weren't for Auto-Pilot. Highly recommended.

PortalX

I'm not on Portal, so I don't know about PortalX -- other than that Steve Tibbett wrote it, and he writes some good stuff, so if you are on Portal, you should definitely have a look. Portal's blurb on it reads:

"Our exclusive PortalX by Steve Tibbett, the graphical "front end" for Portal which will let you automatically click'n'download your waiting email, messages, Usenet groups and binary files! Reply to mail and messages offline using your favorite editor and your replies are sent automatically the next time you log into Portal. (PortalX requires Workbench 2.04 or higher)"

BBS

If you want to run a serious public access BBS, there is a lot to learn. Among other things, there is a lot of software you'll have to evaluate in order to choose the system you want to use. That is beyond the scope of this book. Many people find that they'd like to be able to access a few files on their computer from a remote location sometimes, or would like their friends to be able to. If you are interested in such a limited system, here are a couple of options to consider.

Scripts

Earlier we mentioned the extensive scripting abilities of some terminal emulator programs. Some are so extensive that whole BBSs can be written as a script. The standard NComm distribution, for example, comes complete with a BBS host script.

AuxCLI

If you could access an Amiga shell in a terminal program from a remote location, you could use the computer just as if you were there, right? Well, not really. You could use the program c:eval, for example, which prints on the screen the result of some operation you give it (like 2+2). You can't, however, use sys:tools/calculator. If you tried, a calculator window would open on the Amiga you were dialed in to, but you wouldn't be able to see it, nor would you be able to close it. Remember, your terminal program can display text and can send text. It doesn't know about windows, and it doesn't know about mice.

Still, sometimes it is useful to be able to do things from a remote shell. The device AUX: (in the standard mountlist or sys:storage/ dosdrivers) goes a long way toward giving you this. Several freely redistributable files include utilities and explanations for using of AUX: as a simple sort of BBS.

Games

Computer games are great. Playing with yourself can be satisfying, but it is usually more fun to play with someone else. Modems and networks make playing with someone else much more convenient -- you don't have to be geographically co-located in order to play. You might not even have to play at the same time. In a game like chess, you might log in and make a move, hoping that your opponent will have a chance to do the same before you log in again the next day (or the next week, or whatever).

The games available as part of a BBS or online service are really beyond the scope of this book. As soon as you start calling the BBSs, you'll find out about the games and how to use them.

ASCII chess boards are not the ultimate in high-tech. Two Amigas, connected with modems (or null-modems), can play some really wonderful games in real-time with GUI interfaces. Here are just a few of the great commercial games out there capable of modem play.

Driving Games

Many racing games let you play against a second player, either with an aerial view or with a split screen. Extending this to work with two computers is a natural. If you're into racing games, Richard Daniel has this to say to you:

"Lotus Esprit Challenge 2. This is a car racing game, which when connected via the null (or modem) lets you play up to four players in one race (Split screens). This makes for a very entertaining game, especially if all players are evenly matched."

"The second is STUNT CAR RACER. This is another racer [racing game] in which you drive against another person (or computer with single computer) on a roller coaster type track. You can push each other off the highest points [roller derby with autos?] and such like. Not quite as good as Lotus but still very good via a link-up."

Flight Simulators

Dog fighting against a computer is boring. Dog fighting against an opponent with his own computer is a blast. Some of the programs you might try are: Falcon, Flight of the Intruder, and Mig 29 Super Fulcrum.

RoboSport

Most modem games are one-player games first, but have a two-player option. Some games were created for modem use, but aren't up to the same standard as many others. RoboSport is a great modem game, and was probably designed primarily for modem or network use.

In it, each of up to four players controls four armed robots. Simple mouse-clicks are used to program the robots to move or lay down fire over the course of the coming turn. When each player has finished programming his robots, the turn is resolved by the computer. The computer creates a movie to watch of the action which occurred during the turn. Various scenarios include steal-the-flag and baseball. The types of weapons used by the robots and many other parameters are all configureable.

If you have AS225r2, you can have four-player RoboSport. After seeing RoboSport on the Mac over AppleTalk, the author selfishly made very sure that the programmers for the port to the Amiga would have access to Amiga Ethernet cards and documentation for AS225r2. Unfortunately, AS225r2 didn't become available to those who weren't registered developers until well after RoboSport had peaked in the market.

Other

War games, board games and other strategy games are usually adaptable to multi-player setups over a modem. Some of the titles include: Global Effect, Global War, Hack 'n' Slash, Populous 2, Populous, Powermonger, Stormball, and Vroom.

Buying and Using Modems

Just as is the case with RAM and harddrive capacities or with processor speeds, modems have gotten simultaneously less expensive and more capable over the years. At one time, 300 baud was the best you could get, and it was deadly expensive. Later, 1200 baud modems were almost affordable, and things started to take off with the 2400 baud models. Finally, they'd gotten fast enough to be really usable, and the price had come to be less than that of a printer. 9600 bps and 14.4kbps came into widespread use a few years ago. Today, a 14.4kbps modem can be had for around US$100.

Another leap is here, though. 28.8kbps modems are now available. Some have been around for a year or so, but haven't followed a standard such that they are all compatible with each other. The pseudo-standards V.FC and V.Fast have confused many a consumer, but basically mean that you only get better than 14.4 when connecting to a similar modem. The v.34 standard ensures that any v.34 modem should be able to communicate on good lines at 28.8kbps with any other v.34 modem. When you buy a new high speed modem, be careful to make sure that it is really v.34 and not some other odd-ball "standard." These modems can be purchased at the low-end for well under $300, perhaps closer to $200.

Naturally, as prices continue to come down, the difference in price between 14.4 and 28.8 will narrow. Just as it makes no sense at all to "save" money (and waste time) by buying less than a 14.4 modem, in the near future, less than 28.8 will not have any economic justification.

In selecting a modem, there are many things to be aware of. There is more to it than just speed. Some modems work better with line noise or otherwise poor signals. Some modems have fax capabilities in Class 1 or 2. Some have voice capability. Some modems are easily upgradable. In fact, some modems can receive new programming through a special phone call! Other modems can be upgraded with a new ROM chip, while some are virtually impossible to upgrade. With all of the complexities of the new v.34 standard, the fax commands and the voice processing, bugs and glitches are bound to be found, with the possibilities for improvements through upgrades being an important consideration for some people.

If you know you aren't likely to use your modem to make long-distance calls, how well it handles poor line quality may not be important. If you are unlucky enough to have a long physical loop, however (basically, if the line to your house is borderline), you might have the same problems that others have only with long-distance lines. If you know you aren't likely to use fax or voice capabilities in a modem, those features won't be important to you, and the upgradability of the modem may be less important.

Basically, if your needs are likely to be minimal, you can probably save money by buying an inexpensive modem, perhaps even a 14.4. If you know that you might be seriously using your modem, paying the extra money for higher speed, higher quality, better upgradability, more reliability and more features is a good idea.

Voice Capability

Some modem brands which currently have voice models include Dolphin, LineLink and ZyXEL. More are sure to come later, so you'll have to check around. The modems with voice capability are often DSP-based, which means that the modem has a special processor (specifically, a Digital Signal Processor) running code out of some kind of ROM rather than having everything permanently etched in stone (silicon, to be specific). DSP-based modems are more easily upgraded than other types.

Parameters and Settings

With the first cars, you had to know a lot about how they worked to get them to go -- you needed to be a mechanic every few miles. With computer telecommunications, you used to have to know a lot of details. Today, you can often ignore those details. The defaults with most terminal emulation software, modems and BBSs work with each other as-is. To make things work best, though, you still need to know what the jargon is, what it means, when and how to change the settings. For those with the desire to know more, or for unusual situations, here is a jumping off point. This is really a section of hints and tips. For more details, see the recommended reading list.

XON/XOFF and RTS/CTS

These are terms for handshaking. Handshaking is how your computer lets your modem know that it needs a little time to catch its breath (or vice-versa). If handshaking isn't set up correctly on a high-speed connection, lost data may cause various errors and slower data transfer rates. Technically, handshaking is set both on the modem and the computer, but, in practice, you usually just tell your software what kind of handshaking to use. The software then configures the modem automatically. If your terminal program or other software doesn't do it, consult your modem's manual to find out how to do it yourself. RTS/CTS handshaking (hardware handshaking) is preferred (and sometimes necessary) for all high-speed connections. By the way, some old or cheap modem cables don't carry the RTS/CTS lines between the modem and computer, so if you have problems, make sure that you have what is known as a "hardware handshaking cable."

DTR

One of the lines on the serial connection between your modem and computer is DTR. It stands for Data Terminal Ready, but it means that, depending on how your computer is configured, it will hang up when your computer does not have the serial port active. By most defaults, running a terminal emulator or similar software will make DTR active and keep the modem on the line. When you exit the terminal emulator, the modem will disconnect if it was still on the line. If you need this to work differently for some reason, you can configure most modems to ignore DTR. See the documentation that came with your modem.

Call Waiting

If you have call waiting with your telephone service, you may find your computer calls being terminated when someone calls you. To fix this, use *70 as the first part of the numbers you dial, or check with your phone company to find out how to temporarily turn off the feature before you make a call.

About Null-Modems

To connect two computers via their serial ports, you need a modem at each end. Or a null-modem in the middle.

With a null-modem, you don't have to dial or do anything else special to establish a connection. You plug the computers' serial ports together and you are going. Bring up a terminal program on each machine, for example, and you can immediately see on one computer what you type on the other (make sure you've matched baud rates and other parameters -- use half-duplex if you want to see what you are typing on both computers).

A null-modem crosses the wires of a serial cable so that the send wire on one machine is connected to the receive wire on the other, and vice-versa. Other wires must be changed or jumpered as well to provide for specific software or hardware handshaking requirements.

Null modem adapters are readily available from computer, electronics and office supply stores. Special cables are also available or may be constructed by hand. It is generally preferable to use a null-modem adapter for a few reasons, though. First, it is usually more clearly labeled -- you may confuse a null-modem cable with a standard cable. Second, it is more flexible. Depending on how you may need to connect things at some point, having straight through cables with various gender and null-modem adapters lets you rearrange cabling without buying or making new custom cables.

Part III. Amiga LANs

In this section, we examine the software, products and packages available for various aspects of networking using the Amiga. Ethernet and other LAN hardware, cables and supplies and various software are covered. Where available, current pricing and other information are provided. Contact information for many vendors is provided in an appendix. In addition to purely factual information, I've included subjective information about some of the software. Take this with a grain of salt -- you might like something I don't.

Besides the author's own experience, information is provided from manufacturer's advertising, spec sheets or answers to questions. As well, some information was culled from the comp.sys.amiga.datacomm Amiga Networking FAQ, author's descriptions of freely redistributable files and from various other sources.

Ethernet

By far the most common standard LAN hardware is Ethernet. There are several implementations available for the Amiga. Macintosh computers come standard with Ethernet, as do most Unix computers. Most new PC networks are based on Ethernet, even though few PCs include it.

Ethernet flexibly provides high speeds and easy installations. Technically, Ethernet is a broad standard, but only three implementations are common. The major difference between the three common types of Ethernet is the cabling used. The signals carried by the cables are still the same, though, so it is easy to create a single physical Ethernet which contains multiple cabling types. For the technically inclined, more details on Ethernet standards are provided after the product information below.

Of the several Ethernet products available for the Amiga, most are Zorro-II cards. There is, however, a bridgeboard option and a PCMCIA option. If you need to use Ethernet on an Amiga 500, consider the Slingshot from R&D Microsystems (about US$45) or the Bodega Bay Expantion unit. Both reportedly work with the A2065, and probably with other cards.

Commodore A2065, Ameristar

Ameristar produced the first Ethernet boards for the Amiga (and created the first Amiga TCP/IP implementation -- a port from BSD). They later sold these products to Commodore, which turned them into the A2065 and AS225. The Ameristar card has been out of production for a long time. The A2065 has been of short supply for about a year as of this writing and may be available no longer. Its US street price was under $300.

Both cards are identical in most respects. These Zorro-II cards each have an AUI (Thick Ethernet) port and a BNC (Thin Ethernet) port. Only one port may be used at a time and the desired port must be selected with a jumper block. The cards have 32k of buffer RAM. Neither card was sold with a SANA-II driver included, because they predated the standard. A SANA-II driver for the A2065 also works with the Ameristar cards and is included with the SANA-II spec and most network software. Oxxi supports both of these cards in their ACS.

If you can find one, you can't go wrong with the A2065. For those who like such things, here is Commodore marketing's idea of the technical specifications for the A2065:

Function: Full ANSI 802.3 type Ethernet protocols over either Type A (Thick Ethernet) or Type B (Thin Ethernet/cheapernet) connections. 32K onboard RAM Buffer provides shared RAM between Am7990 processor and the Amiga.
Card Type: Amiga bus (100 pin), Autoconfig
Interface Specs: 15 pin female "D" connector for Type A (Thick Ethernet) networking with 100 nodes per segment Female BNC coax connector for Type B (Thin Ethernet/Cheapernet) networking with 30 nodes per segment.
Speed: 10Mbps CSMA/CD interface DMA data reading and writing to shared RAM
Card Size: Full size Amiga board

EB920
ASDG

Also known as the LanRover, this is another Zorro-II Ethernet card. It only directly supports thin Ethernet. ASDG included a SANA-II driver. Oxxi supports this card in their ACS. This card has a long history as a solid and reliable card. ASDG claims that it is a bit faster than the A2065, but the author doesn't have one to test.

Unfortunately, as with the A2065, this card is no longer manufactured.

GoldenGateII
Software Results Enterprises

This isn't an Ethernet board. It is a special bridge card. It provides an interface to PC slots for use as Amiga peripherals. You cannot use it to run PC software (though it does allow software PC emulations running on the Amiga to access PC cards). One of the drivers supplied is a SANA-II driver for NE2000 Ethernet cards. These Ethernet adapters are available for much less than Zorro-II Ethernet adapters, well under US$100. Since the GoldenGateII is only US$120, this can be the least expensive Ethernet option for the Amiga. It has the disadvantages of taking two slots (one for the bridgecard and one for the NE2000 Ethernet card), as well as being less solid than the Zorro-II Ethernet cards. If you're getting a GoldenGateII for access to internal modem or other I/O cards, though, this is a great way to get inexpensive Ethernet. Note that Oxxi ACS does not support the GoldenGateII.

The GoldenGate was in short supply for a long time, but has been picked up by Software Results Enterprises and should now be readily available.

QuickNet
Resource Management Force US$299

This Australian Zorro-II Ethernet card contains a ROM with a standard SANA-II driver proprietary Amiga peer-to-peer software which you can use instead of SANA-II. Boards for systems without Zorro slots are expected in the future.

Hydra
This Zorro-II Ethernet card is manufactured in the UK. In the US it is distributed by Oxxi. It is thinnet only.

I-Card
Interworks, $299

This is a standard PCMCIA Ethernet card bundled by Interworks with an Amiga SANA-II driver. Versions for thin Ethernet and 10-Base-T are available. Oxxi is working on ACS support for I-Card. If you need to Ethernet an A600 or A1200, this is the way to get it.

A4066

Ameristar CEI

This was a new Zorro-II card from Ameristar, scheduled to be introduced in 1994. In addition to the features of the A2065, it provides a status LED and a 10-Base-T port. Ameristar doesn't directly sell or support the card, so it is available only through CEI (Creative Equipment International, not to be confused with Creative Computers, the mail order dealer). Unfortunately, only a very small quantity were produced, and they sold out.

Ariadne

VillageTronics

I haven't personally used this board, but have seen good reports on it. It comes with 10-Base-2 and 10-Base-T connections and a SANA-II driver as well as two high-speed parallel ports for a cost of approximately US$300.

Technical Details and Cabling Choices

10-Base-5, thick Ethernet, is the least common and is mostly obsolete. The expensive and cumbersome cable allows a longer network (500m), but this is more easily achieved with other technology (such as bridges and repeaters or glass).

10-Base-2, thin Ethernet, sometimes called cheapernet, uses cable that looks much like cable-TV cable with BNC connectors. Each Ethernet card must be connected to a T which has a cable or terminator on each side. There must be exactly two terminators (obviously, one on each end). There may not be any branches or stubs. Each machine must be 2m apart, and the total length of a single Ethernet without repeaters is 200m. This is probably the most common type of Ethernet. It is well suited to smaller installations. It has the disadvantage that any break in the cable disrupts communications between all machines.

10-Base-T is the newest Ethernet standard. It uses cable that looks like standard phone cable, but the connectors (RJ-45) are larger than the telephone's (RJ-11). Machines cannot be directly connected together with 10-Base-T. Each computer is connected to a central hub. If there is a cabling problem, only machines directly connected to that cable are affected, and the rest of the network continues to function. 10-Base-T cards are less expensive to produce than 10-Base-2 cards, and the cable is less expensive too. The hubs cost money, though, so 10BaseT is usually not a win for networks with six or fewer machines. Because of enhanced reliability, and the future options it allows (special hubs can give each computer the full bandwidth of Ethernet, for example), 10-Base-T is often the best choice for larger networks.

Converters are available to change between different types of cabling. If, for example, you have an established 10BaseT network that you'd like to add an Amiga to, you can do it without a 10BaseT card. Relatively inexpensive transceivers can turn the AUI port on an A2065 into a 10BaseT connection.

In any Ethernet, the MTU is 1500 bytes. Each of the three runs at a theoretical maximum of 10 MBPS. In practice, two fast Amigas can typically transfer files at more than 300k/s over Ethernet. Ethernet cards come with a hardware address unique to the card. No two cards have the same physical address. Hence, there are no addressing dip switches or other configuration for Ethernet cards in most networks.

Other Hardware

If Ethernet won't work for you for some reason, other solutions are available. For general purpose LANs, they are mostly less desirable than Ethernet, but they are generally less expensive, and many work with A500s or A1000s for which Ethernet is not readily available.

Parallel Port Solutions

Perhaps the most common alternative networking hardware for the Amiga is to (mis?)-use the parallel ports. By creating a special custom cable and using custom software, this allows networking at up to about 50k/second. This works best if you only need to connect two machines and you don't need the parallel port for a printer and a digitizer and other peripherals. But hey, the price is right.

The original alternative parallel network was ParNet from the Software Distillery, and parallel solutions are sometimes generically referred to as ParNet, even when a different cable or software is used. For a stand-alone parallel solution, Olaf Seibert's ParNFS is generally considered superior to the aging original ParNet software. There are, however, applications for the original that may not work with the replacement. As well, there are SANA-II drivers which allow you to use other networking software. When that software allows internetworking, this can be a great way to connect a lone machine without Ethernet to an Ethernet network (by connecting it to a machine which is on the Ethernet via parallel port).

The various solutions usually include instructions for how to create your own custom cable. The commercial solutions include professionally constructed cables.

Martin Schwanke has done quite a bit of experimenting with parallel port networking on the Amiga. When asked about using ParNFS and AmiTCP over the parallel port, he went on to add several general comments about parallel networking. His thoughts were this (printed with permission):

"I can confirm that ParNFS is: 1) Completely compatible with AmiTCP 3.0, and 2) Far better than ParNet in general."

"One thing that I did notice is that both ParNet and ParNFS seem to need to be set at a fairly high priority. If you are requesting files from a remote machine that has a lot of GUI (Mouse/Gadget) activity for example, ParNet will just hang, and ParNFS will cause a requester. It's obvious from this which is better."

"ParNet already had a priority entry in it's mountlist entry as I recall, but ParNFS did not and I had to add one. A priority of 20 seemed to resolve the problems I mentioned above."

"One problem I could not resolve was when one machine guru'd and had to be rebooted. Neither ParNet or ParNFS would recover their link to the rebooted CPU. This meant I usually had to reboot _both_ machines whenever one died. Better networking packages such as Envoy will recover the links to remote file systems automatically after a reboot of any of the machines on the net."

PLIP
Freely Redistributable Oliver Wagner

PLIP v38.11 is a network device driver conforming to the SANA-II standard. It allows linking of two Amigas using their parallel ports. Transfer speed is around 50kb/sec. The complete low level transfer protocol is integrated in the device driver, including port arbitration handshaking and interrupt driven reads. Although the transfer process itself is CPU intensive, the device needs no CPU resources when no transfer is in progress. PLIP is intended as a low-cost networking solution. Note that PLIP uses different cables than ParNet and SPAR.

Spar
Freely Redistributable v37.2

A SANA-II network device driver. Requires "ParNet" cable. Includes source.

ParNFS
Freely Redistributable v1.0 Olaf 'Rhialto' Seibert

ParNFS is intended to be a replacement for the well-known ParNet file system by the Software Distillery. Includes complete 'C' source.

MultiFace Card
Pre'spect Technics

According to the manufacturer, with the extra parallel ports on these Zorro-II boards, you can create fast ParNets with up to 256 machines. If you need the extra ports anyway and your network demands are few, this may be worth looking into.

ParBench
Shareware v3.2

If you want the original ParNet software, this is probably the best current distribution for it. A collection of utilities and install scripts for setting up a ParNet between 2 Amiga computers. This disk has all files needed to connect 2 Amigas via their parallel ports or to connect an Amiga to a CDTV to use as a CD-ROM drive. ParBench uses Installer and comes with AmigaGuide-based documentation.

Parallel Solution Utilities
The original ParNet has been popular for long enough that several utilities have become available. Here are three.

MShell
Freely Redistributable v0.2 Massimo Brogioni

A remote shell program to use in conjunction with ParNet. You can use the remote Amigas exactly like the local one.

PNUTEH.LHA

A small collection of AmigaDos scripts that, used with ParNet, let you synchronize clocks, send pop-messages, and send NetMail.

NetMount
Freely Redistributable by Tobias Ferber

Allows you to mount a ParNet client with a simple icon click. Net-Mount is configureable via ToolTypes and generates a temporary mountlist for NET: according to your settings. You also need the ParNet distribution to use NetMount.

Twin Express
Freely Redistributable 1.1a

Command line driven serial transfer program. Includes software for Amiga and PC, to allow the quick and easy transfer of files. This isn't the same as a network filesystem, but it is good enough for many people.

Link It!
Legendary Design Technologies, US$59.95

Not yet available at the time of this writing, once available, Link It! may be the solution to many needs. Here is an edited description from the publisher:

"Now you can link your machine to others for fast file transfer and conversions with a few simple mouse clicks. If you've ever upgraded from your present computer to another, you know what a hassle it can be to transfer all of the information from your old harddrive to your new one. Or, if you happen to own both an Amiga and a PC, you've probably wanted to share data easily. There are solutions; but putting large amounts of data on floppies is cumbersome, and trying to hook up both machines with null modem cables can be frustrating. Now there is a solution for all of these problems: Link It! from Legendary Design. A unique pack-age, Link It! comes with a high-speed parallel cable and both Amiga and Windows version to work flawlessly between platforms. Or you can use it Amiga-2-Amiga or PC-2-PC."
Update: as of this printing, Link It! seems to be shipping in only limited quantaties, with the supply of cables being the limiting fac-tor. Some customers have complained that they received only a serial cable -- no parallel cable.

AmigaLink

Distributed in the North America by AmiTrix for about US$300 to connect two machines.

AmigaLink is networking hardware for your floppy port. It uses Ethernet type cabling and connectors and allows up to 300 feet of cable with 20 machines on a single network. It includes a SANA-II driver and basic networking software (primarily useful when you need to network with 1.3 machines, otherwise separate software should be considered). This kind of network is fairly slow compared to Ethernet, but is comparable to ParNet without the hassles of giving up your parallel port, constructing strange cables or being limited to only two machines a short distance apart.

ISDN

Integrated Services Digital Network is a fancy acronym for a simple concept. The copper that connects your home (or office) phone to the telephone company's local switch carries a low-tech analog signal. Usually, though, everything is converted and carried as a digital signal from the local switch all the way to the last switch before the phone you are calling. For voice communications, you don't notice and you don't care. For data communications, this sucks.

By making the local loop digital as well, much more data can be carried over a single voice-grade line. As well, more voice services can be provided on a single line. ISDN makes the local loop digital. Instead of being limited to 14.4kbps or 28.8kbps, it is easy to get service at or exceeding 56kbps.

In many parts of the world, ISDN service costs about the same or just a little more than POTS (plain old telephone service). Many BBSs and other systems are now being set up for ISDN, so it is a real and affordable option for telecommunications.

There are devices which are, basically, ISDN modems. You could attach one of these to the serial port of your Amgia. Because of the speeds involved, though, it is probably better to get a card for your computer. BSC Buroautomation makes the ISDN Master Zorro-II card for the Amiga. It costs about US$500.

There is a lot more you might want to know about ISDN before using it, but that is really beyond the scope of this book. There haven't been many good sources of consumer information about

ISDN because it is so new, but there should be more information available soon in new books and articles. Another good place to look would be in the newsgroup comp.dcom.isdn.

Communicator
Eureka

Here is some of the information provided in Eureka's press release for the Communicator:

The Communicator enables CD32 to communicate with other Amigas. With the Communicator, you can use CD32 as intelligent CD-ROM drive. Control your CD32 from Scala and start Audio or even MPEG tracks (if you have an MPEG module). Or View IFF AGA/PCX/GIF and other CD's even on non-AGA machines. Uploading and starting programs on the CD32 is possible making CD32 a powerful stand alone Computer with communication and graphics capacities far better than CD-I! The Communicator plugs in the keyboard plug and doesn't occupy the expansion slot.

The Communicator package contains: the Communicator hardware with MIDI/Serial/keyboard plug; a CD crowded with the Communicator program, utilities and PD software, an Amiga disk for installing the Amiga side and a manual in English/German and Dutch.

LocalTalk
Since 1984, Macintoshes have come with a serial port well suited for networking. With a theoretical maximum of 230KBPS, it is slow by most LAN standards. When used for networking, these fast serial ports are called a LocalTalk network. Mac's also come with AppleTalk networking software.

Some of the Macintosh emulators available for the Amiga (Emplant and Amax) may be configured with LocalTalk ports. Unfortunately, there is no Amiga AppleTalk software to take advantage of these ports when not running under emulation.

Progressive Peripherals & Software provided Amiga versions of the LocalTalk hardware and AppleTalk software. Progressive suffered a disastrous fire, and while the company came back together for a while afterwards, it seems not to have fully recovered. I haven't heard of anyone being able to reach them (and I haven't been able to, either) in some time. The specs looked like this:

DoubleTalk - Progressive Peripherals & Software
Compatibility: Amiga 500, 2000 and 3000. Apple File Protocol
used in standard AppleTalk networks.
Functions: Share files, printers on existing AppleTalk network. For
Amiga-only networks, has a high-speed mode (twice AppleTalk
speeds) and allows any Amiga to function simultaneously as a file
server, printer server or client.
Hardware: Network interface card with 512K ROM and phone jack
network adapter. Network card provides an additional serial port
for the Amiga.
Software utilities: Network Manager, AutoLogoff, AutoPublish,
password security, NetMail.

A2060

Commodore

ARCNet is a networking hardware standard which was very popular on PCs for a few years, but which is no longer common in computer networking. It has a maximum transfer rate of 2.5 Mbps,
but guarantees that bandwidth to be available. Hence, in some
heavy use conditions, it performs better than you might otherwise
expect. ARCNet uses cables and connectors which look just like
those for 10-Base-2 Ethernet but which are different. They are a
different impedance. Be careful not to mix Ethernet and ARCNet
cables and terminators, because doing so usually causes all kinds
of flakiness rather than simple (and easily diagnosed) failure.

The A2060 is a Zorro-II ARCNet card which has been around for a
while. As with the A2065, Commodore isn't making the board any-
more. Unlike the A2065, it may be relatively easy to buy one. The
demand just isn't as high as for Ethernet. Dealers have been selling new ones for well under US$75. Many of the new packages
include a short ARCNet cable, a T and a terminator -- a nice
bonus. The board never shipped with a SANA-II driver, but an
A2060 driver is included with the SANA-II archive and the Envoy
distribution. There are three of problems with the A2060 which
you should be aware of if you have or are considering an A2060:

First, you have to know about setting hardware addresses. With
most networking software, you have to set the hardware addresses
on the ARCNet cards to correspond to the number with which you
have configured the network. Many A2060 dip switches used to
control the hardware addresses are documented and labelled
incorrectly. Most are upside-down (0's are 1's and vice-versa) and
backwards (the LSB is numbered 8 and the MSB is 1). I'm told

that some are just upside-down or just backwards, but I haven't heard of any A2060s which are correct. If you are electronically-adept, you may be able to determine what you have by examining the boards, otherwise you'll have to experiment.

The other hardware problem is hybrids. The small black-epoxied daughter board on the A2060 is a hybrid. Various hybrids were used at different times during the production life of the A2060. Hybrids should all function identically, but apparently some are buggy. If your ARCNet network works with two machines but not with three, you may have a buggy hybrid.

The SANA-II device available for the ARCNet cards was released from Commodore as beta. It has not been thoroughly tested and is not supported by anyone. Some users have reported problems with the A2060 that cannot be duplicated with other hardware. Some bugs in the A2060 have been fixed, and a new release of the driver should be available through Intangible Assets Manufacturing by the time you read this.

Cables and Supplies

Finding cables and supplies for networking can be difficult since many LANs are set up by dealers or consultants who specialize in networks and get their supplies from distributors rather than retail outlets. Here are some hints.

Redmond cable. While there are many companies who specialize in standard and custom computer cabling, this US company appears to be the most familiar with the particular needs of Amiga users. For anything which isn't a standard cable, they are a good place to start (see the vendors section at the back of the book for more details).

Most Amiga Ethernet cards are sold without the necessary cables and connectors. They can be a little difficult to locate if you don't know where to look. Actually, even Radio Shack (Tandy) carries thin Ethernet cables. Unfortunately, they seem not to know it. You may get further if you ask for RG-58 coax cable with BNC male connectors, BNC F/M/F Ts, and male BNC 50-Ohm terminators.

Many of the computer "superstores" don't carry any networking equipment at all (MicroCenter just started carrying networking equipment and now has a good selection). Looking in the phone book under computers ought to help you to locate several local dealers who sell Ethernet cabling and equipment. If you can't find a local dealer to help you, there are many mail order places you can resort to. Check pricing, though. Some of the mail order outfits cater to corporate data processing shops and gouge on networking equipment. In the US, one vendor of various networking hardware which has good pricing on many items is "Data Comm Warehouse" at 1-800-328-2261, or 1-908-363-4823 fax.

In the US, you should be able to get a two-machine thin-Ethernet setup -- 2m cable, 2 Ts and 2 terminators -- for under $20. On the other hand, a single six-foot 10-Base-T cables runs about US$3, and 8-Port hubs can be had for as little as US$200.

Peer-to-Peer

There are several products which bring peer-to-peer network filesystems, printer sharing and other utilities to the Amiga. The products in this section are designed specifically for that purpose. The next section discusses products which connect Amigas to other kinds of computers over a network. Some of them are suitable for Amiga peer-to-peer use as well. The Other Hardware section above discussed some solutions which include software and are appropriate for consideration for some Amiga peer-to-peer networking needs.

Envoy

Commodore/Intangible Assets Manufacturing
Current list price: US$59.95

Amiga Envoy is the standard Amiga peer-to-peer networking software developed by Commodore's Amiga Networking Group. Its performance, user-interface and API are consistent with the philosophy of the Amiga Operating System. Amiga Envoy provides a simple messaging interface for the easy development of reliable network applications. Included applications enable connected Amiga computers to share hard disks, CD-ROMs, and printers transparently. Third-party applications can provide functionality such as electronic mail, remote computer access, multi-user databases and multi-player games.

Intangible Assets Manufacturing has licensed Amiga Envoy from Commodore to make it available to end-users. The author of this book is one of Amiga Envoy's original designers and wrote IAM's manual for Envoy (included in an Appendix here).

Requirements: Workbench 2.04, Kickstart 2.04, 512k RAM, SANA-II compatible networking hardware (see compatibility). Recommended: Workbench 2.1 or later, Kickstart 2.1 or later, 1MB RAM, Hard disk with 300k free in SYS:.

Compatibility: Any SANA-II networking hardware may be used with Envoy, including Ameristar A2066, AmigaLink, ASDG Lan-Rover, Commodore A2065 or A2060 and SLIP (serial port).

Envoy is IP-based, as are AmiTCP and AS225. AS225r2 runs cooperatively with Envoy on the same hardware simultaneously. Hardware with current (SANA-II r 2) drivers (i.e., A2065) can use two IP-based protocol stacks simultaneously (i.e., AmiTCP and Envoy) without special cooperation from the protocol stacks.

There are several freely redistributable applications and utilities available for Envoy, and more are coming soon (a setup for integrating Toasters is expected soon!). Here are three interesting ones:

NetProbe
v3.11, Cardware (send a postcard), Hakan Tandogan

This utility lets you gather information about all of the active hosts on your Envoy network. It is a great tool for troubleshooting and is a neat toy. NetProbe is available in two versions: one with a great MUI interface and one with a plain text interface.

Don't forget to send a postcard to the author if you use NetProbe. He likes unusual cards and stamps.

Talk/Conf
Freeware, Jeffery Litz
If you want to chat over an Envoy network with two people or with more, these programs from Jeffery Litz will make it easy. Source code is included with the distributions for these two programs, so those who want example code for Envoy services should look here. (Mr. Litz is multi-talented. He also produced the cover art for this book.)

Ventriloquist
v1.1, Shareware, US$30, Dan Barrans

A remote control utility for Amigas on an Envoy network. It lets you control any of several Amigas using the keyboard and mouse of any one of them. In effect, this lets you use several Amigas as if they were a single computer with several screens. VPrefs, a preferences program, is included to help in configuring Ventriloquist.

Alan-FS
Canadian Prototype Replicas

An Amiga peer-to-peer filesystem from a company with years of experience in Amiga filesystems. It has an AmigaGuide context sensitive help facility. Uses AS225r2 (also available from CPR) for TCP/IP network transport. Includes NetAdmin GUI network administrator and installation utility. Password protected for security.

Amigo EtherNet, MultiNet and SerNet
$250 to $325 (three users), Amigo Busines Computers

Despite the suggestions of the names, this is software, not hardware. Three versions are available, one for each of several Ethernet boards, one for a Parallel solution, and serial ports. The software provides peer-to-peer networking with "bi-directional communication."

Enlan-DFS
v2.0 $265 (five computer license), Interworks

Peer-to-Peer networking for the Amiga which provides diskdrive, file and peripheral sharing. It is easy to install and use, and (like the other Amiga network filesystems) is transparent to your application software. Interworks is focused on high-end environments like Toaster render farms.

Heterogenous
When you need to connect an Amiga to something else, here is the software you need to look at. Make sure you also look at TwinEx and Link It! (covered in Other Hardware, above). Internet considerations and the use of TCP/IP are addressed further in the Amiga Internet section.

SAMBA
Microsoft uses the SMB protocol for it's peer-to-peer networking in Windows for Workgroups, Windows 95 and Windows NT. A freely redistributable program called SAMBA lets Unix machines connect as clients or servers to Windows machines on such a peer-to-peer

network. The SAMBA program has been ported to the Amiga, and is available for download from AmiNet. The port was not completed as of the time of this writing (the available version is labeled as a beta), and the author did not know whether he would be able to continue the work. So while this is a promising possibility, it isn't currently easy to use or bug-free and reliable, and may not improve.

TSSnet (DECNet)
Thunder Ridge, Inc. v2.5

Following is (edited) information provided by Thunder Ridge.

TSSnet brings DECnet, the Digital Network Architecture, to Commodore Amiga personal computers. With it, Amigas become Phase IV end nodes in a DECnet network. TSSnet from Thunder Ridge is a licensed implementation of the TSSnet originally developed by Thursby Software Systems for the Macintosh, now sold as Path WORKS by DEC. TSSnet was originally released by Syndesis, and was maintained by Syndesis until January, 1993. At that time, Syndesis split and Thunder Ridge was formed. Thunder Ridge is owned by the original developers of TSSnet for the Amiga.

With TSSNet, the Amiga becomes a cost-effective and powerful workstation ideally suited to today's interactive, graphics-oriented environment of DEC computing. An Amiga TSSNet user can run local applications such as a desktop publishing program while logged in to several DECnet nodes to retrieve data to be added to a report. Users can run remote applications and start new programs on the Amiga.

Support applications add to the power of TSSNet. NCP, the Network Control Program is an intuitive application for complete control of each TSSNet node. It controls line speed, network state, buffer sizes and numbers, node access data, network access control and more. The NCP statistics screen dynamically displays all system tracing counters and error conditions. NetMail is compatible with DECnet's electronic mail and VMS Mail, and allows full mail access to DECnet networks. Mail can be sent to and from the Amiga node asynchronously, while other applications run or even while the Amiga is unattended. Network Virtual Terminal lets you log on to other nodes on the DECnet network. If you like, you can open multiple sessions on other nodes using the DECnet CTERM facility. TSSnet provides a VT100 terminal emulator for use with the Virtual Terminal facility. In addition, any Amiga terminal program can use the Virtual Terminal feature if it supports VT family terminal emulation. NFT (Network File Transfer) allows copy, dir, delete, type, rename, print and submit of files on any node in the network. Print files on remote VAX/VMS printers, or submit command files for execution on the Vax. Task to Task Communications provides an AmigaDOS device that allows Amiga programs to communicate with tasks on other DECnet nodes. Full documentation is available for this easy-to-use programmer's interface to TSSnet. Finally, File Access Listener allows other DECnet nodes to access files on your Amiga directly. Security is maintained through a username and password protection mechanism, as other DECnet hosts use.

TSSnet can use an Ethernet or serial connection and supports SANA-II devices. It fully supports X11 from GfxBase.

Amiga Client Software for Novell Netware
Oxxi

If you have a Netware network and want your Amiga to join, you really only have two choices. Get a Netware NFS server and use TCP/IP on your Amiga or get ACS from Oxxi. Most people I've heard from who are using ACS like it. A few have complained that Oxxi's refusal to support SANA-II creates problems for them, restricting which cards they can use (to those Oxxi has written a driver for) and keeping them from running peer-to-peer software for letting Amigas access each other directly.

DNet
Freely Redistributable, Mattew Dillon

If you have a serial connection to a Unix box, and you want the power of SLIP or PPP with less complexity, DNet might be an answer for you. You'll need to be able to run the Unix binary for DNet on the Unix side (usually with a shell account) as well as using the Amiga side software. Several applications can use DNet in the same way a standard TCP/IP connection could be used. Among them are an IRC client, a special sendmail, a terminal shell and a special version of Mosaic.

AmigaUnixWindows
v3.0, Begware, $10, Ezra Story

Amiga UnixWindows (AmigaUW) is a package designed to allow a person to have multiple concurrent sessions open on a UNIX host over a single serial connection. It is similar to DNet. The package consists of a server on the UNIX host, a server on the Amiga, and a serial device emulator which uses the server on the Amiga to open up sessions on the UNIX host using ordinary terminal programs.

AppleTalk

See the discussion above about LocalTalk. Note that Macintosh emulators like the ShapeShifter do allow the use of an Ethernet card by the Mac emulation.

TCP/IP

TCP/IP the open standard for connecting multiple platforms. Two TCP/IP protocol stacks and dozens of applications are available for the Amiga. The section on Amiga Internet, below, discusses these.

Programming Tools

Besides the products covered here, GfxBase's X-Windows is available with various programming tools.

TorqueWare

AugmenTek

TorqueWare is a programming tool for the Amiga. It allows you to share data and computation across multiple processors. It is based on the Linda programming model. TorqueWare for the Amiga interoperates with Torque Systems products for Mac, SGI and other systems. A 'C' preprocessor, link libraries, support tools, example programs, a GUI and online documentation are included. These tools allow development of parallelized application using multitasking on one CPU.

Part IV. Amiga Internet

If you think you aren't interested in the Internet, please skip to the resources section, then come back here.

Whether you already have access to the Internet or would like to get it or are thinking about upgrading your access, this section contains important information for you: what your options are and what Amiga Internet applications are available. You might be able to access many of the Internet's valuable resources with a lowly mail-only account!

We will start with a look at what kinds of service (accounts) are available.

Next, we will look at Amiga TCP/IP protocol stacks along with Amiga versions of Internet applications. We discussed TCP/IP and Internet applications generally in Part I. Here, we pay special attention to Amiga-specific versions. To cover all of the Internet applications in detail, or to even start a list of general resources would easily consume a book larger than this one. An excellent book to pursue for more help with the applications and a good list of general resources is the "Whole Internet Users Guide and Catalog." We stretch the definition of Internet applications a little so that we can include mail and news readers, as well as UUCP in this section.

Having provided the general information in the first part of this book, we provide details about the Amiga specific resources that are available out there. What they are and where to find them. As well, we will give some alternatives in case you don't have access to a full Internet shell or network account: ways to access resources from mail and how to get mail and news delivered directly to your computer.

Shell Account or Network Account

An account on a system with just Internet mail and/or news is not an Internet account, but you can use it to access several features of the Internet. Many Internet applications have various ways to interact with users via mail. An account with only mail or mail and news might be referred to as a mail-only account.

UUCP connections are somewhat like mail-only accounts. With a UUCP connection, your Amiga is capable of sending and receiving mail and news, but is not part of the Internet and can not use other Internet applications (except through mail gateways).

A shell account is, technically speaking, an account that gives you a Unix (or other operating system) shell prompt rather than a menu or some other interface. An account on an Internet BBS or online service may be functionally equivalent to a shell account if it provides access to a number of services.

An account which lets you make your computer part of the Internet is a network account. If it is not on a dedicated line, it is a dial-up account. These accounts are also referred to by the names of the protocols used -- a SLIP account, a PPP account or just a dial-up IP account (which could be SLIP or PPP).

Whether you have a shell account or an IP account, how you will use the Internet will mostly be the same. The basic applications all work the same. One difference is, when you FTP from a shell account, the file will be in your directory on the host. You will then have to use zmodem or another file transfer protocol to get the file to your Amiga. Similar examples may apply to some other applications. Another difference is that with an IP account, you might do most of your net access through Mosaic, and you might use Amiga programs with GUIs for some functions like reading mail or news. Even then, the GUIs don't really change how the applications work, just the face on the applications.

MLink or TIA

Since the first edition of this book was published, a few new programs have come along to try to work in some specialized situations to provide Internet access. Two of them to note are MLink and TIA. Both include a program to run in an Internet shell account. TIA just turns a shell account into a SLIP account, requiring you to run one of the TCP/IP packages below. MLink has a program which runs on the Amiga side and which emulates a TCP/IP package, to allow you to run TCP/IP applications on the Amiga.

Both of these programs can be useful solutions for some people, but they have many little problems and incompatibilities. The best solution for almost everyone is to use one of the full TCP/IP packages connected to a true SLIP or PPP account.

AS225, AmiTCP, and Miami

These are the three important TCP/IP packages for the Amiga. A fourth, AmigaNOS, has a specialized purpose (ham packet radio). If you are going to connect your Amiga directly to the Internet, or to another TCP/IP network, you'll need one of these packages. It is some of the more complex software you may use on your computer, and it will take considerable background knowledge to use. The information in this book will be helpful, but you'll need to actually read the manual for the software you use. Don't even try to just run it before reading the documentation, with the hope of referring back to the manual occasionally when you get stuck.

"I need help installing AmiTCP or AS225." (Miami is a new package, not yet shipping at the time of this writing, but is similar to both AmiTCP and AS225.) Often heard, it usually isn't true. AS225 and AmiTCP are easy to install. Configuring and using them requires understanding TCP/IP and SANA-II and may require understanding SLIP or PPP and the Internet generally. That's not simple, but a little work makes it very possible. There isn't anything special about either of these software packages. They are all ports of the Berkeley (see below) networking code and utilities. For the most part, little of the ports are Amiga-specific. They work and are configured about the same as TCP/IP on most Unix machines, and not all too differently from on Windows or OS/2 or a Mac. If you need to know how to use or configure TCP/IP on an Amiga, you just plain need to know how to use or configure TCP/IP, not how to install AmiTCP or AS225.

I mention this for three reasons. First, it is important to realize that you are going to have to know TCP/IP and that most of the good books about TCP/IP and the Internet are good resources for most Amiga users if you don't get everything you need out of this book. Second, many users of the Internet have a system administrator who magically ensures that everything is set up and works. Those with PCs or Macs are often handed pre-configured software to use for a particular connection. Most system administrators say "Amiga, what's that?" So for those with Amigas, there is more to learn and more to do for yourself. Fortunately, Amiga users are usually more resourceful and better able to learn technical details for themselves. Finally, once you understand well how to use TCP/IP on the Amiga, you'll understand most of how to use it on any other platform (and vice-versa).

The University of California at Berkeley is filled with nerdy computer students. Bunches of them created (and keep expanding on) a version of Unix known as Berkeley Unix. Lots of people outside Berkeley help, too. Many of the students originally involved with Berkeley Unix went on to found or work for Sun Microsystems. SunOS, of course, is based on Berkeley Unix. Sun's motto has been "the network is the computer" and their systems have had some of the best integrated connectivity since day one.

The Berkeley code is not public domain, but the source code is freely redistributable, and it may be used freely so long as proper notices and credit are given. Hence, many Unices use the Berkeley networking code, as do many other implementations. It is probably safe to say that more machines on the Internet are running a Berkeley-derived TCP/IP than any other single implementation.

Over the years, the Berkeley Unix code has undergone many revisions. As with most other software, each revision has made the software a little nicer, with more features and fewer bugs. With so many people using the software and looking at the source code, a lot of feedback has gone into the improvements.

The Berkeley software consists of two parts -- the protocol stack and the applications. The protocol stack is just IP, ICMP, UDP, TCP, domain name resolver, etc. The applications include the 'r' commands (rlogin, rcp, rsh), Telnet, FTP, finger and others. Several utilities are used for configuring and monitoring the networking software: netstat, ifconfig, traceroute and others. Sun's NFS (Network FileSystem) is the standard network filesystem for Unix, and it is also available for the porting.

Not all of the parts are part of any given port. Sometimes the way configuration files are used is different, and sometimes where they go is different (on Unix, /etc is where most configuration files are, but on the Amiga, the tend to go in the subdirectories 's' and 'db'). Once you've figured out the few major differences (read the manual), though, configuring the Berkeley ports to the Amiga is just like doing it under Unix or on other systems. If you don't know how to configure it under Unix, you might be able to work with someone who does.

The implementations for the Amiga use shared libraries for the protocol code. AS225r2 has a shared library socket API, while AS225r1 has no (released) API and AmiTCP has a link library socket API. There is a shared library for AmiTCP which emulates the AS225r2 socket.library. Miami is also supposed to work with programs written for either AS225 or AmiTCP.

About NFS on the Amiga

The Amiga makes a great NFS client. The NFS client software in AS225 has undergone extensive testing and has been to two separate week-long sessions of interoperability testing with dozens of other NFS implementations.

The Amiga running AmigaOS makes a lousy NFS server. The standard for NFS requires that files be uniquely identified in a small finite number of bytes. Under Unix, inodes are used for such identification. There is no Amiga equivalent. To implement NFS on the Amiga with the standard filesystems requires building a table of all the files to be exported so that a unique identifier is created for each. This table slows down access and takes a painfully long time to construct. Any local writes direct to the filesystem (not through the table) require a rebuild of the table.

In a nutshell, don't bother with NFS servers for native AmigaOS. If you want Amiga peer-to-peer connectiveity, run something like Envoy at the same time you run TCP/IP. If you want to run an alternative OS (like AmigaUnix or NetBSD), that's a different story -- NFS works fine there. A good NFS server for the Amiga would want to use an alternative filesysetem -- like the Berkeley filesystem which has been ported to the Amiga.

By the way, a fairly common problem Amiga NFS users have is their MaxTransfer. With AS225r2, MaxTransfer is set with nfsmgr maxread=n.

About Internet security and the Amiga

If you are going to put your Amiga on the Internet, make sure you understand the security implications. See the security chapter. The important part is that Amigas are pretty unsecurable. If you are on the Internet, you might choose not to run servers on your Amiga at all, unless you are behind a firewall or have only boring and unimportant stuff on your machine.

AS225

AS225 is the name of Commodore's TCP/IP package for the Amiga. As with the A2065, it started as an Ameristar product, but Commodore bought it. Commodore did a lot of work with it before releasing it as AS225 (now known as AS225r1 for "release 1"). It has a fairly long history, and has been available in one form or another for more than five years.

AS225r1 was released in 1991. Three software engineers (the author among them) worked on it full time at Commodore for a year or two after that, creating AS225r2. Unfortunately, Commodore never released AS225r2. Various betas were made available to developers. Eventually, Commodore made AS225r2 source code licenses available. The terms were unacceptable to some interested third parties, but, finally, a third party has licensed AS225r2 and made it available. It can currently be ordered as a new package (US$150) or an upgrade from AS225r1 (US$100 until AS225r3 is released) from Canadian Prototype Replicas (CPR). CPR's initials seem appropriate, since they may have managed to revive AS225r2. On the other hand, Commodore's licensing terms don't allow the use of Commodore's name in the advertising or promotion of the licensed software, so CPR's package is called "CPR TCP/IP Internet Networking Software package, Release 2."

AS225r2 includes a shared library socket API (AS225r1 didn't include an API) and support for SANA-II (AS225r1 was released before SANA-II). It includes servers for rsh, FTP and RIP. Clients include finger, NFS, ping, rlogin, rcp, rsh, FTP, and Telnet. While an NFS server was created for AS225r2, it is not currently included in CPR's distribution, and it is not particularly useful anyway (see NFS and the Amiga below). CPR includes AmigaGuide documentation and an Installer script.

AS225 is also made available with yearly support contracts through GfxBase along with its Amiga X-Windows package.

AS225 is a more mature product than AmiTCP, and is more stable in many respects. For those who need professional support, it is the only option (short of hiring a consultant). But for those on an extra tight budget or who don't mind fixing bugs themselves, there is another option...

AmiTCP
AmiTCP is now a commercial product with a freely redistributable demo version. Originally, the authors ported the BSD software as a project at Helsinki University of Technology. Source code for older versions of AmiTCP was distributed as part of the project. Eventually, the students formed a company to commercialize AmiTCP. Now, you can download the demo version from AmiNet, or get it as part of a disk set from IAM (see page 256). Once you've

seen that the demo is to your liking, or if you'd prefer to start with a printed manual and more support, you can order the commercial version from your Amiga dealer or direct from NSDi.

The client applications included with AmiTCP are Telnet, NFS , ping, rsh, and rlogin, and other. Clients and servers are included for finger and for an Amiga-only peer-to-peer network filesystem called NetFS.

Setting up TCP/IP on the Amiga

AS225r2 and AmiTCP are a little easier to set up for an Ethernet connection than for a dial-up connection. There is more work to do with a dial-up connection. If you have the chance, configure your software on a LAN before you do a dial-up connection. You have to do all of the same basic work anyway, and the experience will make the dial-up configuration easier.

First, read the manual. You can probably install a word processor and use most of its basic functions without ever removing the manual from its shrink-wrap. You simply can't do this with a networking package. There are too many things which are too variable for different sites, and that means that significant configuration is required before anything will work at all. Second, talk to your service provider or network administrator if you have one. She'll have details about the specific environment that you are in, and may have hints about setting up software in that environment. I can provide general guidelines here, but depending on your specific software and environment, you'll have to fill in some of the gaps. As long as you're convinced that its not hard and you carefully read the material available to you, you'll be fine and will come out looking like an expert.

The configuration could be made a little easier with good graphical preferences editors, but you shouldn't be intimidated by the fact that you may have to use a text editor on several files. It really is easy to do.

A lot of configuration may be done for you by an install script which asks you questions. Some of the things that might be set up this way: the name of your host, its IP address, the domain you are in (iam.com is a domain, calvin.iam.com is a host in that domain), the SANA-II device and unit number you'll be using and your user name.

Whether or not the installer script handles this configuration for you, you should know where this information is stored and have some idea of how it is used. Some of the most important files are explained below.

(AS225r2) inet:s/sana2_devs(AmiTCP) amitcp:db/interfaces
This file contains the names and unit numbers of the SANA-II device or devices you are using to connect to your network. If your computer has an Ethernet card, that card's driver should have an entry here. If you are using a dial-up connection, your SLIP, CSLIP or PPP driver should have an entry here. You might use more than one interface at a time. Having extra entries here is not a problem because they will be ignored. AS225r2 automatically names the interfaces as s0, s1, s2, etc. AmiTCP requires names for the interfaces in the file.

(AS225r2)inet:s/inet.config(AmiTCP)amitcp:db/AmiTCP.config
Whether your machine is a gateway and whether to use DNS for name resolution are configured here. AS225r2 also uses this file for user name, host name, netmask, broadcast mask and other information.

(AS225r2)inet:db/hosts(AmiTCP)amitcp:db/hosts
This is a table of IP addresses and host names. For hosts that you access very frequently, you should probably have an entry here whether or not you also use DNS name resolution. If you don't use DNS, you must have an entry here for each host you use on your network.

(AS225r2)inet:db/passwd(AmiTCP)amitcp:db/passwd
Each user of your machine has a name and password and other information in this file. If your Amiga is only used as a client, you may not need to edit this file. If you are on the Internet and you do run any servers, you need to be careful with this file. If someone can read it or write to it, they will have free access to your Amiga. See the section on Amigas as Servers for further details.

Once you've got your machine configured on a LAN or dial-up link, you need to make sure that things are working. Rather than starting with the fanciest software you have, start simple.

The program "ping" is one of the most basic tools available to you. It sends a packet which requests a reply. It uses the "echo" feature of a protocol called ICMP (Internet Control Message Protocol) which all Internet hosts are required to run. Get the IP address of a machine near yours. Ping that IP address. If you get a message that the host is alive, you're connected! If not, your hardware isn't configured or connected properly, or your software isn't configured right. The section on hardware troubleshooting in Appendix C may be helpful, and rereading the documentation or parts of this book may be helpful. If this fails, try to find an expert like a network administrator or a support person with your service provider.

Now that you have ping to an IP address working, try pinging the host by name rather than IP address. If it is alive, at least some of your name resolution is working -- you've either got a correct entry for the host in your hosts file or you have correctly configured DNS. Make sure that your routing is set correctly by trying to ping the addresses of a few remote hosts. If you'll be using DNS, make sure that you can ping a host not in your host table. If you can't, make sure DNS name resolution is turned on in inet/AmiTCP.config and that you've set the servers correctly. With everything working this far, you're probably set. The last test you might want to try is to FTP or Telnet to a remote site.

Once you know the basics are working, getting a particular application to work is usually simple. Again, make sure you've read all of the documentation for the application and know what you need to configure. You'll be able to get it working if you pay attention to the details.

Setting up and Using SLIP or PPP
Make sure you understand all the previous details about TCP/IP and the Internet before you pursue this chapter. You have to do the same setup as for a LAN, and then a little extra. Setting up SLIP or PPP isn't difficult, but it does require some basic background and attention to detail.

If you want to connect your Amiga to the Internet but you don't have an Ethernet or other LAN to connect to the Internet, you'll have to connect using a serial connection with a modem to an Internet service provider. If you want more than a shell account, you'll have to have a SLIP or PPP connection. SLIP stands for Serial Line Internet Protocol. It is a very simple but inflexible way to make the connection. PPP, Point-to-Point Protocol is the official standard for Internet serial connections and is easier to use, if a little more difficult to implement. If you have a choice, use PPP.

On the Amiga, SLIP and PPP are implemented as SANA-II drivers. You must also have protocol software (AS225r2 or AmiTCP) to run on top of the drivers to connect to the Internet. As well, you'll need an IP (SLIP or PPP) account from a service provider. You can get leased-line service that will be connected full-time, but it is more likely that you will get a dial-up account. The leased-line options require special equipment and are beyond the scope of this book. Note that if you can get it, you can also use ISDN instead of standard voice dial-up lines with many service providers. ISDN works in much the same way, only you'll use an ISDN Zorro-II card or special ISDN "modem" and it goes much faster. You'll often have to pay a higher rate to the service provider for ISDN service, and you'll have to pay to have ISDN phone service installed.

To find a service provider, look in the appendix. For the SANA-II drivers, they are available from various sources of freely redistributable software (or may be ordered from IAM). The basic SLIP and CSLIP drivers are included in the SANA-II standards archive, but enhancements to it have been made and released by various people. PPP for the Amiga is US$15 shareware by Holger Kruse. I use it. He has put a lot of effort into an excellent implementation, and the registered version contains more options and features. His price is very fair; register! (The registered version has several options enabled that aren't in the non-registered version, and this results in higher speeds.)

When you establish an account with the service provider, you'll be told whether you can use SLIP, CSLIP, or PPP. You'll be given a telephone number, an account name and password, a static IP address for your host (or that addresses are allocated dynamically for each connection), an IP address for the host you are dialing, and IP addresses for DNS and other servers. You may be given other information such as special login procedures (sometimes you have to do more than just provide a name and password, like indicate to start PPP), netmask, broadcast mask, etc.

The first thing to do with the information you get is to try it out with a terminal emulator program. Dial the number and enter your name and password and whatever else. You might want to capture this session (using the capture feature of your terminal). You're going to make sure that you've got the information correct so that you don't do something like waste your time with the wrong phone number. Pay attention to what prompts you get. Pay attention to the responses to your input. Make sure that the name and password work. If you have to enter any secondary password or other information to get to SLIP/PPP, do that. Do you get some indication that the remote side is now in SLIP or PPP mode (unin-

telligible stuff is one such indication)? Or did it just get you to a
BBS or shell? Or do nothing? Ok, you can hang up now. If something tripped you up, you may need to talk to the service provider
again, otherwise you are ready to move on.

If you are lucky, your service provider has given you a dedicated IP
number for your host. If so, you can skip this paragraph and the
next. If not, you will have to do a little more work to configure your
TCP/IP connection each time you connect. If you are told to use
SLIP or CSLIP, make sure you can't use PPP. It is much easier to
configure PPP for dynamic IP addressing than to configure SLIP for
dynamic addressing. If you're stuck with SLIP, look at the capture
from your dry run with the terminal program. Did the service provider somehow indicate what your host IP address would be for
the session? If so, great. You just need to make some kind of
script (for a terminal program, perhaps) which is capable of dialing
and getting to that point and saving the IP number before finish-
ing the rest of the configuration. Or, you can do it manually each
time. Otherwise, though, I don't know how you'd get it working
(ask your provider for help).

PPP is much easier to use with dynamic addresses. When the PPP
SANA-II driver is brought online, it automatically creates environment variables with your IP address and the IP address of the
machine you are directly connected to. Even better, the PPP distribution comes with a script generator to make a script to configure
AmiTCP for your session -- bring the device online, run the script
generator, execute the script, and you're set.

Knowing the IP address for your host, you need to configure your
SLIP or PPP driver. Most drivers use files in env:sana2/ to store
configuration information for each separate unit of each device.
Consult your documentation for the details. You'll need information such as whether to use hardware handshaking, what baud
rate to use, etc. Make sure you've added your driver to the inet:s/
sana2_devs or AmiTCP:db/interfaces.

Once you've got your modem connected, you have to start your
TCP/IP software. Put your SANA-II device online and then configure your TCP/IP software to use that SANA-II device. If you are
also on a LAN, your TCP/IP software may be already running, so
skip that step. When you installed TCP/IP, you should have configured some of the static things like your username, etc. Make
sure you have a host name, have told the protocol which SANA-II
drivers to use and things like that (see the earlier section on con-

figuring TCP/IP). To get the SANA-II device online, you use the "online" command. It's a part of many of the SANA-II driver distributions and accepts the name and unit number (usually 0) of the device as arguments.

To configure the TCP/IP software for your dial-up connection, you really only need to do two things: "config the interface" and "add a route." With either AS225r2 or AmiTCP, the basic process and the command names are the same. The command "ifconfig" is used to configure interfaces. An interface is a particular unit of a SANA-II driver. For example, if using AS225r2 with your SLIP/PPP driver as the second line in inet:s/sana2_config and your host IP address for this connection is 192.204.28.87, the interface is config'ed with this command: "inet:c/ifconfig s1 192.204.28.87." Note that your host might have more than one IP address -- one on a local Ethernet network and one with a PPP connection, for example. It's because of this that you must add a route. Otherwise, TCP/IP might not know where to send packets. If the host on the other side of your dial-up connection is 192.204.28.8, you might use this command to add the route: "route add default 192.204.28.8 1." That says the following: create a new route (add); for any packets that don't have some better path (default); through the given IP address (of the gateway on the other side of your dial-up connection); there is only one hop (1) between you and the specified gateway.

When you're done with your dial-up connection, you might also unload your TCP/IP software. If you are also on a LAN, though, you may want to keep the TCP/IP software up but remove the dial-up connection. You take the device offline (using the counterpart to the "online" command: "offline"). Then you bring the interface down (with "inet:c/ifconfig s1 down," for example), and remove the route (using something like "route delete default 192.204.28.8").

You can use your terminal program every time to establish the connection with your service provider. That is painfully klunky, though. (If you insist on doing it manually, don't forget about configuring your modem to ignore DTR) Much better is to use something like Thomas Kobler's freely redistributable "dialup" program. This gem is designed to do the dialing for you and to enter the name and password, etc. It uses configuration information from your SANA-II driver and the command line. Once you've got the command line right, you can save it as a script (or in an environment variable). Dialup shows you its interaction over the serial port in a shell window, so you'll know if something goes wrong.

You might as well grab dialup or something similar and use it after your first dry run with the terminal program. There is, by the way, a similar solution which is even more automatic. You install it as a device which calls the service provider when you try to use TCP/IP to the Internet!

I have a script called 'dial' which invokes dialup with my command line. It then configures the interface on my TCP/IP protocol stack and adds a route to the Internet. Another script, 'hangup,' brings down the interface, removes the route and disconnects me from the service provider.

AMITCP AND PPP: Another Look

[Getting started on the Internet has been tough for many people -- especially so for many of the less experienced Amiga users who've been getting online for the first time in the last year or two of the Internet hype. One piece of software that came to help was Christopher Laprise's iNTERiNSATLL script. After seeing how many people were helped by Chris's software, I hired him to write a section for the second printing of my book. This is that section. Rather than integrate the section I'd written previously with Chris's new writing, I decided to keep them both intact. This way, you've got two chances to figure it all out rather than just one. Hopefully, even if you've been having a little trouble following things to this point, Chris will get you going quickly. And if you have any problems, don't blame them on me, they're all Chris's fault, and you can email him a virtual raspberry. For the rest of this part, 'I' refers to Chris, not to Dale. -dale]

Just as on other platforms, the TCP/IP and PPP combination of protocols have become the definitive way to connect Amigas to the Internet. Indeed, TCP/IP is the set of protocols which forms the foundation for the Internet itself, and using it helps ensure you'll have access to the full range of services that are available. Though somewhat complex, this is proving to be manageable for average users to install and operate with the right kind of user interface and guidance.

Here we will guide you through an actual setup process using the most accessible TCP/IP and PPP protocols for the Amiga, via a simple user interface. A certain familiarity with one's computer is required; this is no different for the Amiga than it is with other platforms. Also, one needs to use available resources: We assume that if you run into an Amiga OS concept that is unfamiliar, that you will consult your Amiga handbook; If you are encountering problems using an archive utility, the documentation for that utility is the best source for help.

INSTALLATION with iNTERiNSTALL

Here we use iNTERiNSTALL, which I wrote to remove the many unnecessary steps normally encountered when configuring a dial-up PPP link. Besides the software requirements, a certain minimum of information is required before you begin.

SOFTWARE COMPONENTS
AmiTCP (version "4.0 demo" used here)
PPP (version "1.30 evaluation" used here)
iNTERiNSTALL 1.51
Amiga OS 2.04 (or greater)

AmiTCP is produced by NSDi, and PPP is by Holger Kruse. Both
are shareware (actually, AmiTCP is now fully commercial), and you
are encouraged to send in your registration fee if these products
perform to your satisfaction. In return, you will receive the registered versions which have additional capabilities. iNTERiNSTALL
is distributed in it's "full" version for free, though I suggest you
send a donation if you find it useful. Refer to the respective documentation of these packages for details.

Start with iNTERiNSTALL itself by de-archiving it: An "iNTERiN-
STALL" drawer will be created in the process. Then, as described
in the iNTERiNSTALL documentation, de-archive both AmiTCP
and PPP into the "iNTERiNSTALL" drawer (from Shell, CD there
before running LHA). Make sure the 'iiMOD' module file for your
access provider is also in this drawer (see "HOW CAN I GET A
MODULE?" below). Then run iNTERiNSTALL from Workbench.

Following is a transcript of an actual installation:

```
iNTERiNSTALL 1.51 by Chris Laprise, Installer for AmiTCP and PPP
    iNTERiNSTALL performs an installation and setup for AMITCP and   PPP that is apropriate
for dialup Internet access. No other   installation should be performed with these two pro-
grams.
    Please make sure you have un-arced them into the iNTERiNSTALL   directory as per the
readme file before proceeding.
68030 CPU detected. Proceed with install? (y/n) :y
    PORTAL.iiMOD.. #MODULE FOR iNTERiNSTALL 1.51 - Portal via SprintNet (portal.com)
NETCOM.iiMOD.. #MODULE FOR iNTERiNSTALL 1.51 - Netcom (netcom.com)   LOGONAMERICA.iiMOD..
#MODULE FOR iNTERiNSTALL 1.51 - Log On America (loa.com)   EMPIRENET.iiMOD.. #MODULE FOR
iNTERiNSTALL 1.51 - EmpireNet (empirenet.com)   COMPUSERVE.iiMOD.. #MODULE FOR iNTERiN-
STALL 1.51 - Compuserve (compuserve.com)
1) PORTAL.IIMOD 2) NETCOM.IIMOD 3) LOGONAMERICA.IIMOD 4) EMPIRENET.IIMOD 5) COM-
PUSERVE.IIMOD select: 5
Enter the device name (ex: serial.device) for your modem : gvpser.device
Enter the device unit# (ex: 0) for your modem : 0
Enter the highest port speed (ex: 38400) for your modem : 57600
Enter the modem initialization command : ATZ&D0
Enter the telephone number for Compuserve : 6741377
Enter your USER ID (ex: 70431,2172) : 70431,2172
Enter your PASSWORD : my-password
Installing from AmiTCP-3.0b2
Enter path where the AMITCP dir is to be created (ex: HD1:COMM). Do not enter iNTERiNSTALL
or its subdirs : dh0:
This will over-write the existing configuration. Proceed? (y/n) :y Please Wait... Install-
ing to Q210:AMITCP

--- Please replace any old 'internet' and 'stopnet' icons --- with the current versions.

iNSTALL COMPLETE.  REBOOT AND TYPE 'internet' TO CONNECT
```

SERIAL DEVICE NAME AND UNIT NUMBER Using the built-in Amiga serial device, enter "serial.device" then "0". Otherwise, you will have to enter the name and unit number that the manufacturer of the serial port has assigned to it. For instance, my serial expansion card has two ports, numbered 0 and 1, and the device name for them is "gvpser.device".

HIGHEST PORT SPEED BOTH COMPUTER AND MODEM CAN SUPPORT
If using a serial expansion board, refer to the manufacturer's handbook for the supported port speeds. If using the Amiga built-in port, be careful not to go too high; this port will accept very high speed settings, but higher ones will not act reliably. A speed of 38400 is a practical upper limit for the built-in port.

Your modem handbook will instruct you what serial port (DTE) speeds your modem can support; don't confuse this with the modem's communication (DCE) speed, which is often much lower. Many have a DTE limit of 57600 or 115200 (while lower speeds like 19200 and 38400 can be used).

My serial port supports over 115200, and my modem supports upto 57600, so I used 57600.

THE MODEM INITIALIZATION COMMAND For this setting, we will assume your modem has basic Hayes compatibility. Two typical commands would be "ATZ" or "AT&F" (the first resets the modem to your personal preset, the second resets to factory defaults-- see your modem handbook for details).

The init. command should do the following:

1) Enable hardware flow control (RTS/CTS) (suitable cable required)

2) Disable software flow control (XON/XOFF)

3) Enable data buffering (ASB) Enable error correction (V.42 or MNP4)

4) If available, enable compression (V.42bis or MNP5)

5) Enable word result codes

6) Cause CD line to track actual carrier-detect state

7) Disable DTR hang-up mode

If the factory defaults do not match the above, you can enter an explicit init. command such as "AT&F&K3&Q5Q0V1&C1&D0", which should work with most modems. My personal preset is nearly the same as this, so I can use "ATZ&D0".

THE TELEPHONE NUMBER TO CONNECT TO This will be your access-provider's data line.

YOUR USER ID OR NAME This is your login identity.
YOUR PASSWORD This setting gets stored in "envarc:sana2/ dial.ppp" in case you're worried that someone using your Amiga might look at it (unlikely).

WHAT'S MORE: What else you must supply without a "module" Other information is necessary which is specific to the Internet access provider you subscribe to, such as: the what the login prompts look like (they often vary from provider to provider), the domain name (which your computer will be a part of), and the IP addresses of the Domain Name Servers (with one or more such DNS addresses, your computer can find out the address numbers of any domain name on the Internet).

The prompts essentially require that a dialup/login script be written for Amiga PPP, while the domain name and DNS are supplied by your access provider.

iNTERiNSTALL modules contain the above PPP login script, domain name and DNS information for specific access providers. These modules are used because login scripts can be difficult to write.

HOW CAN I GET A MODULE?
If you're comfortable altering a login script, a custom module can be made using an included module as an example. This could be as simple as changing one or two prompt strings, and entering your access provider's domain name and name server(s) at the bottom. Details are provided in the iNTERiNSTALL documentation. Otherwise, the author of iNTERiNSTALL (and this chapter) can supply you with a module for a nominal fee. You must supply the three types of information outlined in the iNTERiNSTALL documentation (what the login prompts look like, the domain name, and the DNS addresses). Your provider will give you at least the latter two, though you may have to dial the access number with a

terminal program and login manually in order to look at the prompts.

Once you have a module which gives you a sucessful connection, it's a good idea to upload it to your provider's system in a place where other people can get at it. You probably aren't the only Amiga user on that system.

IMPORTANT FILES

This overview will give you an idea of what script and configuration files that an installer must deal with to get the IP connection working.
ENVARC:SANA2/PPP0.CONFIG Contains the serial device name and unit number, port speed, and name of the dial-up script.
ENVARC:SANA2/PPP.DIAL (depends where ppp0.config points) Contains the modem init. command, dialing and login instructions (incl. provider tel#, user ID, password).
AMITCP:BIN/STARTINTERNET See connection overview below. Directs the whole start-up process for AmiTCP. Also supplies info to AmiTCP that would be in db/hosts and db/networks if the addressing weren't dynamic.
AMITCP:DB/INTERFACES Provides information about various low-level protocols for various hardware interfaces (Ethernet, serial PPP, etc.)
AMITCP:DB/RESOLV.CONF Provides information that AmiTCP needs to resolve the identity of hosts (including our own). Specifically, our domain name and the DNS addresses are stored here.

MAKING THE CONNECTION

AmiTCP and PPP are generalized than you may think. As networking tools, they must be able to satisfy a broad range of uses... just one of which is allowing personal computers to surf the World Wide Web from the home. As a result, they cannot do it all on their own: Scripts must provide a helping hand to each tool, taking care of many details. Whenever you start the connection, you're not running AmiTCP or PPP directly, but executing a script which controls this process. iNTERiNSTALL produces the scripts necessary for such use, so that the details of connecting are transparent to the user. Nevertheless, it can be helpful to understand what's going on.

Normally, you will make the connection by executing or clicking on the 'internet' icon; this, in turn, starts the amitcp:bin/startinternet shell script in such a way that no pesky shell windows remain glued to your Workbench screen.

OVERVIEW OF "STARTINTERNET"

1) Is the serial port already in use? If so, notify the user then quit.

2) Put PPP online: PPP initializes modem, dials, logs in and establishes IP addresses (PPP runs the PPP.DIAL SCRIPT during most of this process)

3) Has PPP notified us what the Host and Gateway addresses are? If not, the dialup or login has failed.

4) Start AmiTCP, if it isn't already running.

5) Notify AmiTCP of our Host address (us), and tell it to route all packets going to addresses not on our local network (LAN) to the address of the Gateway we just connected to.

6) Mount the TCP: handler for DOS, giving easy file I/O access over the network (programs and scripts can use this without having to access AmiTCP directly).

7) If it's installed in amitcp:libs, load the "socket.library" which allows applications written for Commodore's TCP/IP (AS225) to work with AmiTCP.

8) Check that AmiTCP is still running. If it isn't, it may have found an error in the configuration files. Notify the user whether the whole connection process has completed or failed.

ONCE YOU'RE CONNECTED (OR NOT?)

You should expect a completed connection. In iNTERiNSTALL's case, you'll have one or two small notification windows on your WorkBench that you can close. A good thing to try on your first successful connect may be to test things out by running a client program (the user-end of a network application). The AmiTCP 4.0 demo comes bundled with several clients, some of which you'll find useful, such as ncftp and telnet. For example, in Amiga Shell typing "telnet compuserve.com" should connect you to CompuServe's login screen (typing "CTRL-]" then "Q" will quit).

If, however, you get a 'FAILED' message (especially if it takes more than a minute or two for a message to appear), then you need to check the information you entered during the installation (re-install over the old installation if you have any doubts). If checking and re-installing doesn't help, the next step is to determine whether something about your Workbench or system configuration is preventing the scripts from working correctly (this is a common cause for connect failures). Boot from a fresh copy of an original _unmodified_ Workbench floppy disk for both the re-install and the connect phases (using your hard disk for the destination of the installation as before). Only the PPP driver and a few ENV: variables will be placed on the Workbench floppy, so you should have enough room. Whether or not this tactic enables you to connect will tell you if something is awry with your usual Workbench configuration. A misplaced command in s:startup-sequence, or a corrupted or non-standard command in c: are a couple of possible causes (which are beyond the scope of this text).

Throughout this process, keep in mind that your setup and installation may actually be OK. From time to time, your access provider will develop problems with their equipment and may behave strangely for periods ranging from 5 minutes to a whole day. Although your first attempt to connect may have gone well, you may find that things just "don't work" on your next try. Whatever the circumstances, it is important to retry the connection, especially if you're fairly certain that you performed the installation correctly. (In other words: Don't panic.)

BREAKING THE CONNECTION

Most people will access the Internet as they do most other services and applications: In sessions. At the end of each session, we need to 'hangup'. A few people will opt for a dedicated line to their access provider, permitting 24 hour/day access. Most likely, your IP user account will entitle you to a limited amount of hours per month for a flat rate with 'overuse' charges for time used beyond your allotment. Even many accounts which are 'unlimited' usage for a flat monthly rate are not intended to be connected for days on end.

As described [ref. elsewhere], an Internet connection has multiple layers. AmiTCP takes care of the TCP and IP layers. But PPP is another layer (lower than IP) and its being separate from AmiTCP means that our Internet connection can be broken in more than one place.

The best way to break our connection to the Internet is generally through the protocol that initiated the dialing and login in the first place. From an Amiga Shell, entering "offline ppp.device 0" will cause PPP to terminate the software link between you and the provider's gateway, and also terminate the usage of the serial port. Termination of the software link should also cause your provider's modem to hang up, ending the telephone call. Further, it may be desirable to shut down AmiTCP itself once the PPP shutdown is done.

The most convenient way to handle the above is through a 'stopnet' script that you can click on or run from Amiga Shell. iNTERiN-STALL's Stopnet will shut down the PPP link, but also asks: A) do you want to shut down AmiTCP as well; B) do you want to force your modem to hangup. The former isn't important, though the latter may be if you're calling long distance and you want to avoid accidentally leaving the line connected. Typically, running Stopnet and pressing return twice (only shutting down PPP) will be sufficient.

RESUMING A CONNECTION

Should your computer crash while connected, it is possible to immediately resume the connection after rebooting. If your configuration supports this, a reset will not cause the modem to hangup, and PPP is capable of recognizing a pre-existing connection and will resume instead of dialing and logging in. Resume is automatic... simply clicking on the "internet" icon provided by iNTERiNSTALL is sufficient.

Requirements for resume capability: A) The PPP 'CD' option must be set (this is the default with iNTERiNSTALL); B) The modem must be set to "ignore DTR" (described under "THE MODEM INITIALIZATION COMMAND" above). Also, your access provider's equipment must be able to support resume in order for this to work.

Do not try to resume after a connection attempt which did not report as "complete" (hangup first, instead).

GETTING YOUR FEET WET...ON THE WEB!

The World Wide Web's soaring popularity is due to it's ability to make so much so accessible. More than anything else, browsing the Web can give you more confidence and get you acquainted with more forms of information on the Internet than any other application at present. From hypertext documents and forms (HTTP) with graphics and sound, to file archives (FTP), to Gopher searches, and even news and mail... a typical Web browsing program is the Swiss Army Knife of the Internet, offering point-and-click simplicity to boot. Even some seasoned Internet pros (accustomed to specialized, complex and powerful programs) cling to the Web because of its convenience.

Amiga Mosaic (AMosaic 2.0 pre-release used here) is the currently the only Web browser on the Amiga which supports advanced features like graphics and sound. It requires Amiga OS 3.0 or greater, and AGA graphics or better are recommended. Basic installation from Amiga Shell is simple: copy from Mosaic/envarc to envarc: all copy from Mosaic/rexx to rexx: all

...then drag the Mosaic drawer icon to someplace on your hard disk and reboot. Graphics and sound decoding is not built into AMosaic, so you should download and install GIF and JPEG Datatypes into your Workbench to gain this capability (also see the AMosaic installation guide for notes on handling music and animation).

AMosaic requires a system enhancement called Magic User Interface (MUI), "user" version 2.3 or greater. MUI is shareware and can be downloaded via FTP from Aminet. The MUI installation is icon-driven and mainly asks for a destination path, and which extras to add (none of which are required).

Domain names, as with the other Internet applications, are the basis for "calling" or connecting to hosts (or "sites") on the Web. However, web browsers also need to know the mode of the connection (hypertext, file transfer, news, etc.) plus often the particular page or subdirectory being accessed. For this, the Web uses Uniform Resource Locators (URLs) which can contain several such parameters on one line. These are described in detail within the section "Uniform Resource Locators", although you only need to understand their purpose in order to use the Web.

Here we'll demonstrate the use of URLs by using AMosaic to download the GIF and JPEG image Datatypes from the AMosaic support site located at www.omnipresence.com.

Run AMosaic from the Workbench and resize the window as you like. Then enter "http://www.omnipresence.com/amosaic" in the URL gadget at the top. The status at the bottom should say "Looking up www.omnipresence.com", followed by other messages ending with "Data transfer complete". Now we see the "home page" for AMosaic support: It will look like a page of text, some of which is highlighted and underlined. These highlighted words are 'links' which can bring you to other pages (often on different sites!) with a single mouse click. You may also see odd symbols, looking like a highlighted box with shapes inside: This represents an 'inline picture' which hasn't been loaded by AMosaic (we can't yet... no Datatypes, remember?).

Now that we've looked at our first Web page, let's proceed to the archives that contain our Datatypes. Click on the link indicating "HTTP download" and you will jump to a page listing a directory of files and subdirectories. Click on the "support/" subdirectory, then after that page loads look through the listing for the Datatype archives (in this case, "ZGIFDT39.16.lha" and "Jpeg-DataType.lha"). We've located our files!

A note is in order here: Web browsers tend to DISPLAY whatever link you click on, even if it's a binary archive! Newer versions of AMosaic will automatically save to disk, instead, if the link's name ends in ".lha". Yet not everything you will want to download will be named this way. To make certain that the next link you select will be saved to disk, toggle the "Save to local disk" option in the pull-down menu. As long as this option is on (a checkmark will appear next to it in the pull-down menu), links that you select will be sent to disk. At times, you may wonder why a file requester has popped up, due to the fact that you forgot to toggle 'Save..' off following a download. Just about anything can be saved with this feature: web pages, graphics, sound, etc.

Simply clicking on the first file will start the download. When it's done, a file requester will allow to select the directory and filename to save it as. Then click on the second file and that will download as the first one did. To abort any transfer, click on the "busy" button (a bouncing checkered ball).

At this point, you may want to investigate the other links on the AMosaic home page before you un-archive the Datatypes and install them. Instead of re-typing the URL, we can keep clicking on the 'BACK' gadget to retrieve previous pages from our computer's memory. (BACK and FORWARD only work if the "Save to local disk" option is turned off.)

Other sites of interest may be the popular sounding boards for finding information on the Internet: Searches by keyword can be made at "http://www.yahoo.com" (look for any of your interests, hobbies, etc.); The name "Amiga Web Directory" says it all and can be browsed at "http://www.prairienet.org/community/clubs/cucug/amiga.html"; An easy way to use the essential Aminet site is "http://ftp.wustl.edu/~aminet/" where you can search by keyword, directory tree, or look at recent uploads; The home page for

Intangible Assets Manufacturing is "http://www.iam.com" (publishers of this book and Envoy); For public discussion of Amiga networking try "news:comp.sys.amiga.networking" (yes, URLs can point AMosaic to UseNet and other services!). (For a more extensive listing, see the "Amiga Resources" section.)

Stop! Before you grab that pen and start jotting these URLs on a napkin, you should know that it's not necessary. Nor will you have to type in URLs over and over for each visit. AMosaic has a nifty 'hotlist' feature: Just click the "ADD" gadget next to the URL, and the URL of the page you're current looking at will be permanently added to your hotlist for future use. To use the hotlist, click on the expand gadget (which looks like a down-arrow pointing at a horizontal line) also next to the URL. A list will appear where you can double-click on any stored URL to re-connect to that page.

A tremendous time saver is the "Delay image loading" feature (toggled from the pull-down menu). Once you install the image Datatypes, you will discover that many web pages are overladen with graphics and can keep you waiting a great deal. Of course, since the text of a page loads first, we can abort once we see the text (but you still have to wait for the first picture to start). Using "Delay.." will make AMosaic avoid loading images until you either select "Load images in current" from the pull-down menu, or you click on an "unloaded image" icon (which will load that particular image).

MAIL AND NEWS: TIPS ON INSTALLING THOR
Access to electronic mail is crucial with an Internet account, so this section will attempt to get you going with one of the better programs for this. Thor actually combines two applications -- mail and news -- into one program and user interface, eliminating what could be considerable headaches in setting up a second program for accessing Usenet newsgroups.

Version 2.1 is described here, and can be obtained from the Thor support site at "http://www.cs.uit.no/~kjelli/thor.html" as two archives (thor21_main.lha and thor21_inet.lha). Thor is shareware and can be registered for $30. Also, the AS225 emulation (socket.library) is required and is also available from the Thor site. THOR INSTALLER In Workbench, create a drawer called 'Thor' somewhere on your hard disk. After un-archiving the main part, double-click on the "InstallThor" icon and click "Proceed" until it asks you where you would like Thor installed. Using the Installer's file requester, select the 'Thor' drawer you created and click "Proceed". After some copying, you'll be asked if you want to select a language other than English. Then you'll be asked about fonts: leave them all selected and click "Proceed". Next you'll be asked if you want to install modules for Bulletin Board Systems (BBSs): Click "No". When asked about "modules... for the Internet", click "NO"! (This option is desirable, but would not work for me; We will install them from the shell.) Answer "No" to the "download and an upload directory" question. Select the style of icons for Thor (if you don't recognize what the other types are, leave it on "Normal" and click "Proceed"). The Thor installer will notify you that it's finished. THOR INET The Thor Internet modules have yet to be installed. Open an Amiga Shell, and issue the following commands:

```
makedir ram:thorinet cd ram:thorinet
...at this point, un-archive the Thor Inet part; the following line is an example: lha x
dh0:thor21_inet.lha
Copy #? `getenv THOR/THORPATH` all Execute s/cfgtcp Execute s/cfgtcp_online
```

THOR CONFIGURATON
Run Thor from the icon in the 'Thor' drawer you created. It will complain about a missing global configuration: Press "OK" until the small Configuration window appears. For now, select "Global", then "Save". Next, select "Systems" then "New": Now enter a name that is associated with your access provider ("portal.com" for example). Under "Mailpacket" enter a simple name ("portal" for example). Under "Type", select "TCP". Select "Save" and answer "yes" to the conference list question. Select "User Info" and fill in your user name (ex: johnd) and email address (ex: johnd@por-tal.com). Close the User Options window then select "Type Options". Fill in your mailserver address (ex: mail). Remove the checkmark from "Get >From System Config" beside the "User-name" field. Enter your username (ex: johnp). Fill the "Newsserver" field with your news server address (ex: news). For "Sockets" enter 2. Select "Save" (the CfgTCP window will disappear). Close the remaining configuration windows and the Startup window (this will exit Thor).

Thor is now ready for use. The icon-driven ConnectThor program is what actually read/writes mail and news, and is used while you are connected to the Internet.

Caveats: To be on the safe side, always exit Thor before you run ConnectThor, and vice-versa. Accessing a newsgroup using the browse/hotlist feature within ConnectThor does not subscribe you to that newsgroup. The "Join Conference" function within Thor is used to subscribe. Enabling XPR compression to reduce the disk space used by mail and news sounds like a good idea, but I haven't had great luck with it. Leaving this option turned off is probably the best way to avoid corruption of mail and news data. Familiarize yourself with the Thor documentation. In particular, the section on using the editor can be valuable for the beginner.

NOW YOU'RE AN INTERNET DENIZEN

Between AMosaic and Thor, you can access the majority of Internet services. Like a highway, the Internet has many uses: For an extensive list of applications, see [ref]. Also keep in mind that several can be working at the same time (browse the Web while getting mail/news, while downloading via FTP, while periodically monitoring a live text discussion via Internet Relay Chat). You can have multiple Web windows just by running AMosaic more than once. You'll find the Amiga's efficient multitasking at least as valuable on the Internet as with anything else. Using an Amiga does affect your ability to use Internet applications (often for the better), but new types of applications are not always available when they arrive for other platforms (telephone conversation over the net is an example). The key here is to keep a lookout for new ways of using the Internet, and what's being done to bring these applications to the Amiga.

[Thanks, Chris! - dale]

UUCP

In Part I, we discussed the basic idea of UUCP, a store-and-forward network which used to be the network protocol to deliver most electronic mail and news. While UUCP was originally developed for Unix computers, it has been widely ported and is available for the Amiga.

Matt Dillon ported `UUCP' to the Amiga. It is available on `Fred Fish' and `AmiNet.' It has its own newsgroup and its own FAQ. The best source of general information about UUCP is in the software documentation and in the O'Reilly Nutshell UUCP books listed in the reading list at the back of this book.

Typically UUCP is used to connect to the global UseNet. That requires a modem and phone line, a hard drive with several megabytes of free space, and a special arrangement with a UseNet 'feed' -- someone who will store and forward data from your computer to and from the rest of the world. It is generally run only on computers which stay on 24-hours a day (or nearly so).

UUCP is complex to set up and to maintain. There are lots of little details that have to be attended to, probably more than with some simple TCP/IP setups. The software was not written to be user-friendly, and it has evolved over many years, growing in complexity along the way.

If you have an Internet shell account, or an account on a BBS or online service with UseNet mail and news, there probably isn't much point in considering running UUCP on a single-user computer. If you want to try it because you like trying new things, or if you are setting up a BBS (or other multi-user system), go for it.

Until recently, you might run UUCP if you wanted inexpensive (or free) mail and news, or if you wanted to cut back on the time spent online to a long-distance connection (if you didn't have a local system to use). Now, TCP/IP access is almost as inexpensive as UUCP, and it will probably be less expensive soon. UUCP still has its place, but that is in connecting BBSs and remote outposts. For most people, even individuals who'd rather get mail and news directly to their Amiga, using TCP/IP with SMTP, POP and NNTP makes more sense than setting up UUCP.

Mail and News Readers

If you have a shell, BBS or online service account, you'll use mail and news reader software on the remote host. If you get mail and news using TCP/IP or UUCP rather than a terminal session, you'll need your own Amiga software for reading mail and news. There is a wide variety to choose from.

Most Amiga mail and news readers are very flexible. The same program can often use files stored locally, POP or NNTP to read from, and can write to local files, POP, SMTP or NNTP. The flexibility comes at a small cost -- the additional complexity results in interfaces which are less intuitive than they might otherwise be. Setting up your Amiga to receive and read mail and news takes a lot of patience and time, but is not otherwise difficult.

Due to the wide variety of continuously updated software and possible configurations, I can't begin to give you instructions for how to set up and use the software you might choose for your particular situation (though I've included in a previous section a description of using one of the more popular readers, Thor). Make sure that you have the basic underlying software (TCP/IP or UUCP) set up and working well before you mess with mail or news. Then read your software's documentation carefully before starting. You'll need to attend to many details, and there is no way to get through it with a minimum skimming of the docs.

From the current AmiNet index, here are several freely redistributable mail readers and related files:

```
AM1_19beta_bin.lha      comm/mail   158K+Mail system for AmigaUUCP
AM1_19beta_contr.lha    comm/mail   722K needed multimedia/uucp tools for AmigaMail
AM1_19beta_src.lha      comm/mail   172K MUA for AmigaUUCP (plus) (src)
AmigaElm-v3.lha         comm/mail   332K+UUCP Mail-Reader, version 3 (3.99)
avml32.lzh              comm/mail    72K+The AVM mail reader for UUCP version 1.3.2
ems_1_0_docs_eng.lha    comm/mail   114K Documentation to ems_1_0_exec.lha EMS 1.0
ems_1_0_exec.lha        comm/mail   343K+EMS 1.0 - Electronic Mail System - powerfu
ems_register.lha        comm/mail     2K+How to register for EMS in Germany
ListSERV3_0.lha         comm/mail    65K+Mailing list package / unreg. version
metamail-2.3a.lha       comm/mail   210K+Send/read MIME-conformant mail.
MUIEmail_V37.84.lha     comm/mail    39K+GUI frontend for email. Needs 2.04, MUI.
NetIdSMTP10.lha         comm/mail    15K+Sends SMTP Messages from a spooled file.
PGPMIP.lha              comm/mail   135K+integrating PGP into e-mail
pmread.lzh              comm/mail    94K+Integrated news/mail reader system
pmread_dat.lzh          comm/mail     6K+Sample News file for use with PMRead
smail2.lha              comm/mail   207K+Smail Version 2.0
smailsr2.lha            comm/mail   156K+Smail V2.0 sources
spluu_116_beta.lha      comm/mail    20K File EMail/Splitter with UUCP and LhA func
```

Here are the latest news readers available on AmiNet:

```
amiga-nn-2.lha          comm/news     8K+Simplenews, forgotten in Amiga NN dist
amiga-nn.lha            comm/news   293K+Amiga-port of NN 6.4.18
amiga-nn6.4.18.lha      comm/news   307K+Amiga-port of NN 6.4.18apl3 newsreader
AnnR09.lha              comm/news   113K+Ann - an Amiga NewsReader for NetNews
Arn103a.lha             comm/news   272K+Amiga USENET/UUCP newsreader V1.03a
Arn103a_src.lha         comm/news   252K+Source for UUCP/USENET newsreader V1.03a
GRn-2.1.lha             comm/news   232K+Gadtools-based newsreader for AS225R2/AmiT
MassDecode1.1.lha       comm/news    39K+Scans UseNet newsgroups and uudecodes bina
MD100.lha               comm/news    36K+Scans UseNet newsgroups and uudecodes bina
PurgeNews.lha           comm/news    19K+Configurable news purger.
Rn15.lha                comm/news    37K+An update to rn 1.5 (16-Aug-91)
tin122.lha              comm/news   202K+Amiga TIN v1.22 - Full featured Usenet new
```

INetUtils

v1.3, Freely Redistributable, Michael B. Smith

INetUtils is a collection of utilities for Amigas running TCP/IP to use news and mail. I use INetUtils on my Amigas. Included programs areSMTPd, SMTPpost, NNTPpost, NNTPXfer, AmiPOP, and Sabot (a newmail activity program). You must still have a newsreader and a mailread to make use of INetUtils -- it just provides the underlying mechanisms.

GRn

v2.1, Freeware, Michael B. Smith and Michael H. Schwartz
All Rights Reserved.

This is the newsreader I choose to use on my Amiga. Here is a description from the documentation:

"GRn is Gadtools Read News, a Gadtools-based newsreader for the Amiga, running Release 2.0 or above. Some special features are available on higher releases. GRn supports locally stored news (via AmigaUUCP, C News, or NNTPxfer) and NNTP in a variety of ways (AS225r2, AmiTCP 2.2 or above, DNet, AUW and direct connection via serial.device or serial clone)."

While GRn 2.1 is freeware, future versions will likely be shareware or commercial.

Other Internet Applications
Using WAIS
Many Gopher servers provide an interface to the Wide Area Information Service. You won't even leave Gopher to type your query. You can also use Telnet to "quake.think.com" (or various other servers) and log in as "wais" to use their link for an alternate interface. Mosaic also offers an interface to WAIS.

WWW Update
If you have IP connectivity to the Internet, you will want to have a look at AmigaMosaic or other graphical browser. Otherwise, you'll need to use the interface available from your service provider. If you have a shell account, you probably have access to Lynx and/or WWW. Lynx is probably the nicer interface.

When this book was first written, there was only one graphical web browser for the Amiga. Now there are a dozen, all in various states of testing and public pre-release. There's even a port of the Lynx text-based browser to run on the Amiga. AMosaic is still a good way to get started, and once you're on the Web, you can easily search for information about newly available browsers to decide if you'd like to try one of them.

AmigaMosaic
Freely Redistributable
Amiga Port by Michael Fischer, Michael Witbrock, Mike Meyer

This is a great port of the original (NCSA) Mosaic to the Amiga. It is not, however, distributed by the University of Illinois or the National Center for Supercomputing Applications. (I think the authors should have named the Amiga port MMM, after their initials. Maybe they worried that Campbell's Soup might sue them.)

AmigaMosaic is a great Web browser. It uses MUI for a graphical user interface, and has an extensive ARexx interface. Datatypes are used to provide extensible multimedia capabilities, so AmigaOS version 3.0 or later is required for using all of Mosaic's capabilities (but it does work with 2.04). Versions are available for use with AmiTCP, AS225r2 and DNet. It can also be used stand-alone for reading local documents only. Unfortunately, the current version does not support forms, which are required for some Internet shopping malls and the like.

Make sure you read all of the Mosaic documentation, either in the docs directory of the distribution or online at the AmigaMosaic home page. If you're reading the docs locally in Mosaic, start with the index file. As with other complex software, setting up AmigaMosaic may take a little patience, but it is not difficult.

GNUEmacs

As I may have mentioned before, there are people who use Emacs all day. They never do anything else. This isn't because they never do anything but edit text, it is because Emacs is not just a religion, it is also darncd near a full operating system!

The GNUEmacs port available for the Amiga has scripts for Amiga IRC and Gopher clients (and probably for other clients as well).

X-Windows

In general, if you don't know what X-Windows is, you don't need it. For the curious, however, it is basically a way to allow one computer (or special terminal) to be the display and input device for a distant computer. The display is generally at least 1024x800, often 24-bit, and the input is usually assumed to include a three-button mouse. X-Windows names clients and servers a little backwards -- the "terminal" is referred to as a server and the computer is referred to as a client (there is a technical explanation which sounds reasonable for this naming convention, but it is still counter-intuitive to most people). X-Windows is very network and resource intensive, and is generally only used with Unix machines in a LAN environment, but it is occasionally used in other ways. X-Windows usually runs on top of TCP/IP and has complex installation and configuration requirements.

DaggeX
Freely Redistributable

I haven't tried DaggeX, but the comments I have seen and heard about it indicate that it is an adequate but slow port of X-Windows to the Amiga. It is available on AmiNet and from various other sources.

Amiga X-Windows
X11R4 - GfxBase, Inc.

A commercially ported and supported version of X-Windows for the Amiga. `X11R4' full color for the Amiga is available from `Gfx-Base, Inc.'. Also available are XView, OpenLook, Motif, programmers toolkits, and Berkeley sockets library. X Windows supports Commodore TCP/IP and Syndesis DECnet for Ethernet and serial connections, SANA for local. A demo version is available on `Ami-Net' in /pub/aminet/gfx/X11. The author, Dale Luck, wrote much of the original Amiga graphics code while he was part of Amiga, Inc. Hence, his implementation is solid and takes good advantage of the Amiga's special graphics features. It has probably been upgraded since these stats, and I believe the current version is able to take advantage of AGA and several of the available graphics cards.

Compatibility: AS225(tcp/ip) TSSnet(DECnet) Local(Sanal), all Amigas. WB1.3 and WB2.0
Requires: min 1M ram for server, 7M harddisk, more ram for local clients
Graphics: lowres (up to 32 colors), hires (up to 16), super/productivity (up to 4) All resolutions up to 2kx2k. A2024(Hedley) at 1024x800(1024/pal), interlace
Includes: pbmplus utilities, X11R5 fonts, xpr for Amiga printers.
Input: international keyboard support, 3 button mouse.
Other graphics cards: GDA-1 (upto 1024x768 256/16M colors), Ameristar 1600GX (upto 1600x1280 256/16M colors)

Amiga Resources
Whether you use a local BBS, a large Online Service or join the Internet, there are a set of common text resources you should be able to get at from most places. More and more, many of these resources appear first on the Internet and spread from there. Some of these resources are only readily available from the Internet.

Large collections of freely redistributable files are another important resource for the Amiga, as are various newsgroups and mailing lists.

Uniform Resource Locators

The URL is a way of spelling out where any given resource on the net is located. It indicates the type of application used to access the resource and the host of the resource. URLs are constructed differently for different types of resources. Rather than telling you a comprehensive explanation of how to read or write them, I'll give you some examples with an explanation for each.

From a Web browser, you can go to a specified URL. If the URL is for a file (for example), it will be automatically FTP'd.

file: //host/path/file
This says that the file "file" is available from the Internet machine "host" in the directory "path" for standard anonymous FTP. A file URL could point to a directory rather than a file (even to a root directory). By specifying a username (and possibly even a non-standard anonymous password), URLs can refer to files on non-standard servers. An example might be: file://ftp@host:passwd/path/file.

A disadvantage of specifying files by URL is that alternate servers (or even local copies) can't be referenced. On the other hand, the file pointed to might be known to be the current revision, while copies might not be.

telnet://host:port
This is pretty self-explanatory: there is a Telnet resource on a given host at a given port. The port might be left out if the resource is for the standard Telnet port.

gopher://host:port
Just like a Telnet URL, only for a gopher hole rather than a Telnet service. Gopher URLs can refer to specific directories in a hole, but that is really only useful from a browser.

news:group
Used to refer to a specific newsgroup. "news:comp.sys.amiga.networking" is one URL worth checking out.

http://host/path/document
"http:insti.physics.sunysb.edu/Amosaic/home," for example
specifies a hypertext document on the World Wide Web located on
the host insti.physics.sunysb.edu in the directory Amosaic, specifically, the "home" document.

Web Pages

From these starting points, it's pretty easy to get to most interesting Amiga information. Go find a Web browser and give it a try.
You'll be amazed.

The IAM home page is at: http://www.iam.com/
IAM's Amiga links are at:

> http://www.iam.com/amiga/amiga.html

The Amiga Web Directory is at:

> http://www.cucug.org/amiga.html

Another Web page to check out is Mike Meyer's:

> http://www.phone.net/

Meyer's Web server runs on an Amiga 3000 under AmigaOS. Mike
is a consultant and one of the authors of AmigaMosaic.

News

News groups used to be used for the distribution of software and
sources as well as for discussions, but the popularity of anonymous FTP servers has pretty much eliminated this practice. A few
Amiga newsgroups for source and binary distribution may be left
over from the old days, but they are now dormant and ignored.

That a group is moderated means that all posts are filtered by
someone who makes sure that only relevant information is dis-
seminated. The signal-to-noise ratio in these groups are excellent,
and if you can, you should subscribe to all the moderated Amiga
newsgroups. It'll take you about five minutes a week to read the
messages. (A signal-to-noise ratio is the number of articles with
good information versus the number of articles you couldn't care
less about.)

By the way, when you are new to news, you should read news.newuser for a while to get your bearings. It is a moderated group with postings introducing you to the net and the rules.

comp.sys.amiga.advocacy
Where the noise-to-signal ratio is at its highest. If you want to complain about how awful something is (either the PC or Commodore's management over the years), do it here. If you want to tell everyone how to think, do it here. If you want a good laugh, you may be able to find it here -- there are people who take this stuff seriously.

comp.sys.amiga.announce
Moderated. Announcements of new products, etc.

comp.sys.amiga.applications
Discussions of Amiga applications, which are suitable for particular purposes, how to use, etc.

comp.sys.amiga.audio
Digitizers, mod players, music and other audio topics are here.

comp.sys.amiga.cd32
All about your favorite console.

comp.sys.amiga.datacomm
Telecommunications with the Amiga. Used to include networking.

comp.sys.amiga.emulations
AMax, Bridgeboards, Emplant, PC-Task and more are discussed here.

comp.sys.amiga.games
You can guess what is discussed in this group.

comp.sys.amiga.graphics
Graphics programming, graphical accelerators and other Amiga technical graphics discussions happen here.

comp.sys.amiga.hardware
Now what does that jumper do?

comp.sys.amiga.introduction
If you are new to news or the Amiga, make sure to read this group for at least a little while.

comp.sys.amiga.marketplace
For Sale and Wanted ads for Amiga hardware, software and peripherals.

comp.sys.amiga.misc
General Amiga discussions that don't fit somewhere else happen here. The fanatical and religious discussion belong in .advocacy.

comp.sys.amiga.multimedia
Scala, AmigaVision, CanDo and similar products are discussed here, as are the presentations made with them.

comp.sys.amiga.networking
AmiTCP, AS225, Envoy, other protocols and the applications for them are all discussed here. If you're interested in this book, you're also interested in this group.

comp.sys.amiga.programmer
How to program your favorite machine -- in assembler, C and more.

comp.sys.amiga.reviews
Moderated. Reviews of Amiga products written by volunteers.

comp.sys.amiga.uucp
All about the Amiga port of UUCP and how to use it.

comp.unix.amiga
About Unix (AmigaUnix, BSD, etc.).

Mailing Lists

Mailing lists are a way to have ongoing discussions about highly-specialize topics, in semi-private, or with a wider audience than just those who have access to news (some people have Internet mail, but not news). Some mailing lists have small amounts of traffic, like a message or two a week. Others may fill your mailbox in a day. If you choose to subscribe to a mailing list, make sure that you save the message which tells you how to unsubscribe and pay close attention to the details of those instructions if you do need to unsubscribe. As well, you'll find details about the nature of the list and what questions or comments would be appropriate or inappropriate.

This compilation of Amiga mailing lists started as the work of Aaron Weiss, who published an earlier version in the May 1994 issue of Internet World magazine and has graciously given permission for me to update this list and freely reprint it. Maintaining the list on IAM's Web site, I've received numerous additions and updates. The version here was last updated in March of 1996. The latest version is available at http://www.iam.com/amiga/lists.html.

The list is in no particular order, except that I tend to add new entries to the top of the list.

NOTES:
1) For subscribe@xamiga.linet.org servers, please respond to welcome message to become an active subscriber.
2) Message between quotations is what should be written in email to mail list address. The word "Body:" preceding message means that the message should appear in the body of the email rather than the subject line. The rest are generally assumed to be subject line messages, but I always put the message in both places just to be sure.

Amiga Announcements from IAM (new products, updates, etc.)
registration-server@iam.com
"subscribe"

Grapevine Support list (IRC Client)
majordomo@gv.warped.com
subscribe grapevine [your email address]

AmiGate Support list (Fido<>UseNet Gating Software)
listserv@boble.ping.dk
ADD Amigatelist

Juggler List (pre-release Web Browser)
majordomo@ua.pt
subscribe juggler [your email address]

Slipcall (Dialup-Tool)
egge@canit.se
SUBSCRIBE sclist <address> <full name>

AFS mailing-list
emailurl@flevel.co.uk
subscribe afs me@my.domain

CyberGraphics mailing-list

Post: cgraphx@colombo.telesys-innov.fr
Sub: listserv@colombo.telesys-innov.fr
    subscribe cgraphx Firstname Lastname

Oberon-A Mailing List
oberon-a-request@wossname.apana.org.au
ADD [your email address]

ACE Basic
listserver@appcomp.utas.edu.au
subscribe ace [your name]

Amiga Oberon & Modula-2
majordomo@virginia.edu
subscribe amiga-m2 [your email address]

The PageStream user's mailing list
PGS-request@ramiga.cts.com
ADD [your email address]

lwplugin-l (for lightwave plugin software development info)
listserv@netcom.com
subscribe lwplugin-l

ami-sci (Scientific/engineering software and related homebrew
hardware)
majordomo@phy.ucsf.edu
subscribe ami-sci
http://keck.ucsf.edu/~jwright/ami-sci/

Amiga Formula One Grand Prix (World Circuits in the US)
amigaf1gp@math.ohio-state.edu
unknown

Blitz Basic 2 Programming
majordomo@cc.helsinki.fi
subscribe blitz-list user@domain

Golden Gate 2 (bridgecard for using PC peripherals in your Amiga)
GG2-list@kumiss.infinet.com

AMOS
subscribe@xamiga.linet.org
"#amos username@domain;"

CDPub (CDROM publishing and systems) - All platforms
Mail-Server@knex.via.mind.org
"SUBSCRIBE CDPub FirstName LastName"

Commodore-Amiga
subscribe@xamiga.linet.org
"#commodore username@domain;"

CSAA (comp.sys.amiga.announce) (Product or other)
announce-request@cs.ucdavis.edu

Emplant List (APPEARS TO BE DEFUNCT June, 95, NEW INFO
APPRECIATED)
subscribe@xamiga.linet.org
"#emplant username@domain;"

Excelsior! BBS System
subscribe@xamiga.linet.org
"#excelsior username@domain;"

GodlyGraphics - Christian Computer Graphics esp. using Amiga
GodlyGraphics-request@acs.harding.edu

Hyperami - AmigaVision, CanDo, DeluxeVideo, Director, etc...
listserv@archive.oit.unc.edu
"subscribe hyperami"

Imagine - the 3D Rendering package
Listserv@sjuvm.stjohns.edu
old?: imagine-request@email.eag.unisysgsg.com
old?: imagine-request@email.sp.paramax.com
"subscribe" in subject line and body

Lightwave - Video Toaster and related hardware
1. subscribe@xamiga.linet.org
    "#lightwave username@domain;"

2. lightwave-request@bobsbox.rent.com
    body: "subscribe lightwave-l your_address {your_name)"

Video Toaster
toaster_request@bobsbox.rent.com
body: "subscribe toaster-l your_id@your_address (your_name)"

ParNET - Amiga<->Amiga networking system
parnet-list-request@ben.com
questions to: parnet-list-owner@ben.com

SupraFAX
subscribe@xamiga.linet.org
"#supra username@domain;"

Amiga Misc (bit.listserv.i-amiga)
i-amiga@rutvm1.rutgers.edu

Comp.Sys.Amiga.Hardware
ami-hard%mainecs@cunyvm.cuny.edu

Comp.Sys.Amiga.Tech
ami-tech%mainecs@cunyvm.cuny.edu

EGS Mailing List (The 3rd party RTG system for 24bit graphic
boards)
listproc@okcforum.osrhe.edu
body: "SUBSCRIBE EGS <yourname>"

Piccolo (The 24bit Graphics Board)
pks-list-request@ben.com

Linux (680x0 channel)
linux-activists@niksula.hut.fi

Amiga SLIP List
amiga-slip-requests@ccs.carleton.ca

Amiga Mosaic
subscribe to: witbrock@cs.cmu.edu

Amiga Mach List
mailserver@lists.funet.fi
"sub amiga-mach firstname lastname"

Amiga X11 Info
mailserver@lists.funet.fi
"sub amiga-x11 your_first_name your_last_name"

Amiga GNU C info
mailserver@lists.funet.fi
"sub amiga-gcc-info your_first_name your_last_name"

Amiga GNU C Compiler Internals
mailserver@lists.funet.fi
"sub amiga-gcc-port your_first_name your_last_name"

Amiga Reviews Request Info
amiga-reviews-requests@math.uh.edu

Aminet Weekly Uploads
listserv@wunet.wustl.edu
"SUBSCRIBE aminet-weekly" OR
"SUBSCRIBE aminet-daily"

NetBSD Port
majordomo@netbsd.org
"subscribe port-amiga"

listserv@gu.uwa.edu.au
"subscribe real3d firstname lastname"

AmiTCP
amitcp-request@hut.fi

Picasso II Gfx Board
Picasso-Request@Terrapin-Station.umd.edu
"subscribe picasso"

Amiga LISP
amigalisp-request@contessa.phone.net

UMS (Universal Message System)
request@umshq.dfv.rwth-aachen.de

PGP Encryption for Amiga
listserv@peti.gun.de
body: "ADD [your_email_address] PGPAmiga" or "HELP"

FAQs

For many of the Amiga UseNet newsgroups there are one or more FAQs. An FAQ is a list of Frequently Asked Questions (with answers). Most are created because there are certain common questions that are being asked all the time. In the hopes that new participants in a newsgroup will find answers there rather than immediately asking the most basic questions to thousands of newsgroup readers, the FAQs are painstakingly assembled and posted regularly.

A great newsgroup, misc.answers, is a common place for all (and only) FAQs to be posted. You'll find lots of answers to questions you didn't know existed in this newsgroup. It is a good way to find out what kind of resources and topics of discussion are available through UseNet.

There is a comp.sys.amiga.datacomm networking FAQ (which will probably become the comp.sys.amiga.networking FAQ), an AmiTCP FAQ, an AmigaNOS FAQ, a general Amiga FAQ, and many others. They can be found in the newsgroups, on some FAQ archive sites and on many BBSs and other sources of freely redistributable files. Here were the FAQs stored on AmiNet recently (several others are in existence, you'll have to check the newsgroups, misc.answers, or the mailing lists):

```
anetfaq.lzhdocs/help77K+Amiga Networking FAQ
AmigaFAQg140794.lhadocs/misc329K+Frequently asked questions (german) concer
AmigaSciSchUnix.lhadocs/misc22K+Amiga_Science/School/UNIX_FAQ 4.03
ImagFAQ5.lhagfx/3d23K Imagine FAQ #5
NetBSD-info.lzh misc/unix25K+FAQ on NetBSD-Amiga (11.Jan.94)
modsFAQ12.lhamus/misc3K+FAQ S3M/MTM/FT mod formats in Amiga V1.2
merlin.lhapix/illu49K Pic and FAQ about merlin gfx board, German
```

'Zines

There are several on-disk or network magazines published about various topics at various (often irregular) intervals. These are sometimes referred to as 'zines. Some are excellent sources of timely information, others are adolescent ramblings. Among Amiga 'zines, one really stands out...

Amiga Report

A great online weekly magazine, free for the taking. Includes press releases, product reviews and other features. Often contains more details than a print magazine could afford space for. Amiga Report can be found on many BBSs (look at the BBS list), Internet FTP sites, the WWW, etc. The editors and authors of Amiga Report deserve a lot of credit for an excellent job of bringing up-to-the-minute news to the Amiga community for free.

RFCs

Internet standards (and recommendations and other information) are available in documents called RFCs. The acronym stands for "Request For Comments," but why isn't important. What is important is that the technical details of all standard protocols are spelled out in detail and are available for free. There are also recommendations, suggestions and other kinds of information. Each RFC is a stand-alone document (though it may reference other RFCs) and is referred to by number. The RFCs can be FTP'd from numerous sites. If you are on the Internet, you should at least obtain a current index to the RFCs (available from the same places as the RFCs themselves) so that you know what information is available in case you need it.

FTP by Mail

If you cannot use FTP at all, there is a service called "ftpmail" available from a few sites. You can send e-mail to one of these machines and it will use FTP to retrieve files for you and send you the files back again via e-mail. To find out more about the ftpmail service, send a message to "ftpmail@decwrl.dec.com" or "ftp-mail@doc.ic.ac.uk" or "ftpmail@vm.gmd.de" whose body consists of the single line "help".

Jargon File

There are so many technical words and special meanings in the computer community that a large file has been created with definitions for all of them. Many terms are regional or specific to particular institutions. Some are truly slang rather than merely technical. The style of the jargon file is light and humorous, so it is fun while it is informative. A must. By the way, I think that "The Hacker's Dictionary" is just a published version of one edition of the Jargon file, but I haven't checked my facts on this one.

Technical Support Areas

Many companies provide some level of technical support through the Internet and other online areas. It ranges from top-notch official support from paid support personnel assigned to answer questions in a vendor area to employees (or even users) who volunteer to answer questions in a general forum. Keep this in mind as you try to get technical support online. In either case, you may get a higher level of support with more convenience than you can by calling voice, but don't expect that every problem can be (or will be) resolved online. Make sure you've started by looking at the manual and have considered whether your question or problem can be resolved well with a voice call. If not, and you do post, be polite and be patient. Then, if your questions go unanswered or your problem goes unsolved for a few days, it's time to make a voice call. Even if you aren't happy with a technical support area, it is not the place to flame everyone in the world for lamely failing to help you.

BIX, CompuServe and several of the other online services have official vendor support areas for many Amiga companies. You can expect most questions in these areas to be answered within 24 hours by a representative from the company. Unfortunately, some companies are better than others about this, but you'll quickly learn which companies those are.

Many companies maintain their own BBS for customer support. This is often the best place to get the fastest answers and latest patches, even though it means paying for a long-distance call and learning a new system. The reason that the BBS is often better supported (than other online areas) should be obvious -- employees don't have to do anything special or go anywhere to do things with the BBS in their offices. The BBSs often have message areas for users, and these can also be quite worthwhile -- the only users are those who are really interested in the product, so the signal-to-noise ratio for messages about the product tends to be good. You might want to try both company BBSs and other vendor areas. You may find that you don't have any need for the BBSs -- or that you prefer them.

Finally, many developers and engineers have accounts with UseNet news access. They tend to read groups in which their products are discussed. If they see questions about their products, they'll often try to answer. This is a lot more hit-and-miss than the above methods, because when there are deadlines to be met, reading news might be the first thing to go, or someone may just not feel like answering a question they don't have to.

Fish Disks

If you've had an Amiga for very long at all, you surely know about the Fish Disks. Over one thousand floppies filled with freely redistributable software from the beginning of the Amiga's history up to the present day. Fred Fish devoted large amounts of his time to sorting through submissions from around the world, choosing those worthy of belonging to his collection and distributing his disks. These days, Fred distributes things on CD-ROM rather than on floppy. The one-thousand floppies are available individually for free copying at many Amiga user's groups, and for a small charge from many Amiga dealers. The CD-ROMs are inexpensive, and make the investment in a CD-ROM drive worth while.

For many types of freely-redistributable files you might be interested in, a good index of the Fish Disks is the place to start! The CD-ROMs include complete indexes, AC's Guide contains an index, and indexes are available as downloads from many sources.

AmiNet

Though AmiNet is easiest to access from the Internet, it is available in other ways, and it is a very important source of current freely redistributable software.

AmiNet is a set of interconnected FTP sites and other file accessing services for Amiga software. Each of the sites is referred to as a mirror (though one site could be considered the main site). Moderators examine incoming files before adding them to the public area. When they do, the mirrors are usually updated that day (three times a day).

All mirrors have the new files but most delete old files, however ftp.wustl.edu and ftp.cdrom.com keep all files. Whenever possible, use a mirror that is the close to you (generally, one on the same continent). A list of mirrors appears below.

There are thousands of Amiga files on AmiNet, with dozens added each week. What the Fish Disks were to the distribution of Amiga software five years ago, AmiNet is today.

Because gigabyte harddrives and CD-ROMs are used to store the AmiNet files, a logical organization is possible. Here is the current top-level directory structure to give you an idea of what kinds of files are available and how they are organized. There are subdirectories within each of the directories.

new/	New files, upload here.
	(See new/README.BEFORE.UPLOAD)
priv/	Private uploads.
	(See new/README.BEFORE.UPLOAD)

biz/	Business software	hard/	Hardware related
comm/	Communications	info/	Site information
demo/	Euro style demos	misc/	Miscellaneous
docs/	Text documents	mods/	Music modules
dev/	Developer software	mus/	Music software
disk/	Disk tools	pix/	Pictures
game/	Games software	text/	Text related
gfx/	Graphics software	util/	Utilities

To find a file on AmiNet, the best thing is to access it through the WWW or gopher servers. Next best is to download the INDEX file and to search it (using c:search, for example).

To Access AmiNet from the Internet

http://ftp.wustl.edu/~aminet/ or ftp://ftp.wustl.edu/pub/aminet. From there, you can find help files, an index and a list of mirror sites so that you can choose a machine closer to you. Intercontinental network links tend to be much slower than other links, so it is important to minimize your impact on them. Here are some of the current mirrors (if you are in Europe, start with one of the European mirrors instead of wustl):

USA (MO)	ftp.wustl.edu	128.252.135.4	pub/aminet/
USA (CA)	ftp.cdrom.com	192.153.46.2	pub/aminet/
USA (TX)	ftp.etsu.edu	192.43.199.20	pub/aminet/
Scandinavia	ftp.luth.se	130.240.18.2	pub/aminet/
Switzerland	ftp.eunet.ch	146.228.10.16	pub/aminet/
Switzerland	litamiga.epfl.ch	128.178.151.32	pub/aminet/ (*)
Germany	ftp.uni-paderborn.de	131.234.2.32	pub/aminet/
Germany	ftp.uni-erlangen.de	131.188.3.2	pub/aminet/
Germany	ftp.uni-bielefeld.de	129.70.4.55	pub/aminet/
Germany	ftp.uni-oldenburg.de	134.106.40.9	pub/aminet/
Germany	ftp.uni-kl.de	131.246.9.95	pub/aminet/
Germany	ftp.uni-stuttgart.de	129.96.8.13	pub/aminet/
Germany	ftp.uni-siegen.de	141.99.128.1	pub/aminet/
Germany	ftp.cs.tu-berlin.de	130.149.17.7	pub/aminet/
UK	ftp.doc.ic.ac.uk	146.169.2.1	pub/aminet/

(*) closed 6:30am to 4pm weekdays

To Access Aminet without the Internet

If you don't have Internet access, get it. Barring that, many BBSs carry up-to-date Aminet files. If you have Internet mail, you can use an FTPMail service. Finally, CD-ROMs are pressed regularly with a snapshot of Aminet, and even if you have Internet access, the CD-ROMs are an inexpensive way to speed up access to older files and to reduce the usage of network bandwidth. If you want to get the list of new uploads mailed every week, send mail with 'SUBSCRIBE aminet-weekly user-name@domain.name' in the body to listserv@wunet.wustl.edu. If you want daily updates, just use 'SUBSCRIBE aminet-daily' instead. Replace user-name@domain.name with your email address, of course and keep the welcome mail in case you forget how to unsubscribe.

172

Projects like Aminet are undertaken by volunteers who put in a lot of hard work. If you use Aminet, do your part to help out. Make sure to read the help files and policies. Make an effort to follow the guidelines provided to reduce your impact on the resource. Read the upload policies and to upload new files if you can. If you have institutional resources, consider working with the moderators and mirror administrators to add a new Aminet mirror.

Five people who deserve recognition for their Aminet involvement: Urban D. Mueller, Chris Schneider, Matthias Scheler, Peter Sjostrom, Brian Wright. Urban Mueller, in particular, has made some really wonderful things happen (like the gopher and WWW interfaces)!

Besides the AmiNet sites, you might want to know about an archive of AmigaUnix software at litamiga.epfl.ch and the collection of ARexx code at ftp:arexx.uwaterloo.ca:/pub/arexx.

For Programmers
I had originally hoped to have enough space and time to include tutorials in developing applications for AS225/AmiTCP and Envoy. Unfortunately, I ran out of both. Hopefully, there will be enough demand to warrant an expanded second edition of this book which includes that information.

See the suggested reading list for several places to look for the information you need for programming. Envoy, AS225r2 and AmiTCP all include API and some programmer documentation. The DevCon notes and AmigaMail articles contain some introductory information. Various sources are available, and that seems to be how most Amiga programmers prefer to learn things anyway.

The number of applications with source for TCP/IP is very large. Source is available to all of AmiTCP and to most of it's utilities. Source is available to many utilities for AS225r2. Get on AmiNet and look around until you find something you like.

Jeffrey Litz has kindly made available the complete source to his CONF and TALK clients and servers for Envoy. CONF is quite similar to conferencing on multi-line BBSs such as Dialog Pro, Paragon, and others. But CONF is an Envoy service that lets an unspecified number of people "talk" in an unspecified number of conference areas. TALK is just a simpler, two-person-only version. If you can't find these files at your source for freely redistributable files, you may order them from IAM (see page 256).

SANA-II

The SANA-II standards archive (currently SANA2_r2.lha) is the place to start if you need to write a SANA-II driver or a protocol stack which will call SANA-II drivers. The archive includes sample source for a SANA-II driver. Few other sources are publicly available, but the archive should be sufficient.

The author of this book is still actively interested in SANA-II. After all, he wrote much of the current specification documents. If you develop Amiga hardware with a SANA-II driver or if you develop protocol software which calls SANA-II, please consider sending evaluation units to IAM. IAM hopes to be able to continue to evaluate various products and to do some degree of testing for SANA-II compliance and interoperability.

If you have specific questions about the SANA-II standard or if you need consulting services related to SANA-II, please contact IAM.

Part V. Security, Privacy, etc.

Keeping systems from being tampered with and keeping your private information from being read is an important consideration in using the networks. Whether you just need to make sure that the homework paper you're writing isn't deleted by someone else and that your love notes are only read by your lover, or to make sure that State Secrets are kept from The Enemy, the basic things to be aware of are the same.

Using computers and networks with social responsibility and an eye toward democratic goals is also a topic of this section.

Selecting and Protecting Passwords

If you think your passwords aren't important because you aren't a spy or army general, guess again. With your password to a BBS, for example, a malicious hacker can impersonate you to cause all kinds of trouble, or can generally snoop around your correspondence, etc. Someone with your password may cause you to lose access to a system or may be able to destroy files or other information. Worse, on a pay system like an online system, they may rack up serious bills for you. Remember, your PINs (personal identification numbers) for ATM (automated teller machines) cards or credit cards are also passwords.

Passwords are useless if they can easily be guessed. You'd be surprised how fast a computer program can guess at passwords. If you have a choice about your password (you often don't with PINs, for example), choose a password which is at least six characters long and which includes mixed-case and non-alpha characters (numbers or symbols, for example). Simple words out of a dictionary are the first to fall under attack. Don't choose things that are easy to guess about you. If you post all over the nets about Star Trek and choose "Picard" as your password, you aren't being very secure.

Don't use the same password on multiple systems. Not all sysops are completely honest (most are, but not all). Also, many BBSs are not as secure as you might like. So if you use the same password on a few systems, and one of those systems is compromised, all of the systems you use may be compromised. Those who try to circumvent security measures know that many people use the same password in many places, so if they want access to a more secure system (like a pay-service), they may try to get your password from a less secure system (like a local BBS).

In a similar vein, be careful about what you mis-type. Many systems keep logs of failed login attempts. Such logs are often less well protected than the rest of the system. If you miss the correct password by one letter, someone may easily be able to easily guess your password from what you entered. If you type the (correct) password for the wrong system, someone with access to the log could try that password on other systems they know you are on until they find one where it works.

Don't write your passwords down and leave them out for anyone to see. For the most important and secure systems, you should have passwords memorized. This may not be realistic for every single password you have if you are on several systems. Most terminal emulators and similar programs allow you to store passwords and to create macros which automatically enter the correct username and password for the system you are calling. If your machine is physically secure and you are pretty sure that no one untrustworthy is going to be able to snoop around on it, take advantage of these features. They keep you from entering incorrect passwords (see above) and keep you from advertising your passwords by putting them on Post-It notes.

Viruses and Virus Checkers

The general media have made sure that you are aware of computer viruses even if you don't have a computer. They've perhaps been a bit alarmist about the whole thing, but hey, their job is to sell papers. Even if you don't use a modem or connect to the networks, you should be aware of the potential problems created by some malicious creatures and what you should to protect yourself to some degree.

A computer virus is a program which tries to spread itself somehow. It may write itself to every floppy disk inserted into a machine, for example. Clearly, once a virus author unleashes a virus, it might spread pretty quickly between many thousands of machines. As you can see, the telephone lines don't need to be involved. Taking a floppy from one machine to another may be all that is required.

Some viruses don't do anything at all besides spread. Others display silly messages. Some are downright mean, and may do nasty things like erase your files.

Many people are paranoid that using a modem or connecting to a network is going to make them vulnerable to catching a virus. There is no way to get a virus from just connecting to a modem or a network. Some people think that getting (or using) freely redistributable files makes them vulnerable to viruses. They are partially correct. Any time you run a program on your computer, you might run into a virus. Fortunately, the files put in the large public collections and on most BBSs and online services are all tested before being made available for download.

You can protect yourself from viruses by running a virus checker. This is a program which knows about many specific viruses and about the kinds of things that viruses do generally. By running such a program in the background all the time, you are much less likely to have a problem. Get at least your first virus checker from a source with a well-established reputation (like a Fred Fish CD-ROM) so that you know your virus checker isn't infected.

You should also make sure that you keep good backups of any important files (which you would want to do even if there were no viruses).

The documentation of most virus checkers provides additional information that you will want to have if you are concerned about viruses.

By the way, while you do need to be cautious, viruses aren't as wide-spread as you might believe. Among those who are reasonably cautious and who don't swap hundreds of disks of pirated software, they are relatively rare. In many years of computing, I've seen a couple of viruses, but I haven't been infected by any. I've been a little lucky, but so have many others. Keep a look out, but don't lose any sleep over it.

Piracy

If you choose to break the law, that is your choice. I'm not a judge or a cop. I'm not going to try to tell you what to do, or what you should do. I'm not going to play Big Brother and try to catch you doing something that I can turn you in for. I just want to make sure you understand the whole story before you make your decision.

People who write programs deserve to be paid. I've never heard from anyone who disagrees with that statement. Some people believe software should be free -- that something other than a price on software is how programmers should be paid. I agree with that general sentiment, but I'm not sure how to make it work (or if it can be made to work). Until and unless such a system is in place and is working, it is theft to use a commercial program without purchasing it (or to continue to use shareware without registering it).

You may quickly find in the online world that there are many people who believe the theft of software is somehow less immoral than the theft of jewelry or cars. Whole BBSs exist just to distribute commercial software illegally. Sometimes the software is exactly as it comes on the install disks, sometimes it is altered to remove any copy protection or to give "credit" to someone who thinks they are doing something neat by uploading the software.

By the way, you should be aware that many pirates are so busy copying programs that they don't notice things like viruses. The incidents of viruses seem to be much higher among pirates than among everyone else.

There is plenty of great free software out there. There is lots of good commercial software out there that is worth every penny of its cost. As more people realize that software is worth paying for (or, at least, that programmers should be paid), there will be even more.

Pretty Good Privacy

I originally wrote a couple of paragraphs about PGP, not having

time to add much more without taking away time from some of the
more Amiga-specific things I was writing about. I felt so strongly
about these issues, though, that I wanted to add more. So I
obtained permission from Andre Bacard to include his PGP FAQ in
this book in order to replace what I had originally written. Mr.
Bacard is the author of "Hunger for Power: Who Rules the World
and How." He also writes a "Technology & Society" column and
has been interviewed on hundreds of radio talk shows. The
remainder of this section (to "PGPAmiga") is Bacard's.

Bacard's Overview of Computer Privacy and PGP

This article offers a nontechnical overview of PGP to help you
decide whether or not to use this globally popular computer software to safeguard your computer files and e-mail. I have written
this especially for persons with a sense of humor. In Winter 1994,
my book on computer privacy will be published. Details are avail-
ablefrom abacard@well.sf.ca.us

IMPORTANT DISCLAIMER
PGP is controversial, politically and legally. Persons reading this
document may reside anywhere from South Africa to Finland, or
from Japan to the United States. Abortion, alcohol, and firearms
are legal in some countries and illegal in others. Similarly, PGP's
legality varies depending upon where you reside. If you have legal
questions about PGP, you can consult someone who knows your
nation's computer laws. If PGP sparks political questions, you can
check the News Groups listed later in this text.

What is PGP?
PGP (also called "Pretty Good Privacy") is a computer program that
encrypts (scrambles) and decrypts (unscrambles) data. For example, PGP can encrypt "Andre" so that it reads "457mRT." Your
computer can decrypt this garble back into "Andre" if you have
PGP.

Who created PGP?
Philip Zimmermann <prz@acm.org> wrote the initial program.
Phil, who lives in Boulder, Colorado, is a hero to many pro-privacy
activists. He works as a cryptographic consultant. Phil Zimmermann, Peter Gutmann, Hal Finney, Branko Lankester and programmers around the globe have created subsequent PGP
versions and shells.

PGP is based upon the RSA public-key encryption system. RSA
has been around since 1977, when it was first announced by its

inventors: Ronald Rivest of MIT, Adi Shamir of the Weizmann Institute in Israel, and Leonard Adelman of USC. It is called "RSA" after the initials of its inventors.

Who uses PGP [or other RSA-based systems]?
Persons who value privacy use PGP [or other RSA-based systems]. Politicians running election campaigns, taxpayers storing I.R.S. records, therapists protecting clients' files, authors negotiating contracts, entrepreneurs guarding trade secrets, journalists unveiling corruption, singles seeking spouses, and spouses pursuing singles are a few of the law abiding citizens who employ PGP to keep their computer files and their e-mail confidential.

Businesses also use PGP [or other RSA-based systems]. Suppose you're a corporate manager, and you need to e-mail an employee about his poor job performance. You may be required by law to keep this e-mail confidential. Suppose you're a saleswoman, and you must communicate over public computer networks with a branch office about your customer list. You may be compelled by your company and the law to keep this list confidential. These are a few reasons why businesses use encryption to protect their customers, their employees, and themselves.

Thomas G. Donlan, an editor at BARRON'S [a financial publication related to THE WALL STREET JOURNAL], wrote a full-page editorial in the April 25, 1994 BARRON'S entitled "Privacy and Security: Computer Technology Opens Secrets, And Closes Them."

Mr. Donlan wrote, in part:

RSA Data Security, the company founded by the three inventors, has hundreds of satisfied customers, including Microsoft, Apple, Novell, Sun, AT&T and Lotus. Versions of RSA are available for almost any personal computer or workstation, many of them built into the operating systems. Lotus Notes, the network communications system, automatically encrypts all it messages using RSA. Other companies have similar products designed around the same basic concept, and some versions are available for free on computer bulletin boards.

Donlan continues:

Without security, the Internet is little more than the world's biggest bulletin board. With security, it could become the information supermarket of the world. RSA lets people and banks feels secure putting their credit card numbers on the public network. Although it still seems that computers created an age of snoopery, the age of privacy is at hand.

Aren't computers and e-mail already safe?
E-mail is notoriously unsafe. Your typical e-mail travels through many computers. The persons who run these computers can read, copy, and store your mail. Many voyeurs get their kicks out of intercepting mail. Sending your business, legal, and personal mail through computers is even less confidential than sending the same material on a postcard. PGP is one secure "envelope" that keeps busybodies, competitors, and gossips from victimizing you.

I have nothing to hide. Why do I need privacy?
Show me a human being who has no secrets from her family, her neighbors, or her colleagues, and I'll show you someone who is either an extraordinary exhibitionist or an incredible dullard.

A college student wrote me the following:

"I had a part-time job at a dry cleaner. One day I returned a diamond ring that I'd found in a man's coat pocket to his wife. Unfortunately, it was NOT her ring! It belonged to her husband's girlfriend. His wife was furious and divorced her husband over this incident. My boss told me: 'Return jewelry ONLY to the person whose clothes you found it in, and NEVER return underwear that you find in pockets!' Until that moment, I thought my boss was a finicky woman. But she taught me the need for PGP."

Privacy, discretion, confidentiality, and prudence are hallmarks of civilization.

I've heard police say that encryption should be outlawed because criminals use it to avoid detection. Is this true?

The next time you hear someone say this, ask him if he wants to outlaw the likes of Thomas Jefferson, the "Father of American Cryptography."

Many governments, banks, corporations, and law enforcement agencies use encryption to hide their operations. Yes, a few criminals also use encryption. Criminals are more likely to use cars, gloves, and ski-masks to evade capture.

PGP is "encryption for the masses." It gives law abiding citizens the privacy rights which governments and corporations insist that they need for themselves.

How does PGP work?
PGP is a type of "public key cryptography." When you start using PGP, the program generates two "keys" that belong uniquely to you. Think of these keys as computer counterparts of the keys in your pocket. One PGP key is SECRET and stays in your computer. The other key is PUBLIC. You give this second key to your correspondents. Here is a sample PUBLIC KEY:

```
- -----BEGIN PGP PUBLIC KEY BLOCK-----
Version: 2.7

mQA9Ai2wD2YAAAEBgJ18cV7rMAFv7P3eBd/cZayI8EEO6XGYkhEO9SLJOw+DFyHg
Px5o+IiR2A6Fh+HguQAFEbQZZGVtbyA8ZGVtb0B3ZWxsLnNmLmNhLnVzPokARQIF
EC2wD4yR2A6Fh+HguQEB3xcBfRTi3D/2qdU3TosScYMAHfgfUwCelbb6wikSxoF5
ees9DL9QMzPZXCioh42dEUXP0g==
=sw5W
- -----END PGP PUBLIC KEY BLOCK-----
```

Suppose the above PUBLIC KEY is yours, and you e-mail it to me. I can store your PUBLIC KEY in my PGP program and use your PUBLIC KEY to encrypt a message that only you can read. [You read it by using PGP and your PRIVATE KEY to decrypt it. -d.l.] The beauty of PGP is that you can advertise your PUBLIC KEY the same way that you can give out your telephone number. If I have your telephone number, I can call your telephone; however, I cannot answer your telephone. Similarly, if I have your PUBLIC KEY, I can write you mail; however, I cannot read your mail.

This might sound a bit mysterious at first. However, it is very straightforward when you play with PGP for awhile.

How safe is PGP? Will it really protect my privacy?
Maybe your government or your mother-in-law can "break" PGP messages with super computers or pure brilliance. I have no way of knowing. Three facts are certain. First, top-rate civilian cryptographers and computer experts have tried unsuccessfully to break PGP. Second, whoever proves that he or she can unravel PGP will earn quick fame in crypto circles. He or she will be applauded at banquets and attract grant money. Third, PGP's programmers will broadcast this news at once.

Almost daily, someone posts a notice such as "PGP Broken by Omaha Teenager." Take these claims with a grain of salt. The crypto world attracts its share of paranoids, provocateurs, and UFO aliens.

To date, nobody has publicly DEMONSTRATED the skill to out-smart or outmuscle PGP.

Is PGP available for my machine?
Versions are available for various Unixes, Macintosh, Amiga, Atari ST, OS/2, MS-DOS, and CompuServe's WinCIM & CSNav. Many persons are working to expand PGP's usability. Read the Usenet alt.security.pgp newsgroup for the latest developments.

What is a PGP signature?
At the end of this document, you will see a PGP signature. This "digital signature" allows persons who have PGP and my PUBLIC KEY to verify that 1) I, Andre Bacard, (not a SPORTS ILLUS-TRATED superstar pretending to be me!) wrote this document, and 2) Nobody has altered this text since I signed it. [*Actually, the FAQ has been edited, so the signature has been invalidated and deleted. If the signature had been left here, you could have used it to determine that this exact text was not authenticated by Andre Bacard. -d.l.*]

PGP signatures may be helpful for signing contracts, transferring money, and verifying a person's identity.

How difficult is it to learn PGP?
PGP comes with a manual. It took me a weekend of trial and error to feel comfortable with this program. PGP has around two dozen commands.

Where can I learn more about the PGP and related subjects?
The following News Groups are a good place to start:

alt.privacy	to hear about electronic privacy issues
alt.security.pgp	to learn everything known about PGP
comp.org.cpsr.talk	to connect with Computer Professionals for Social Responsibility
comp.org.eff.talk	to touch base with the Electronic Frontier Foundation
talk.politics.crypto	to keep abreast of legal & political changes

Anything else I should know?
Andre Bacard is publishing a book about computer privacy in Winter 1994. Check your bookstore around Christmas. You will be amazed and shocked by what you read. You can reach him at abacard@well.sf.ca.us.

Andre Bacard
Box 3009
Stanford, CA 94309
abacard@well.sf.ca.us

Bacard supports the Electronic Frontier Foundation and Computer Professionals for Social Responsibility. Info at <info@eff.org> and at <cpsr@cpsr.org>.

"He only earns his freedom and existence, who daily conquers them anew." [Goethe, FAUST (1832)]

PGPAmiga
Freely Redistributable, v2.3a patch level 3, Amiga port by Peter Simons

PPGAmiga 2.3a.3 is capable of reading and generating the new packet-type used by PGP 2.6, because PGP 2.6 is not available outside the USA or Canada. This archive contains the latest alt.security.pgp FAQ and full AmigaGuide documentation, along with related programs like AmigaELM, PGPMore, PGPSendMail and StealthPGP.

Amiga as Server

In a day when personal computers didn't really have operating systems (just program loaders), the Amiga had a fully multi-tasking OS. But it was a single-user system. Combined with the fact that the Amiga has no memory protection, this virtually is a death blow to the notion of a flexible and secure Amiga server on a network.

With a simple BBS, where all remote user access is through a single program, security isn't as difficult to enforce. The situation is very different on a network, especially a public network like the Internet.

First, anyone with physical access to the Amiga console can do anything at all to the system, and there is pretty much no stopping them. Sure, there is a Zorro-II card which requires a password on boot, but, even assuming that works perfectly, it is undesirable for most Amiga owners. Even if your Amiga server is physically secure (i.e., in a locked room), there are still problems (see below).

Next, the Amiga has no way to indicate that certain files belong to certain people and shouldn't be accessible to other people. Extensions to the standard protection bits have provided some relief in this regard, but it is not well-integrated with the rest of the operating system.

Any user who can run an arbitrary program on an Amiga can load and run a program which reads and writes anywhere in memory. This allows the circumvention of any measures to protect files or other resources from being world readable and writeable. Even if you think you've configured your system not to allow programs to be run remotely, if you provide any kind of network services, there is some risk. A bug might somehow allow remote execution of programs under certain (often convoluted) circumstances. These kinds of bugs are the ones routinely exploited by hackers. Running servers may also allows for very simple Trojan horses. A user just uploads a program that he hopes you will run eventually, and when run, it does something to break security.

At least on a Unix (or other multi-user) system, there are some protections against any user running completely amok. A Trojan horse must be run by a superuser to grant superuser access, and superuser accounts are used carefully in an attempt to avoid this. On an Amiga, a user with any access at all can get access to everything -- every program is run as if by a superuser.

If your Amiga network is isolated -- a few Amigas at work or in a classroom, this probably isn't important. If it is on the Internet, you should strongly consider not running most servers or making sure that you are behind a good firewall. Some servers are relatively safe to run, but you'll have to use your own discretion and the degree to which security is important to you to determine which ones.

MultiUser

While the OS filesystems don't enforce the extended protection bits, the Envoy Filesystem server does. If you want some degree of multi-user file protection bits on the local filesystem, MultiUser is a freely redistributable software package you can use.

Before you rely on MultiUser for security, make sure you've read the section above explaining some of the difficulties with securing an Amiga.

Some people think MultiUser is great and turns the Amiga into a perfect multi-user system. I tend to agree with Mike Meyer, who said: "the problem was (and is) that AmigaDOS was not designed as a multiuser
platform. While there exists various kludges to make it look like one, they work about as well as the kludges for multiTASKing on platforms that weren't designed for it."

Anonymous News and Mail posting

Sometimes the only way to have privacy is to have anonymity. Sometimes, as in the case of violent political repression, anonymity may be a matter of life and death. While it is subject to abuse, many believe that it is important that anonymity be available.

On the Internet, the way to get anonymity is obvious -- anonymous mail servers.

Some BBSs and online services may have a means of obtaining anonymity, but most do not, at least not in any serious fashion (graffiti walls don't count).

Social Responsibility

The rapidly expanding "InfoBahn" is bringing social, political and ethical challenges at a hectic pace. The potentials for abuse, misuse, accident, and other calamities are real. Vigilance over this growing technology is required. Whether at a political or a merely personal level, you owe it to yourself and your society to know some of the issues involved.

If you don't want your privacy invaded or your other civil rights trampled, if you don't want to see a further disparity between the technology-rich and technology-poor, if you don't want to fly in a plane whose computers cause a crash or bank with an institution with computers that lose your deposits, here are a few places you can get information and learn about actions you can take. Some of the information here consists of direct quotes shamelessly stolen from the organizations themselves.

Forum on Risks to the Public in Computers and Related Systems

ACM Committee on Computers and Public Policy, Peter G. Neumann, moderator

The newsgroup comp.risks is an excellent source of general information about the risks of computing. It is a moderated newsgroup containing digests of the risks mailing list. Topics have included: aeronautical computing (especially fly-by-wire and air-traffic control); banking; ergonomics; electronic voting and much more. This is one of the best signal-to-noise newsgroups you'll find.

Privacy Forum Digest

Moderated by Lauren Weinstein
Vortex Technology, Woodland Hills, CA, U.S.A.

The PRIVACY Forum digest is supported in part by the ACM Committee on Computers and Public Policy. The Internet PRIVACY Forum is a moderated digest for the discussion and analysis of issues relating to the general topic of privacy (both personal and collective) in the "information age" of the 1990's and beyond. The moderator will choose submissions for inclusion based on their relevance and content. Submissions will not be routinely acknowledged.

Subscriptions are by an automatic "listserv" system; for subscription information, please send a message consisting of the word "help" (quotes not included) in the BODY of a message to: "privacy-request@vortex.com".

Computer Professionals for Social Responsibility

P.O. Box 717
Palo Alto, CA 94302
415-322-3778
415-322-4748 (fax)
email: cpsr-info@cpsr.org
http://www.cpsr.org/home
comp.org.cpsr.announce

CPSR's Web Pages cover issues related to the organization's mission to provide the public and policymakers with realistic assessments of the power, promise, and problems of information technology. These issues include the National Information Infrastructure, Civil Liberties and Privacy, Computers in the Workplace, Technology Policy and Human Needs, Gender and Minority Issues, Reliability and Risks of Computer-Based Systems and Community Networking. There are also links to many reports and other sources of information.

CPSR was founded in 1981 by a group of computer scientists concerned about the use of computers in nuclear weapons systems. CPSR has since grown into a national public-interest alliance of information technology professionals and other people. Currently, CPSR has 22 chapters in the U.S. and affiliations with similar groups worldwide. The National Office is in Palo Alto, California.

Electronic Frontier Foundation
1001 G Street NW, Suite 950 E
Washington DC 20001 USA
+1 202 347 5400 (voice)
+1 202 393 5509 (fax)
+1 202 638 6119 (BBS - 16.8k ZyXEL)
+1 202 638 6120 (BBS - 14.4k V.32bis)
Internet: ask@eff.org
http://www.eff.org
news:comp.org.eff.news

From their Web pages:

"The Electronic Frontier Foundation (EFF) was founded in July of 1990 to ensure that the principles embodied in the Constitution and the Bill of Rights are protected as new communications technologies emerge.

Since its inception, EFF has worked to shape our nation's communications infrastructure and the policies that govern it in order to maintain and enhance First Amendment, privacy and other democratic values. We believe that our overriding public goal must be the creation of Electronic Democracy, so our work focuses on the establishment of:

* new laws that protect citizens' basic Constitutional rights as they use new communications technologies,

* a policy of common carriage requirements for all network providers so that all speech, no matter how controversial, will be carried without discrimination,

* a National Public Network where voice, data and video services are accessible to all citizens on an equitable and affordable basis, and

* a diversity of communities that enable all citizens to have a voice in the information age.

EFF is active on the Internet, the WELL, CIS, GEnie, BIX and other places."

The Association for Computing Machinery
1515 Broadway
New York, NY 10036
(212) 626-0500
email: ACMHELP@ACM.ORG

As you can see from their sponsorship of the Risks and Privacy forums, ACM is involved with several of the important issues facing computing and networking. Among benefits to their members are networking services (like inexpensive email accounts in the acm.org domain). It is an organization primarily for computing professionals, but others can join as student or associate (non-voting) members.

Appendix A: Choosing Providers

To decide what kind of services you need and where to get them, here are some guidelines, as well as information about particular providers.

Which Type of System is Right for You?

If your Amiga is connected to the Internet, you might never use another BBS or online service. If not, you will likely be interested in using a BBS or online service in addition to any network to which you may connect your Amigas.

The key to selecting a system (or systems -- many people use more than one) is deciding on a budget and evaluating your needs. Remember in making your budget that the systems you pay for aren't just an expense. They are also a savings. You might find a product review that steers you away from a bad purchase, a utility that saves you hours of time, or a bit of advice that tells you how to do something you couldn't figure out from reading a manual.

Below are several aspects of service to consider in evaluating your needs for the type of system you will connect to.

Email

If you want to use email, decide what you need. Do you want to be able to send mail to a particular group of people (perhaps your local Amiga user's group), or to a large number of people throughout the world? Is speed important to you, or is it OK if a message takes several days to be delivered? Do you plan to use email on a regular basis, checking your mailbox daily (or more often), or do you plan to check it more sporadically?

Most people have a few email addresses that they use for different purposes. They may, for example, have an Internet address which anyone can use to reach them, and an account on a local BBS which is used by members of a local user's group (not all of whom have access to Internet mail).

If you can afford it, the best email is usually Internet email. Systems which are connected to the Internet can reach millions of users and usually deliver mail very quickly. Most on-line services and some BBSs are directly connected. See "Connecting to the Internet" for information on costs and locating access.

If you are on a really tight budget but still want to be able to send email to a large number of people, look for a BBS which is connected to FidoNet or a similar BBS network. These tend to deliver mail much more slowly, but often can deliver mail to most of the same people the Internet can. There is often some charge for email sent outside the system you log into.

If you only want to be able to send email to a particular group of people, a BBS which is devoted to that group may be all you need (and may be free). Most computer user's groups have their own BBS, and many BBSs exist for special topics -- ranging from antique collectors to zydeco music lovers.

Messages

The quantity and quality of messages varies widely between systems. Some BBSs have little message traffic at all. Most BBSs have a much smaller user base than the online services, so unless they are connected to a network like Fido or the Internet, they aren't the best place to look for anything but specialized information (for example, local interest).

If you are interested in messages about Amiga computers, there are several excellent places to look. BIX has a lot of US Amiga developers online, many of whom answer questions from other users, though perhaps it has been on the decline with the Commodore situation. CompuServe has an active Amiga area with a good signal-to-noise ratio. There are many Internet newsgroups which carry hundreds of messages about Amigas each day, and these groups are accessible from many online systems. Unfortunately, most of these messages are noise. With a good newsreader to filter out undesirable messages and allow selection from subject lines, it is still a good resource.

Games

Entertainment is a primary use for many computers. BBSs and online services can add a whole new dimension to computer gaming.

Many BBSs, even single-line BBSs, contain simple games. One example is chess between humans with a turn made each time the other player logs in. Some games are complex and involve many other players. For example, trade wars allows each player to move between systems, buying and selling goods. Turns are made each day with only so many moves being allowed per player per day.

Most of these games use ASCII graphics and keyboard input as a user-interface.

Online services and networks sometimes offer more complex games, sometimes with rich graphical user-interfaces. GEnie seems to be the online service with the most emphasis on games. (Actually, there are a few services devoted almost entirely to games, the Sierra Network, for example, but these require software not currently available for Amigas). There you can dog-fight against dozens of humans in fighterplanes or command a giant fighting robot. It looks like an arcade game, but your opponents might be anywhere in the country or the world.

Systems which have the best game features tend to lack in other areas and vice-versa. If you are a serious game player, you might choose a game-oriented system, or vice-versa. To get the best of both worlds, you might join two, choosing one online service for entertainment and another for your other communications needs.

Information

The large online services provide access to information, articles and research databases in many specialized fields. Access to many of these services is at a premium surcharge. CompuServe, for example, includes more things that I could list. Here are a few: bibliographic databases, Consumer's Reports, encyclopedias, financial information (like stock quotes, Dun and Bradstreet's, and Standard and Poor's), Health Database Plus, news wires (like Associated Press and Reuters), and much more.

If access to these kinds of information is important to you, you may have to do a detailed comparison of what is available and where it is available. Make sure to closely check the surcharges for accessing the information you are interested in, as it can vary considerably from one database to another and can be quite expensive.

For general information, BBSs are not an option (though some BBSs are run for the sole purpose of disseminating specialized information, by the government, for example). The online services usually present their expensive information on an easy-to-use platter. Most information is available on the Internet, but takes more skill and knowledge to find. This is changing, and more information providers are making databases available over the Internet for a fee.

Internet Service Providers

The number of Internet service providers and the areas in which they provide service are growing rapidly. The following are just a few of the largest national Internet service providers in the U.S (and a couple of local providers). Wherever you live in the world, you'll want to investigate local options, because there is often someone undercutting the large providers on price. Of course, you have to be careful, because you sometimes get what you pay for! The three major U.S. providers listed here provide various levels of service from shell accounts and SLIP/PPP dial-in accounts to ISDN accounts and 56k or T1 leased-line service.

Prices are always coming down, but they tend to be a little higher in less densely populated areas and outside of the U.S. In early 1996, in a U.S. metropolitan area, you can expect to pay as little as $10 a month for a shell account or as little as under $20 for a SLIP/PPP account. That's generally for several hours per day or even unlimited usage! In the U.K., Demon offers dial-up SLIP/PPP accounts starting at #10 per month. (I've seen several strong recommendations for Demon, so they are well worth looking into if you are in the U.K.)

Another point to note is that the online services have started offering full internet connectivity as part of their packages. So you can get PPP from CompuServe and many others now. In large cities, the cheapest Internet service tends to come from the local Internet provider who offers nothing but PPP, but in smaller locales, you may not have that option. As well, if you want to use the extra value of an online service, you may be better to use one account for both purposes. While you'll be charged a higher rate for your hourly Internet time, you may make up for it by paying only one monthly premium, and in the convenience of getting it all in one bill. On the other hand, if you have the option and are a particularly heavy Internet user, you'll want to reduce or eliminate hourly charges for for your Internet access.

Finally, you'd be well advised to pick up the book "Connecting to the Internet" to get more background on types of service, evaluating service and lists of service providers.

Demon Internet Limited

42 Hendon Lane
Finchley
London

N3 1TT
081-349 0063 (London)
031-552 0344 (Edinburgh)
081-343 3881 (HelpLine)
email internet@demon.net

Netcomm
1-800-501-8649
info@netcom.com
4000 Moorpark Avenue
Suite 200
San Jose, CA 95117

Performance Systems International
1.800.82psi82
703.709.0300
info@psi.com
510 Huntmar Park Drive
Herndon, VA 22070

UUNet Technologies, Inc.
3110 Fairview Park Drive, Suite 570
Falls Church, VA 22042 USA
+1 800 258 9691
alternet-info@alter.net

Additionally, here are a few of the U.S. regional or local service providers worth looking into:

Online Orlando Internet Services
info@oo.com
modem: 407-647-6461 (or telnet to oo.com)
P.O. Box 4037
Winter Park, FL 32793
Currently, their BBS is run entirely with Amigas and provides access to many Internet applications. Worth checking out for that reason alone!

NetAccess
Philadelphia, PA

Current (as of this writing) pricing was $12.50/month for a 24 hour/day shell account with 10mb storage. Six hours/day of SLIP/PPP was $20/month. Telnet to unix1.netaxs.com, call 215-

576-8669, or email support@netaxs.com. NetAccess is rapidly adding points-of-presence throughout the SE PA and Southern NJ area.

Online Systems

I haven't been on all of these systems recently, and haven't been on some of them at all. So in some cases I offer my opinions or impressions, but in other cases, I had to rely on others or on the vendors themselves for information. I asked some of the systems to send me additional information and received no response. For most services, I've provided the form of the Internet address of users of the service.

America Online (AOL)
username@aol.com

AOL is now the largest online service. It has a reputation for being easy to use, but also for being somewhat braindead. If you have a PC or Mac, you might want to play with AOL, or maybe not. But don't bother trying it with an Amiga sans Bridgeboard or Mac Emulator -- AOL uses special software not available for the Amiga. Update: Apple's eworld has closed, and Apple announced that AOL is now its online service of choice. So if you're an Emplant or ShapeShifter, maybe you'll want to check out AOL after all.

BIX
username@bix.com
1-800-227-2983

Official support for Amiga registered developers in the U.S. was long handled through BIX. You'll therefore find many developers represented on BIX and a strong Amiga community. This may be on the decline, especially as CATS has been defunct for some time, and that was what kept many people there. The interface for BIX is lousy, and there aren't any readily available easy-to use Amiga OLRs to improve the situation.

On the other hand, I spend so much time on the Internet and CIS that I may not be able to give BIX a fair shake. It might be great for you.

CompuServe (CIS)
first.second@compuserve.com (just replace the comma in the user ID with a period)

1-800-848-8199

I've mentioned some of the features of CIS at several places in this book. I've been on CIS for a few years. I don't like the user names (all numbers, though they're in the process of adding optional character-based user names), the pricing used to be outrageous, some of the policies are brain-dead, but, overall, CIS is probably a good place to be. The signal-to-noise ratio is much better in general than on most other systems. The people on CIS tend to be professionals who aren't necessarily "computer people." The wide variety of databases, the electronic mall, and many other features add more value to a CIS account. Whether CIS is a good place for you depends on your budget and your interests, but CIS is probably suitable for many more people today than it was a few years ago. It's also an easy-to-find widely-available Internet provider.

CIX
username@cix.compulink.co.uk

In the UK, CIX is one of the places to be. Not to be confused with the Commercial Internet Exchange, also abbreviated CIX (but not an end-user organization, but part of the commercial infrastructure of the Internet), the Compulink Information Exchange is an online system with many conferences in a wide variety of areas. The Amiga has at least twenty conference areas on CIX, and UK developer support is done through CIX (in much the same way as BIX is used in the US).

Delphi
user@delphi.com

I haven't been on Delphi, so the following information is taken from Amiga Report. Delphi is run by the same people who run BIX:

Amiga Report International Online Magazine is available every week in the Amiga SIG on DELPHI. Amiga Report readers are invited to join DELPHI and become a part of the friendly community of Amiga enthusiasts there.

Using a personal computer and modem, members worldwide access DELPHI services via a local phone call. Via modem, dial up DELPHI at 1-800-695-4002. When connected, press RETURN once or twice. At Username: type JOINDELPHI and press

RETURN, at Password: type AMIGAREPORT and press RETURN. DELPHI's best plan is the 20/20 plan. It gives you 20 hours each month for the low price of only $19.95! Additional hours are only $1.50 each! This covers 1200, 2400 and even 9600 connections! For more information, and details on other plans, call DELPHI Member Services at 1-800-695-4005

Complete Internet connection -- Telnet, FTP, IRC, Gopher, E-Mail and more! (Internet option is $3/month extra), SIGs for all types of computers -- Amiga, IBM, Macintosh, Atari, etc., Large file databases! SIGs for hobbies, video games, graphics, and more!, Business and world news, stock reports, etc., Grolier's Electronic Encyclopedia!

GEnie

username@genie.com

Although pricing for online services fluctuates often, GEnie is often the least expensive major service. There are active Amiga areas there, but I've never visited.

Joining GEnie is easy. Use half duplex at 300/1200/2400 baud. Dial 1-800-638-8369 (Canada 1-800-387-8330). Type HHH at CONNECT. At the U#= prompt, type AMIGA and press Return.

Prodigy

PCs and Macs are welcome, but the required custom software, like that of AOL, isn't available for the Amiga.

Portal

I also haven't been on Portal, but here is some information (again, taken from Amiga Report):

The Portal Online System is the home of acclaimed Amiga Zone, which was formerly on the People/Link System. Plink went out of business in May, 1991 and The Amiga Zone's staff moved to Portal the next day. The Zone has just celebrated its second anniversary on Portal.

You can reach Portal through any SprintNet (formerly Telenet) indial anywhere in the USA. If you have an account on another Internet-connected system, you can connect to Portal using the UNIX Telnet programs, from anywhere in the industrialized world. Delphi and BIX users can now Telnet into Portal for a flat $19.95 a month, with *unlimited* use.

Over 1.5 GIGabytes of Amiga-specific files, The entire Fred Fish collection of freely distributable software, online. Fast, Batch Zmodem file transfer protocol. Twenty Amiga vendor areas with participants like AmigaWorld, ASDG, Soft-Logik, Black Belt, Apex Publishing, Stylus, Prolific, NES. Amiga Internet mailing lists for Imagine, DCTV, LightWave, HyperAmi, Director and Landscapes are fed right into the Zone message bases. Free unlimited Internet Email. Portal has the Usenet. Portal features an exciting package of Internet features: IRC, FTP, TELNET, MUDS, LIBS. Internet Services is a menu driven version of the same kinds of utilities you can also use from your Portal UNIX shell account.

Portal Signup or for more information: 408-973-9111 (voice) 9a.m.-5p.m. Mon-Fri, Pacific Time   408-725-0561 (modem 3/12/ 2400) 24 hours every day 408-973-8091 (modem 9600/14400) 24 hours every day or enter "C PORTAL" from any Sprintnet dial-in in the USA, or telnet to "portal.com" from anywhere.

The WELL
1750 Bridgeway Suite A-200
Sausalito, CA, 94965
USA
Voice: (415) 332-4335
Fax: (415) 332-4927
Email: support@well.sf.ca.us

The Whole Earth 'Lectronic Link is one of the less-well known gems of the online community. If interacting with other people is your primary interest in an online system, check out The Well. Headquartered in the San Francisco bay area, it attracts all kinds. By the way, the founder of the Well is a member of the EFF board of directors.

BBSs
The following list of Amiga-supporting BBSs around the world is an abridged list from AmigaReport (with the permission of the editor, Robert Niles). The editing I've done doesn't reflect on the quality of the boards (because I haven't been on most of them) but on geography -- I've tried to include BBSs from many countries, and removed several BBSs which had many duplicates for a given country (as well as editing some of the longer entries).

Once you've found one BBS near you, it will be easy to find many others, since they usually contain list of numbers for other local sites. If a BBS in your country isn't listed, make an international call or two and you'll probably bc ablc to find the number for some local BBSs.

IN THE MEANTIME BBS
Official Amiga Report Distribution Site
Running AXShell
Robert Niles, Sysop
rniles@imtired.itm.com
509-966-3828 Supra V.32bis 24hrs - 7 days
Yakima, Washington

BIOSMATICA BBS
Official Amiga Report Distribution Site -- Portugal
Running Excelsior/Trapdoor/UUCP
Celso Martinho, Sysop
FidoNet 2:361/9
+351-34-382320 V.32bis 24hrs - 7 days

AMIGA JUNCTION 9
Official Amiga Report Distribution Site -- United Kingdom
Running DLG Professional
Stephen Anderson, Sysop
Sysop Email: sysadmin@junct9.royle.org
Line 1 +44 (0)372 271000 14400
         V.32bis/HST   FidoNet 2:440/20
Line 2 +44 (0)372 278000 14400
         V.32bis only FidoNet 2:440/21
Line 3 +44 (0)372 279000 2400
         V.42bis/MNP
Internet: user_name@junct9.royle.org

BITSTREAM BBS
The BBS of the Nelson (NZ) Amiga Users Group
Official Amiga Report Distribution Site
Running Xenolink 1.0 Z.3
Glen Roberts, Sysop
FidoNet 3:771/850
+64 3 5485321 Supra V.32bis 24hrs - 7 days
Nelson, New Zealand

REALM OF TWILIGHT BBS
Official Amiga Report Distribution Site -- Canada

Running Excelsior! BBS
Thorsten Schiller, Sysop
Usenet: realm.tdkcs.waterloo.on.ca
UUCP: ...!uunet.ca!tdkcs!realm
FIDO: 1:221/302
Fish: 33:33/8
24hrs - 7 days
519-748-9365 (2400 baud)
519-748-9026 (v.32bis)
Ontario, Canada

METNET TRIANGLE SYSTEM
Official Amiga Report Distribution Site
UK Support for Mebbsnet
Running Mebbsnet and Starnet 1.02a
Jon Witty, Sysop
FIDO: 2:252/129.0
24 hrs - 7 days
Line 1: 44-482-473871 16.8 DS HST
Lines 2-7: 44-482-442251 2400 (6 lines)
Line 8: 44-482-491744 2400
Line 9: 44-482-449028 2400
Voice helpline 44-482-491752 (anytime)

OMAHA AMIGANET
Official Amiga Report Distribution Site
Running DLG Professional
Andy Wasserman, Sysop
24 hrs - 7 days
FidoNet: 1:285/11
AmigaNet: 40:200/10
Line 1: 402-333-5110 V.32bis
Line 2: 402-691-0104 USR DS
Omaha, Nebraska

AMIGA-NIGHT-SYSTEM
Official Amiga Report Distribution Site - Finland
Running DLG Professional
Janne Saarme, Sysop
24 hrs - 7 days
InterNet: luumu@fenix.fipnet.fi
FidoNet: 2:220/550.0
+358-0-675840 V.32bis
Helsinki, Finland

RAMSES THE AMIGA FLYING
Official Amiga Report Distribution Site -- France
Running DLG Professional
Eric Delord, Sysop
Philippe Brand, Co-Sysop
Stephane Legrand, Co-Sysop
Internet: user.name@ramses.gna.org
Fidonet: 2:320/104
+33-1-60037015 USR DS 16.8
+33-1-60037713 V.32bis
+33-1-60037716 1200-2400

THE GATEWAY BBS
Official Amiga Report Distribution Site
Running Excelsior! BBS
Stace Cunningham, Sysop
Dan Butler, CoSysop
24 hrs - 7 days
InterNet: stace@tecnet1.jcte.jcs.mil
FidoNet: 1:3604/60.0
601-374-2697 Hayes Optina 28.8 V.FC
Biloxi, Mississippi

Amiga BBS
Official Amiga Report Distribution Site
Running Excelsior! BBS
Alejandro Kurczyn, Sysop
FidoNet 4:975/7
First Amiga BBS in Mexico
(5) 887-3080   9600 V32,MNP
Estado de Mexico, Mexico

AMIGA DO PC BBS
Official Amiga Report Distribution Site - Brazil
Running Excelsior! v 1.18
+55-192-33-2260
Weekdays: 19-07 (-3 GMT)
Weekends: 24 hours
Internet: fimoraes@dcc.unicamp.br

COMM-LINK BBS
Official Amiga Report Distribution Site
Running Excelsior Pro
604-945-6192 USR DS 16.8
InterNet: steve_hooper@comm.tfbbs.wimsey.com

Steve Hooper, Sysop
Port Coquitlam, B.C. Canada

Tierra-Miga BBS
Software: CNet
Gib Gilbertson
24 hours 7 days
FidoNet: 1:202/638.0
AmigaNet: 40:406/3.0
Internet: torment.cts.com
Line #1: 619.292.0754 V32.bis
City: San Diego, CA.

FREELAND MAINFRAME
Offical Amiga Report Distribution Site
Running DLG Professional
John Freeland, SysOp
206-438-1670 Supra 2400zi
206-438-2273 Telebit WorldBlazer(v.32bis)
206-456-6013 Supra v.32bis
Internet - freemf.eskimo.com
Olympia, Washington

LAHO BBS
Official Amiga Report Distribution Site -- Finland
Running MBBS
Lenni Uitti, SysOp
Tero Manninen, SysOp (PC-areas)
Juha Makinen, SysOp (Amiga-areas)
+358-64-414 1516, V.32bis/HST
+358-64-414 0400, V.32bis/HST
+358-64-414 6800, V.32/HST
+358-64-423 1300, V.32 MNP
Seinajoki, Finland

FALLING BBS
Official Amiga Report Distribution Site -- Norway
Running ABBS
Christopher Naas, Sysop
+47 69 256117 V.32bis 24hrs - 7 days
EMail: naasc@cnaas.adsp.sub.org

COMMAND LINE BBS
Official Amiga Report Distribution Site -- Canada
Canada's Amiga Graphics & Animation Source

Running AmiExpress BBS
Nick Poliwko, Sysop
416-533-8321 V.32 24hrs - 7 days
Toronto, Canada

LEGUANS BYTE CHANNEL
Official Amiga Report Distribution Site -- Germany
 Running EazyBBS V2.11
Andreas Geist, Sysop
Usenet: andreas@lbcmbx.in-berlin.de
Line 1: 49-30-8110060 USR DS 16.8
Line 2: 49-30-8122442 USR DS 16.8

STINGRAY DATABASE
Official Amiga Report Distribution Site -- Germany
Running FastCall
Bernd Mienert, Sysop
EMail: sysop@sting-db.zer.sub.org.dbp.de
+49 208 496807 HST-Dual 24hrs - 7 days
Muelheim/Ruhr, Germany

T.B.P. VIDEO SLATE
Official Amiga Report Distribution Site
An Amiga dedicated BBS for All
Running Skyline 1.3.2
Mark E Davidson, Sysop
24 hrs - 7 days
201-586-3623 USR 14.4 HST
Rockaway, New Jersey

CONTINENTAL DRIFT BBS
Official Amiga Report Distribution Site
Running DLG Pro software
Murray Chaffer & Andre Lackmann, Sysops
+612 949-4256
24 hours - 7 days

GURU MEDITATION
Official Amiga Report Distribution Site -- Spain
Running Remote Access
Javier Frias, SysOp
+34-1-383-1317 V.32bis
24 hours - 7days
Spain

MOONLIGHT SONATA DLG
Amiga Report Official Distribution Site
DAS ModPlayer Support
Node #1 - +358-18-161763 - ZyXEL V32b 19200
Node #2 - +358-18-161862 - HST DS V32 14400
Fidonet: 2:221/112.0
Keyboards: Erno Tuomainen
Amiga3000 25MHz - 1.3Gigs HD
BBS Software: Dialog Pro BB/OS

REDEYE BBS
Running EXCELSIOR/UUCP/AFAX
"Official Amiga Report Distribution Site Germany/Europe"
Sysop: Thorsten Meyer
Internet: sysop@redeye.greenie.muc.de
Line 1: +49-89-5460535 (V.32b, Zyxel EG +)
Line 2: +49-89-5460071 (USR Courier V32b terbo)
24hrs - 7 days
Munich, Germany

Appendix B: Amiga Vendors

These are the current names, addresses and other information for vendors of Amiga networking products known to the author at the time of this writing. Literature, samples, etc. from new vendors would be appreciated so that future editions of this book can reflect them.

Amigo Business Computers
192 Laurel Road
East Northport, NY 11731
(516) 757-7334
Fax: (516) 757 7234
Products: Amigo EtherNet, MultiNet, SerNet software and Com-Ports multi-serial board.

AmiTrix Development
5312-47 Street
Beaumont, Alberta, Canada
T4X 1H9
phone and fax: (403) 929-8459
web: http://www.networkx.com/amitrix/
email: sales@amitrix.com
products: AmigaLink, SCSI interface for CDTV and A570

AugmentTek
3606 South 180th Street C-22
SeaTac, WA 98188
Products: TorqueWare

Canadian Prototype Replicas
PO Box 8
Ontario, Canada
N0B 1M0
(519) 884-4412
Products: AS225r2, Alan-FS

C-Born Software Systems
59 West Fyans St
Geelong 3220
Victoria, AUSTRALIA
Voice   +61 52 786530 or +61 52 290144
AmigaFax +61 52 786355 or +61 52 290248
Email: sol.ccs.deakin.EDU.AU!drum3!dave
Prodcuts: Fax Software

Creative Equipment International (CEI)
5555 W. Flagler St
Miami, Florida 33134 USA
Phone (305) 266-2800
Products: A4066 Ethernet

EUREKA
Adsteeg 10 6191 PX
Beek(L)
The Netherlands
Tel. +31-46370800
Fax. +31-46360188
Products: The Communicator

Expert Services
7559 Mall Road
Florence, KY 41042
USA
606-371-9690
Fax: 606-282-5942
Products: TrapFax, AmigaOS 3.1

GfxBase, Inc.
1881 Ellwell Dr.
Milpitas, CA 95035
(408) 262-1469
(408) 262-8276 (FAX)
Products: X-Windows, AS225r2

GP Software
21 Aloomba Road
Ashgrove QLD
AUSTRALIA 4060
Voice/Fax: +617 3661402
Email: GREGP@GPSOFT.ASDP.SUB.ORG
Products: GP-Fax, GP-Term

Hirsch & Wolf OHG
Mittelstrasse 33
D-56564 Neuwied
Germany
Voice: +49 (2631) 8399-0
Fax: +49 (2631) 8399-31
Products: Books, DevCon Notes, AmigaMail

Hydra Systems
Wyndrushe House
Red Lane, Kenilworth CV8 1PB
United Kingdom
Products: Hydra Ethernet Card

Intangible Assets Manufacturing
828 Ormond Avenue
Drexel Hill, PA 19026-2604
USA
+1 610 853 4406
fax: +1 610 853 3733
email: info@iam.com
Products: Amiga Envoy, Consulting and More

Interworks
43191 Camino Casillas
Suite B2469
Temecula, CA 92592-3714
phone and fax: (909) 699-8120
Products: I-Card (PCMCIA Ethernet), Enlan-DFS

Ledgendary Design Technologies
25 Frontenac Avenue
Brantford, Ontario N3R 3B7
or
P.O. Box 1147
Lewiston, NY 14092-847
voice/fax: (519) 753-6120
Products: Link It!

Migraph, Inc.
32700 Pacific Highway South
Suite 14
Federal Way, WA 98003
USA
(206) 838-4677
Products: OCR

NSDi
P.O.Box 32
FIN-02151 ESPOO FINLAND
fax: +358 207 34 67 34
email: info@nsdi.fi
products: AmiTCP/IP

Oxxi

Since the first printing of this book, the Oxxi product line (or, at least, Amiga Client Software for Novell) seems to have been taken over by Interworks, above.

Resource Management Fource Pty Ltd

70-74 May Street
St Peters NSW 2044
AUSTRALIA
Tel: +61 2 550 4244
Fax: +61 2 550 4284
Products: QuickNet Ethernet hardware and QuickNet software

Software Results Enterprises

2447 N. 4th St., Suite B.
Columbus, OH 43202-2706
614/262-9146 (voice)
Products: GoldenGate II board

Spectronics International U.S.A.

34 East Main Street #23
Champaign, IL 61820
phone: +1 (217) 352 0061
fax: +1 (217) 352 0063
BBS: +1 (217) 352 7627
Products: AmigaLink

Thunder Ridge, Inc.

N9353 Benson Road
Brooklyn, WI 53521
tel: (608) 455-1039
fax: (608) 455-1317
Products: TSSNet (DECNet)

Appendix C: Recommended Reading

As I may have said elsewhere, this book is just a beginning -- an invitation to explore. In the same way that your first computer book was not your last, hopefully your first networking book will not be your last. There is a lot of ground to cover! These are some of the books, articles and files that I've read and use all the time (one or two aren't on my shelves, but come with recommendations from trusted friends). Unfortunately, I don't receive any kickbacks from any of the publishers or authors of any of these materials.

Books

I include an ISBN for those who need to order one and don't have access to something like Books in Print.

Applied Cryptography: Protocols, Algorithms, and Source Code in C, Schneier, Bruce, Wiley, 1994, ISBN 0-471-59756-2
If you're really concerned about security, you need to know about cryptography. If you need to know about modern computer cryptography, look here.

The Computer Privacy Handbook, Bacard, Andre, Peachpit Press, 1995
A practical guide to e-mail encryption, data protection and PGP privacy software, written for users, not programmers. It doesn't have Amiga specific information (other than a reference to an earlier edition of this book), but it does have loads of general information that will be useful to Amiga users (especially since PGP tends not to be very platform specific).

Connecting to the Internet, Estrada, Susan, O'Reilly & Associates, 1993, ISBN 1-56592-061-9
If you haven't already connected to the Internet but are thinking about doing so, get this book! It explores the different types of connections and different needs as well as how to find and evaluate both dial-up (shell and SLIP/PPP) and dedicated line service providers.

Department of Defense (DoD) Trusted Computer Systems Evaluation Criteria (TCSEC). GPO #008-000-00461-7, DoD 5200.28-STD, 12/6/85

Computer Security Basics, Russel, Deborah, and Gangemi, G.T., O'Reilly
If you're a real nut for security stuff, here you can find all kinds of good reasons why you aren't going to get much security out of your Amiga running AmigaOS.

The Hacker Crackdown, Sterling, Bruce, Bantam Books, ISBN 0-553-56370-X
A natural book to pick up after you've finished Hackers. Explains how and why hackers attracted the attention of U.S. police and Secret Service. More to do with law and law enforcement and the issues thereof than to do with technical computer issues. If you are interested in those topics, this book is an interesting and informative read.

TCP/IP Illustrated, Volume 1, Stevens, Richard W., Addison Wesley, ISBN: 0-201-63346-9
An excellent starting point for people interested in the TCP/IP protocol suite. Provides exercises at the end of each chapter to test what you learned in the chapter. Many problems ask you to get your hands on a computer. You'll have to go to the bookstore and compare this to the "Internetworking with TCP/IP" series to decide which is better suited to your style of learning. Some people say that they find this book easier to understand that "Internetworking with TCP/IP Volume I."

The Whole Internet User's Guide & Catalog 2d, Krol, Ed, O'Reilly & Associates, 1994, ISBN 1-56592-025-2.
If you've got access to the Internet through a shell account or direct connection and you want to know how to use it and all of the things that you can do with it, this is the first (and perhaps best) place to look.

TCP/IP Network Administration, Hunt, Craig, O'Reilly & Associates, ISBN 0-937175-82-X.
If you are going to run your own TCP/IP network (or establish your own connection to the Internet), this is a good place to look for much of the information you'll need. If your network is at all complicated (for example, if you have any kind of internet), you'll want the descriptions of administering mail systems, routing, etc. If you haven't figured it out by now, almost all of the ORA books are highly recommended. ("Almost" is in there only because I haven't read all of them, and don't have expertise in some of the more obscure titles like Japanese computing.)

Internetworking With TCP/IP, Comer, Douglas E., Prentice Hall.
A three-volume set. Volume I covers Principles, Protocols and
Architecture. This is the classic explanation of the nitty-gritty
details of the TCP/IP protocols. If you have to (or want to) understand these details this book may become a bible to you. Depending on what your needs are, either or both of the second to
volumes (co-authored with Stevens) might also be wonderfully
helpful. Volume II is Design, Implementation and Internals, while
Volume III is Client-Server Programming and Applications.

Inca Gold, Cussler, Clive, Simon & Schuster, 1994, ISBN 0-671-
68156-7
You need a break from computing every once in a while. Somehow,
I didn't discover Cussler and his character, Dirk Pitt, until this
year. If you liked Bond, Pitt will entertain you well.
Update: Since the first printing of this book, I've become a scuba
diver, so I enjoy Dirk's underwater adventures even more. On my
way to Australia in Decebmer of 1995, I picked up a copy of Cussler's "Shockwave" in the LA airport. A neat twist (and good reading) since it is mostly set in Australia and on the open sea. I really
enjoyed the week I spent diving in the Coral Sea and the two
weeks I spent in Brisbane and Sydney. Highly recommeded. Even
better if you can find a good book to read on the plane.

X-Window System User's Guide, 3d, Quercia, Valerie and
O'Reilly, Tim, O'Reilly & Associates, 1990,
ISBN 0-937175-14-5.
If you're going to use X, you're going to need this book. This ver-
sion covers X11 R3 and R4. There may be a new version for R5.
This volume is part of a series of guides for X from ORA, and
depending on what you're going to be doing with X, you may want
other volumes, too.

Unix Network Programming. Stevens, Richard W., Prentice Hall,
1990, ISBN 0-13-949876-1
If you have to program sockets (which is to say, if you want to
write software for AmiTCP or for AS225), this is where to learn to
do it. My well-worn copy still has several place-markers raggedly
hanging out from between the pages.

Using UUCP and UseNet, Todine, Grace and Dougherty, Dale,
O'Reilly & Associates, ISBN 0-937175-10-2.
Managing UUCP and UseNet, 10d, O'Reilly, Tim and Todino,
Grace, O'Reilly & Associates, ISBN 0-937175-93-5.
These days, if you need one of these books, you probably also need

the other. If you are going to run UUCP on one of your systems, make sure you have these books. Almost all of the documentation that doesn't come with any of the software packages (which is to say, almost all of it) is in here.

AppleTalk
There is a great series of very good books published by Apple Computer about networking and AppleTalk. Their documentation is excellent. Any of the books has a list of the others, along with a description of who they are for.

NetWare
I don't have a specific book to recommend for NetWare. There are plenty of them. Most administrators of NetWare networks are trained and certified, though, so there isn't much point.

The Cuckoo's Egg. Stoll, Clifford, Doubleday, 1989, ISBN 0-385-24946-2
This is a great (true) story about security on the Internet. It is very readable and enjoyable, even for those with little or no technical expertise. It doesn't provide a huge amount of technical information, but the view that it gives of the communities and bureaucracies of the Internet make it a worth-while read even to networking experts. The entertainment value of the book alone is worth the price of admission.

Hackers: Heros of the Computer Revolution. Levy, Stephen, Delta, 1984, ISBN 0-385-31210-5
A classic of computer literature, this book examines the people behind the origins of computing. Everyone who has anything to do with computers should read this sometime. It is entertaining as well as informative. Understanding the origins of multiuser computing and security make understanding modern systems easier. Understanding the culture of early computing also aids in understanding the current culture of computing. The book is not technically sophisticated, but is still good reading even for experts.

Denny Atkin's Best Amiga Tips and Secrets. Atkin, Denny, Compute Books, 1993, ISBN 0-87455-275-3
Though there aren't any networking tips here, every serious Amiga user ought to go through this book. There are lots of great tips for getting more from your Amiga and using it more efficiently. Whether you are a new user or a former Commodore software engineer, there is likely to be something new and useful to you in this book.

The Amiga Guru Book: A Reference Manual, Babel, Ralph, self-published, 1993, no ISBN (see your Amiga dealer or email rbabel@babylon.rmt.sub.org)
All Amiga programers should have a copy of this reference. The RKMs are still the indispensable final authorities, but the Guru Book provides many detailed explanations beyond what is clear or available in the RKMs. There is no networking-specific information contained herein, just good stuff for all Amiga programmers.

The Internet Message: **Closing the Book with Electronic Mail**, Rose, Marshall T., PTR Prentice-Hall, 1993, ISBN 0-13-092941-7
Marshall T. Rose is one of the (co-)authors of many Internet mail standards. If you want to understand the technical details of how any aspect of Internet mail works theoretically, you'll probably find it here. If you are going to be implementing any mail system (but especially a TCP/IP based mail system), you ought to read this.

Newton's Telecom Dictionary, Newton, Harry, Telecom Library Inc., 1993, ISBN 0-936648-42-2
More than 1100 pages of definitions and explanations for telecommunications terms. Set in an informal, non-technical style, it makes for great learning. If you need to talk to the phone company, but can't understand what they say, this book should set you straight. It includes many networking and computer terms along with the telecom lingo.

Connect Your Amiga: A Guide to the Internet, LANs, BBSs and Online Services, Larson, Dale L., Intangible Assets Manufacturing, 1994, ISBN 1-885876-02-5
A wonderful introduction and a great collection of advanced information all rolled into one. Recommended without reservation. Buy two copies and beg the publisher for new updated editions so that you can buy more.

Periodicals (magazines)

I include the ISSN for the same reason I give ISBNs for books. Since so much changes so quickly in the online world, I strongly suggest that you find at least one magazine you like and subscribe. You may be missing out on something new and not even know it. General Amiga magazines sometimes carry information about networking, but more often they provide only limited coverage of online services and freely redistributable files. (Actually, that has improved a lot during the last two years -- most Amiga magazines now have regular decent coverage of networking in general and of the Internet in particular.) Of course, you already subscribe to those magazines anyway, don't you?

Internet World, Mecklermedia, ISSN 1064-3923
meckler@jvnc.net
This magazine has provided a good mix of coverage from the highly technical to the introductory. Definitely worth the price of admission. Find a library which has it or order the back issue for May 1994 -- there is an article about the Amiga on the Internet.

Wired, ISSN 1059-1028
info@wired.com
Somehow, I was lucky enough to be on the list of people who got the first issue free. This magazine has style. You probably will feel something strong about it. You might not like its style (I don't always). I find that it always has something worth reading. I also find the artsy layout a good break from the plain presentation of most other technical magazines -- of course, sometimes it is a humor break. If you are going to surf the nets and want to be hip, get Wired.

Byte, ISSN 0360-5280
Byte is a fairly good general magazine for those interested in personal computing. Whatever you may say about its non-coverage of the Amiga, it provides a fairly good mix of technical and high-level or introductory articles. Recently, it has had several good articles on networking technologies, including a detailed introduction to the workings of PPP (June, 1994), William Stallings' piece on PGP (July, 1994), a review of the Telebit NetBlazer router/modem (June 1994) a now-dated-but-likely-to-be-updated-in-a-future-issue evaluation of "V.34" modems (July, 1994), and more.

Other

DevCon Notes, Commodore, 1991 and 1993; and AmigaMail, Commodore.
The 1991 DevCon notes contain detailed information on socket programming and an early version of the SANA-II standard. The 1993 DevCon notes contain detailed information on Envoy. AmigaMail includes articles on SANA-II and socket programming. All of these may be available from Hirsch and Wolf (see the vendors section).

Appendix D: Questions and Answers

There are some questions which are asked so often, that I thought I'd give the quick answers in one place. You could get this information from the main text and some of the sources I've referred to, but this is just to make sure.

I want to get my Amiga on the Web, what do I need?

Besides reading this book to get an understanding of what you are going to have to set up, and what software you're going to get, you're going to need an Amiga with a harddrive running AmigaOS 3 or higher. RAM requirements vary, but I'd say you need more than 2MB.

I can't get my Ethernet hardware working. What am I doing wrong?

I don't know, but here are some questions to ask yourself. For 10-Base-2: is there a T and terminator at each end of the cable? are the cable and terminators of the correct impedance? do you have any branches in the cable? For 10-Base-T: Is your hub operating correctly? Are your cables of the correct type (you're not using phone cables, right)?

I'm trying to hook up a serial connection, but I can't get it working. What am I doing wrong?

Do you have the baud rate set correctly on both devices? Do you have the right kind of cable? Make sure you don't have a null-modem cable connected to a modem, and aren't trying to use a modem cable as a null-modem. Make sure that you have a hardware handshaking cable if you're trying to use hardware handshaking. Also check the length of your cable -- serial connections can often be more than a hundred feet long (though parallel connections need to be kept much shorter).

I have two Amigas I want to network to each other. What is the best way to do it?

There are two parts to consider: hardware and software. As far as hardware, your needs for future expansion and your need for speed and availability of ports today are the primary considerations. If you're plans for future expansion are minimal, then: If you don't need speed and can sacrifice ports, a serial or parallel connection is fine. If you don't need speed but can't sacrifice ports, look at AmigaLink.

If you need speed, or if you'd like to be able to add more machines later, you should seriously consider Ethernet hardware. Ethernet is fast and lets you have lots of machines on a single network. Since Ethernet is available for almost every computer, it will let you connect non-Amigas.

As to software: if you only need Amiga peer-to-peer networking and won't be doing any other networking, there are a few solutions available to you. The free ones are mostly worth what you pay for them. If your budget is tight and you aren't going to depend on your network for much (or aren't going to use it often), go for ParNFS or NetFS (or the software that comes with AmigaLink). You'll have to use one of the above if you are still using 1.3, because the commercial solutions all require 2.04 or better. If you don't care about a standard API (programmer's interface) for the networking software because you aren't going to use any network applications except those provided with the package, any of the commercial peer-to-peer products are good. If you want Commodore's solution which includes the Amiga standard peer-to-peer networking API, get Envoy.

If you might be connecting to the Internet with a dial-up IP account, or if you might otherwise want to network with non-Amigas, see the question about software for that.

I have three or more Amigas I want to network. What is the best way to do it?
You just narrowed down your choices quite a bit. The serial and parallel solutions are much less suitable (or even impossible) to use with larger networks. The kludges that work (barely) with a couple of machines fall apart as you add more. You'll need to pay for a real networking hardware solution.

If you count an A1000 or A500 among the machines you want to network, your choices are very limited. With an internetwork-capable protocol stack, you could use a multi-serial card to connect several machines together in a star topology with the "hub" routing packets as needed. You could also have an Ethernet connecting most machines with a satellite machine or two off serial. This gives you some flexibility. The other option is AmigaLink.

If you've got Zorro and/or PCMCIA slots on all of your machines, the answer is pretty clear. Ethernet.

The software issues are really the same as with a two Amiga network.

I have one (or more) Amigas I want to connect to other computers in a network. What software should I use?
It depends on what your needs are, whether you have an established network, and how much you can afford.

If you are on an extra tight budget, you might be limited to a serial connection or even to SneakerNet.

If you already have a NetWare or DECnet network, the software you want for your Amiga is clear. If you are setting up a new network, the most general-purpose answer is usually TCP/IP. By the way, this doesn't prevent you from using one of the peer-to-peer Amiga solutions.

In my offices, I have an AmigaUnix box, an OS/2 box and many different Amigas. All of the machines have connections to a single Ethernet. The Unix and OS/2 boxes run TCP/IP. The other Amigas all run both AS225r2 and Envoy simultaneously (sharing a single Ethernet card in each machine). Envoy is used for all Amiga-to-Amiga networking, while AS225r2 is used for connectivity with the Unix or OS/2 machines. Since Envoy is also IP-based, any internetworking I do will work for both networking packages.

If you want to try this with AmiTCP and Envoy, you'll have to have a SANA-II r 2 driver (like the A2065 driver in the latest SANA-II archive), but reports are that it does work.

I want to connect my Amiga to a PC. How should I do it?
First, clarify what you mean by connect. Is moving a file once in a while all you need? If so, SneakerNet and CrossDos work well. You use CrossDos (part of AmigaOS 2.1 and later, or available as a separate, third party product) to read and write PC-format disks.

If the files you'll transfer are larger than a single disk, there are several utilities which could help you. One is included with ADPro, another is available separately from AugmenTek.

If you need to transfer files more often or more conveniently, a serial link might be sufficient. You can do it with a terminal program on each side of the link, but something like Twin Express or Link It! is easier to use.

I want to connect to a Mac. How should I do it?

TCP/IP works well. Or get an Emplant or an Amax with AppleTalk and LocalTalk or EtherTalk. You might be able to use TSSNet if you have another DECnet clone such as the Macintosh version of TSSNet on the Mac. Obviously, you'd want to check this last one with the manufacturers before spending so much money.

I want to connect to a Unix box. How should I do it?

TCP/IP. Or a run a terminal session over a serial port (with modem or null-modem). If you do that, have a look at DNet and AmigaUnixWindows.

I want to be on the Internet. How should I do it?

This is a big question. You want to start by learning all you can about the available options. Then you need to decide how "on the Internet" you want to be. Is getting mail and reading news good enough? Is a shell account giving you access to Telnet and FTP and gopher good enough? Would a dial-up IP connection be good enough, or do you need a 24-hour connection?

I'm using NFS and my client keeps timing out. What can I do?

First, don't try NFS with a 14.4 connection, probably not even 28.8. It is too painful. Next, if you are using SLIP or PPP or if you are going through several hops, you may need to reduce your MaxTransfer. In AS225, that is done with an argument to nfsmgr, and 1024 is a value that seems to work well with most SLIP or PPP connections. In AmiTCP, the parameters are RPC_TIMEOUT, MAX_READDIRSIZE, MAX_READSIZE and MAX_WRITESIZE.

I want to use ParNet or PLIP or something similar, but I also want to be able to use my Printer and/or digitizer. Can I use a switchbox?

If you use all of these parallel port devices often enough that turning off your computer and rearranging what is plugged in is not an option, there are really two possible solutions. One is to add parallel ports with an expansion card. The other is to get real networking hardware. While switchboxes can work with parallel ports, they often cause problems by making the connections less reliable (longer total cable length and additional contacts increase noise and signal loss). If you don't get a quality switchbox, it could even damage your computer or peripherals by switching some lines before others or by making contact with one device before breaking all contact with the other. The later can be overcome by only switching with everything turned off. Even if you had a perfect switchbox, much of the software won't properly release the parallel port, so you'd have to reboot anyway.

You get what you pay for, and the parallel port is for free networking, not good networking.

I want to network an A500. What are my options?

Besides using one of the serial, parallel or floppy options, you could use a SlingShot adapter (about US$35) to allow you to attach a single Zorro-II device. Better yet, you could upgrade to a newer machine.

Appendix E: Amiga Envoy Manual

For those of you who've purchased Amiga Envoy (or who want to know more about it), here is intangible Assets Manufacturing's Amiga Envoy documentation. Most of the material in this appendix is as originally published in the Amiga Envoy Manual, by Dale L. Larson, Copyright ©1993-1996 by Dale L. Larson and Intangible Assets Manufacturing.

Commodore Software Engineers Ken Dyke, Brian Jackson, Randell Jesup, Dale L. Larson, and Greg Miller originally developed Amiga Envoy. Amiga Envoy 2.0 has been developed by Heinz Wrobel and Dale L. Larson of IAM.

Heinz Wrobel would like to dedicate his work to Joan Thuesen.

Introduction

Amiga Envoy is the standard networking software package from Commodore. With it, Amigas can transparently share files and printers. Amiga Envoy provides a simple messaging interface for the easy development of reliable network applications. Amiga Envoy's performance, user-interface and API are consistent with the philosophy of the Amiga Operating System. Amiga Envoy only works between Amiga computers.

To make Amiga Envoy available to you, Intangible Assets Manufacturing has produced this manual and licensed the software from Commodore.

To understand Amiga Envoy file and printer sharing, it is important to learn a few terms. A "client" is the Amiga that is accessing files on another Amiga's hard disk (or CD-ROM, etc.) or that is outputting to another Amiga's printer. The "server" is the Amiga with that remote hard disk or printer. The client is said to be "importing" the services that are "exported" by the server. Since Amiga Envoy is a peer-to-peer network, there are no arbitrary limits on which Amigas may be clients or servers or both.

For file sharing, the server is configured to export one or many directories (drawers) or volumes. Each directory or volume exported is referred to as an exported filesystem. Any Amiga on the network may import these filesystems. Each import behaves as if it were a local volume -- it even has an icon on the Workbench. A client may import many filesystems from one or several different servers. A client may also be a server.

For printer sharing, the server is configured to export its printer. Any number of clients may import the printer. A print server may not also be a print client. A client uses the printer as if it were connected locally -- you must even select the appropriate preferences printer driver. Any applications software that prints to the preferences printer driver will automatically print to the imported printer. Applications software which prints directly to the parallel or serial devices using its own printer drivers will not print over the network.

About Hardware and SANA-II

Communications hardware is required for networking. There are several networking hardware products available for the Amiga. Each such product must be programmed differently. Rather than requiring networking protocol software (such as the lower layers of Amiga Envoy) to contain embedded code for all hardware, Commodore developed a standard for network device drivers. This is the SANA-II Network Device Driver Specification (often referred to as just "SANA-II").

Amiga Envoy requires networking hardware with standard SANA-II drivers. This includes most networking hardware.

Your hardware should come with documentation and a SANA-II driver. In case you have Commodore's Ethernet (A2065) or ArcNet (A2060) boards, SANA-II drivers for these boards are included with the Amiga Envoy software, and can be installed automatically.

Third parties developed special SANA-II drivers for the Amiga's built-in serial and parallel ports, allowing them to act as networking hardware. These ports are dramatically slower than specialized networking hardware and are not as easy to use for networking. Though freely redistributable serial and parallel SANA-II drivers are available from BBS's, Fish Disks and other sources, Intangible Assets Manufacturing encourages you to use true networking hardware with Amiga Envoy and does not provide support for serial or parallel SANA-II drivers, except those sold with support by IAM.

Requirements

Sane use of Amiga Envoy requires two or more Amiga computers. (Amiga Envoy can be used on a single Amiga, but talking to oneself is not generally considered sane.) Each Amiga must be running at least AmigaOS 2.04 (2.1 or higher preferred). One megabyte of system memory on each system is recommended, more is preferred. At least one server must have a hard disk. Hard disk installation requires 300k free in SYS:. Each Amiga to be networked must have similar networking hardware with a SANA-II driver. Install your hardware before you attempt to install Amiga Envoy.

Who this is for

This manual is for those needing to set up a simple Amiga Envoy network -- to share files and data on a single physical network with no security requirements.

No networking experience is assumed. You must, however, be familiar with the information contained in the documentation that came with your computer. If you aren't sure what a "drawer" or a "volume" is, or don't know how to use the ASL file requester or the preferences editors, you should learn more about your computer before attempting to install Amiga Envoy.

This manual does not explain how to develop applications for Envoy, how to enable and use Amiga Envoy's security mechanisms, how to use Amiga Envoy with other networking software or how to use Amiga Envoy in an internet (two or more connected physical networks) or with realms. That means that Envoy/Configuration/Users, Groups, and Network Configuration are not documented in this manual. Commodore has included some text files on the Amiga Envoy disk which provide limited documentation on some of these features, but Intangible Assets Manufacturing does not support them. For detailed or advanced information on Amiga Envoy, as well as information on other Amiga networking products, see "The Amiga Networking Handbook" (ordering information is in the section on "Support").

Planning

With many software products, installation consists entirely of copying files. With network software, significantly more configuration is required. Consequently, before beginning installation of Amiga Envoy, you should do a little planning.

You must decide on a name and number for each Amiga. The name will be used by people to refer to that Amiga, so it should be easy to remember and to type. Have fun by choosing a common theme for all your names -- comic strip characters, elements, fruits, liquors, etc. The numbers, on the other hand, will only be used by the computers, not by humans. Each network number must be a unique integer between 1 and 254. Simply start counting from the first name you assign to the last. That way you won't have any duplicates. Remember that you need to purchase one copy of the Amiga Envoy package for each two machines being used on your network.

You should also decide which Amigas will export files or printers to other Amigas. Typically, most Amigas with a hard disk and/or CD-ROM drive will export files. Most Amigas with a printer will export that printer if some Amigas are printerless.

Get a piece of paper. Write a name and number for each Amiga you are going to network. For each Amiga, write down which volumes or directories, if any, will be exported. Make a name for each of these exports (what the filesystem will be called on any clients) and write that down. Write down whether the Amiga will export a printer. If an Amiga will be importing a printer and/or any filesystem(s), make a note of that. Optionally, quickly sketch a diagram of how your Amigas are physically located and connected. Even with the smallest networks, this planning will make installation easier.

Installation

You must now install and configure the Amiga Envoy software on each Amiga in your network. Follow your plan as you carry out the steps below.

To Install to Floppy Disk

Amigas that will act only as clients may run Amiga Envoy from floppy. By importing files, a floppy-only Amiga can effectively get a free but slow hard disk. To create a bootable Amiga Envoy floppy, make a copy of your Workbench disk (2.04 or better). Amiga Envoy will delete files from that disk during installation. Boot from this copy of Workbench. Install per the instructions for Install to hard disk below, but substitute "Install to Floppy icon" below for "Install to hard disk icon." Installing to floppy on a single-drive Amiga is not recommended as it requires excessive disk swapping.

To Install to Hard Disk

Amiga Envoy uses Commodore's standard Amiga Installer program. To use it, insert the Amiga Envoy disk into a disk drive. From the Workbench, double-click the Amiga Envoy disk icon to open a window for the disk. Double-click the Install to hard disk icon. Throughout the installation process, you may access detailed help messages by pressing the help key or by clicking the help button.

Once you've started it, Installer asks whether you are an "Intermediate" or "Expert" user. Click the "Proceed with Install" button, accepting "Intermediate," the default.

If you want to keep a record of what Installer does, then on the Options page, select the "Printer" or "Log File" radio button. Otherwise, accept the defaults. Either way, click the "Proceed" button.

If you are asked "In which disk (or drawer) should the Amiga Envoy drawer be installed or updated?" click the "Proceed" button

to accept the default of SYS:. Remember where you choose to
have Amiga Envoy installed. During configuration, you will frequently have to open the Amiga Envoy drawer, wherever it is on
your system. By default, it is installed to SYS: (usually Workbench:).

Configuration

Once finished copying files, the Amiga Envoy Installer script asks
you questions so that it can configure the software. You should
have already written down the answers to these questions in your
networking plan.

The first configuration question Installer asks is what services you
want to run. In response to "Please select which Amiga Envoy services you would like activated when the Services Manager is run,"
make sure that the "Printer" check box is checked only if this
Amiga will export a printer and that the "File System" box is
checked only if this Amiga will export files. The default is to export
files, but not a printer. Then click the "Proceed" button.

In response to "Please select the type of network configuration you
are using," make sure that Simple Network is selected, then click
the "Proceed" button. This manual does not provide full documentation for complex networks.

Click the "Proceed" button when you see "Please enter the name of
this Amiga's Owner."

Enter the name you've chosen for this Amiga when you are asked
to "Please enter a name for your Amiga." Then click the "Proceed"
button.

Enter the number (1-254) you've chosen for this Amiga when you
are asked to "Please enter a network address for your Amiga." Follow your plan and remember not to use the same number for more
than one Amiga. Then click the "Proceed" button

When you are asked to "Please select what type of network interface hardware you'll be using," determine whether your hardware
is listed. (If you are using a Commodore A2065 or A2060, all the
information required to configure your hardware is already known
to Amiga Envoy. It will automatically set up the hardware parameters.) Select the appropriate box and then click "Continue." Skip
the next paragraph unless you are using other hardware.

If you are using other hardware, you will need to answer additional questions during installation. In response to "Please select what type of network interface hardware you will be using," select "Other" and then click "Continue." You will then be asked to make sure that the SANA-II driver for your hardware is copied to the drawer Devs:Networks before you continue. Once you have done so, Installer asks you to select the appropriate SANA-II driver for your hardware. It uses an ASL file requester displaying the contents of Devs:Networks to let you make this selection. Next, you will be asked to give the packet type number specific to your hardware for IP and then for ARP packets. The default values are appropriate for Ethernet networks. Check your network hardware documentation to determine the packet type numbers for your network hardware.

Installer will inform you that it has completed its work and that it will reboot this Amiga when you click the "Proceed" button.

Once the Amiga has rebooted, you have a little manual configuration work left to do. If this Amiga will be a server, see the sections below on File Sharing and/or Printer Sharing for directions on how to export files and/or a printer. If this Amiga will be a client, make sure the server(s) have been configured first, then go on to the sections below on how to import files and/or a printer. Install and do export configuration on all servers first, since a client cannot import services not yet exported. Then install to clients that are not also servers and configure all the clients for imports. Note that some configuration does not take effect until the computer reboots, so it is advisable to reboot after completing configuration on a given machine. It is necessary to reboot a server after configuration before all of its exports are available to clients.

Now restart the same procedure on the other computers in the network. Be careful not to use the same address for more than one computer.

File Sharing

The part of the Amiga Envoy software package that provides file sharing is EFS -- the Amiga Envoy File System. To use EFS, Amiga Envoy must be installed to and configured on each Amiga that will be sharing files. EFS has client software and server software. Any given Amiga may run just the client, just the server, or both. Each volume or directory a server makes available to remote machines is an exported filesystem. Any number of clients may import the filesystem. On the client, an imported filesystem behaves as if it were a local volume -- it even has an icon on the Workbench. The entire connection between EFS client and server is referred to as a "mount" because the client has mounted a filesystem from the server. A given Amiga may be involved in several mounts as both a client and a server.

Following are directions for how to configure a particular Amiga as a server (To Export a Volume or Directory) or as a client (To Import a Filesystem). To configure a particular Amiga as both a client and server, simply follow the directions for both. Remember that a server must be configured (and rebooted) before a client can mount a filesystem exported from that server.

To Export a Volume or Directory

Open Envoy/Configuration/Filesystem Exports. The "Shared Directories" listview displays all the devices or directories that you have previously exported (none if this is a new installation). Click the "Add" button to select a new volume or directory to export. "Add" brings up an ASL file requester. The file requester will not allow you to select a file, only a volume or directory. Once you've selected and clicked the ASL file requester's "OK" button, your new selection appears in the "Shared Directories" listview.

Click on your new selection in the "Shared Directories" listview. With the selection highlighted, click the "No Security" checkbox. Then enter the name for this export into the "Name" string gadget. This will be the name used by clients importing the volume.

Continue to "Add" more exports as you like. When finished, click the "Save" button to exit Filesystem Exports. Clients will not be able to import added volumes or directories until this Amiga reboots. Once configured, exports are made automatically each time the Amiga is turned on or rebooted.

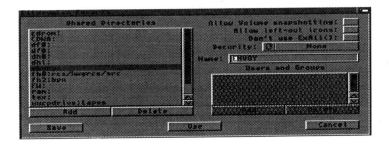

Notes on Volume or Directory Export:

In selecting a volume or directory, you can type the name of a non-filesystem device (i.e., ser: or speak:) into the ASL file requester, but you shouldn't. An attempt to import such a device will result only in an error requester on the client.

If a client can't mount filesystems from this server, make sure that when you installed Amiga Envoy on this Amiga, you checked the "File System" check box when Installer asked you to "Please select which Amiga Envoy services you would like activated when the Services Manager is run." Open Amiga Envoy/Configuration/Services Configuration. In the listview, "Service" Filesystem should have "Status" Enabled. If Filesystem is not in the listview, you did not configure this Amiga to export filesystems during Amiga Envoy installation. Click the "Add" gadget. Using the ASL file requester, select Envoy/Services/Filesystem.service. Click the "Enabled" checkbox to activate the service. Click the "Save" button to confirm your action and exit Services Configuration.

Don't forget that you must reboot the server before the exports become available.

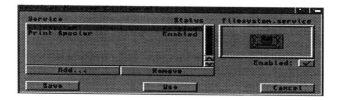

To Import a Filesystem

From the client's side, it doesn't matter whether the server is exporting a volume or a directory. They are both imported as filesystems. A client may import several filesystems from any number of servers, and may import more than one filesystem from the same server. The server for each import must be fully configured for EFS exports before the client can make the imports.

Open Envoy/configuration/Filesystem Imports. You must respond to two requesters before you can use Filesystem Imports itself. A "Host Request" will ask you which Amiga you wish to import a filesystem from. The requester will poll the network for a few seconds, then display in a listview all Amigas currently exporting filesystems. (If no servers are listed, make sure that at least one server has been configured for filesystem exports, then see the Troubleshooting section.) Select a server by double-clicking it. This will close the "Host Request" and bring up an "Enter Username and Password" requester. Type "Admin" into the "User" string gadget, ignoring the password gadget. Click the "OK" button.

Now you may select a filesystem to import. Double-click the file-system you wish to import. You will be asked whether you wish to make this connection permanent. If you respond by clicking the "Yes" button, this filesystem will automatically be imported every time this Amiga is turned on or reboots. If you select the "No" but-ton, this filesystem will not be automatically imported when this Amiga is rebooted or turned on. Once you've selected, another requester informs you that the connection has been established. Click the requester's "OK" button.

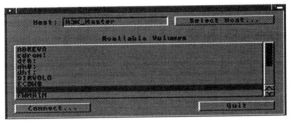

If you wish to add more imports from this host, you may select them now. If you wish to add imports from other hosts, click the "Select Host..." button to bring up the "Host Request" again. Once you are finished adding exports, click the "Quit" button.

Notes

For each permanent filesystem import, a mountfile is added to Devs:DosDrivers (AmigaOS 2.1 and higher) or to Sys:WBStartup (2.04). For temporary filesystem imports, a mountfile is added to SYS:Storage/DosDrivers (2.1 and higher) or Devs: (2.04). Once a temporary import has been made, it may be remade after reboot or power on by double-clicking the mountfile icon. This is much eas-ier than going through the mount process from scratch.

To Stop Exporting a Volume or Directory

Open Envoy/Configuration/Filesystem Exports. Select the volume or directory you wish to stop exporting in the "Shared Directories" listview. With this entry highlighted, click the "Delete" button. This does not delete the volume or directory, it just removes it from the exports list. Click the "Save" button to exit Filesystem Exports.

To Stop All Volume and Directory Exports

Open Envoy/Configuration/Services Configuration. In the list-view, "Service" Filesystem should have "Status" Enabled. Click on Filesystem to highlight it. If you may want to export a volume or directory again in the future, click the "Enabled" checkbox to change the "Status" to Disabled. Otherwise, click the "Remove" gadget to eliminate the Service altogether. Click the "Save" button to confirm your action and exit Services Configuration. The volumes and directories formerly exported are still remembered, so they can be easily exported again by reenabling or adding and reenabling.

To Stop Importing a Filesystem

Filesystem imports will remain mounted until you reboot. To prevent a permanent filesystem import from being remounted on reboot, move or delete its mountfile. The mountfiles will be located in Devs:DosDrivers (AmigaOS 2.1 and higher) or in Sys:WBStartup (2.04).

Printer Sharing

The Amiga Envoy Network Printing system allows an Amiga with a printer to share that printer with other Amigas on the network. The clients behave as if the printer was connected to their own parallel or serial ports rather than to the network. The server can continue to print as if the printer were not exported over the network. Client printing is spooled to the RAM: drive on the server before output to the printer commences.

A given Amiga may import only one printer at a time. All output is directed to the imported printer, even if a printer is attached locally. There is no way to easily select from multiple printers for different print jobs. It is possible, however, to turn network printing on and off easily.

To Export a Printer

During installation, check the "Printer" checkbox when asked to "Please select which Amiga Envoy services you would like activated when the Services Manager is run."

Open Envoy/Configuration/Printer Export. Click the "Add" gadget. Double-click the entry for "Admin" in the listview for "Select a User or Group." Click the "Save" gadget to exit Printer Export.

Don't forget that you will have to reboot the server before the exports become available.

If you did not select the print server option during installation, you may still export a printer without reinstalling. Open Envoy/Configuration/Services Configuration. Click the "Add" gadget. Using the ASL file requester which pops up, select and accept Envoy/Services/Printspool.service. Click the "Enabled" checkbox in Services Configuration to activate the service. Click the "Save" button to confirm your action and exit Services Configuration.

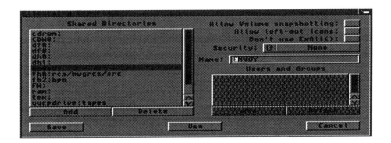

To Import a Printer

To choose which server's printer this Amiga will print to, open Envoy/Configuration/Printer Import. Click the "Select Host..." gadget. The topic "Import a Filesystem" has directions on using the "Host Request" and "Enter Username and Password" requesters Printer Import will bring up. Select a server following those directions. To exit Printer Import, click the "Use" or "Save" buttons. "Save" to select a server for all future network printing, "Use" to override any saved value until the next reboot.

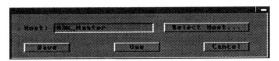

After exiting Printer Import, open Envoy/Configuration/Network Printing. Click the "Install" button to begin directing printer output to the server and exit Network Printing. This setting will survive reboot and power off.

To Stop Exporting a Printer

Open Envoy/Configuration/Services Configuration. In the list-view, "Service" Print Spooler should have "Status" Enabled. Click on Printer Spooler to highlight it. If you may want to export a printer again in the future, click the "Enabled" checkbox to change the "Status" to Disabled. Otherwise, click the "Remove" gadget to eliminate the Service altogether. Click the "Save" button to confirm your action and exit Services Configuration.

To Stop Importing a Printer

Open Envoy/Configuration/Network Printing. Click the "Remove" button to stop directing output to a network printer and to exit Network Printing. Amiga Envoy will still remember the server selected in Printer Import, it just won't do print redirection. Importing the printer again later only requires reselecting "Install" from Network Printing.

Known Bugs

Many high-quality word-processors (i.e., SoftWood's FinalCopy and FinalWriter) ouput text as graphics. With Amiga Envoy print.device version 40.1 and printspool.service version 40.2, large print jobs are prematurely terminated. About one megabyte of data (approximately two or three pages of graphics) is all that will be printed . This is not the fault of the word-processors, it is a bug in Amiga Envoy.

Troubleshooting

No servers listed in Host Request.

Make sure that at least one Amiga on the network is configured as a server for the applicable service. Check that the server(s) are running correctly. Check that the local Amiga is configured prop-erly. Check the network cabling and other hardware.

"Failed to Contact remote printer server" requester when attempting to print.

If you are trying to use a network printer, the host you selected as a server may be turned off or may have stopped exporting print services. Use Amiga Envoy/Configuration/Printer Import to find out or to double-check that server you are using. Then check that server to make sure it is OK and still exporting print services. If you aren't trying to use a network printer, click the "Remove" button in Amiga Envoy/Configuration/Network Printing to disable print redirection.

Graphics or PostScript don't print correctly to a network printer. On the print client, use Preferences/Printer to select the appropriate preferences printer driver for the printer attached to the print server.

Network printing fails from some applications while working with others.
Only applications which use prt: or printer.device work with Amiga Envoy network printing.

"Permission denied to access that printer."
This requester means that you are trying to print on an Amiga that is the client of a printer server but that the name and password you've provided in Envoy/Configuration/Printer Import does not match an account set up in the print server's Envoy/configuration/Printer Export. Unfortunately, Printer Import does not provide error messages when you attempt to import a printer, only when you attempt to print. To fix your problem, cancel the requester, then open Printer Import and click the "Select Host" button. Double-click the print server you desire to use. Then enter "Admin" as the username and click "OK." Finally, click save. Try printing again. If it fails, go to the server and Open Printer Export. Click the "Add" gadget. Double-click the entry for "Admin" in the listview for "Select a User or Group." Click the "Save" gadget to exit Printer Export. Reboot the server and try printing again.

Cannot connect to host 'foo'
Make sure that 'foo' is turned on, has Amiga Envoy installed, is connected to the network and is configured as a server.

Device 'bar' is already mounted.
If you attempt to mount a filesystem a second time, Amiga Envoy complains with this message. If you get this message but still don't have an icon for the filesystem on the Workbench, try accessing the mounted filesystem from the Shell (i.e., "dir bar"). If Amiga Envoy cannot connect to a host initially, it will try again when the filesystem is next accessed. If accessing it from the shell is successful, an icon will appear on the Workbench.

Hardware

If you are using thin-Ethernet (cheapernet), or ArcNet, make sure that your network is properly wired. If your network was working, but stopped, make sure that no connections have been broken. Each system must be connected directly to a T-connector, with coaxial cable running to the adjacent systems on either side. There cannot be branches or loops in the cable. The end systems must have a terminator on one side of the T-connector. Make sure the type and values of the cable and the terminators are correct.

When in doubt...

Reboot every machine on the network, including clients and servers. Servers must generally be rebooted after reconfiguration anyway, and rebooting the clients can't hurt. There are various reasons that rebooting all of the machines may help to clear up or to shed light on a problem you are having.

Support and Bug Reports

Companies other than IAM have also licensed Amiga Envoy. IAM only provides support for copies of Amiga Envoy published by IAM.

This product is not sold with telephone support. Support is available via postal mail and Internet/UseNet electronic mail. Questions may also be answered in the comp.sys.amiga.networking newsgroup, and in the Communications section of the CompuServe AmigaUser forum. You may also send electronic or postal mail.

Note that Commodore (now Escom) does not currently provide any end-user support for Amiga Envoy, so do not contact Commodore (or Escom) directly for support or to report bugs.

Address email to:

envoy-help@iam.com -- For technical support of Amiga Envoy. You must have purchased IAM's Amiga Envoy package.

envoy-bugs@iam.com -- To report bugs in Amiga Envoy;

info@iam.com -- For questions regarding ordering, product availability, specifications, etc.

Advanced Topics

Three features of Envoy have been ignored in this introductory manual: security, internetworking and programming. Some documentation on these topics are included in text files on the Amiga Envoy disk. You should consult those text files.

For security, make sure you've read the "Amiga as Server" section of this book. Then use Envoy/Configuration/Users, and Envoy/Configuration/Groups to edit the users and groups on each server. Using the export preferences editors, grant permissions, as appropriate, on each server for each service.

For internetworking, you should establish a good background knowledge of TCP/IP routing and configuration before you attempt to internetwork Envoy. See the Recommended Reading appendix. As well, note the bug listed in the Known Bugs section. If you have a choice about the networking numbering used in your internetwork, Envoy currently works best with a different class C network address per network.

Programming Amiga Envoy is little different than programming Exec messages. Autodocs and Includes are contained on the Envoy disk. Sample source code is available in the public domain.

Glossary

Glossaries aren't just for when you need to know what a particular word means. Knowing the language of a field gives you a lot of information about that field. I recommend that you read through each definition in this glossary.

The information came from many sources. In addition to the author's own memory and expertise, some of the sources consulted include glossaries from books listed under "Recommended Reading" and several FAQs and other files listed under "Resources." For a more exhaustive dictionary of computer and networking terms, see the jargon file or "The Hacker's Dictionary" or "Newton's Telecom Dictionary."

10-Base-2 -- Also known as thin-Ethernet or Cheapernet, the modern standard coaxial Ethernet in a bus topology.

10-Base-5 -- Also known as thick Ethernet. Interfaces to the computer via an AUI port. The original Ethernet standard. Still used occasionally for long runs of cable.

10-Base-T -- Ethernet on twisted pair in a star topology.

Account -- A computing environment configuration associated with a particular user. Usually includes a username and password, an email mailbox, a record of read and unread public messages, terminal settings, etc. Sometimes includes a directory for the user's own files.

Ack -- Short for acknowledge, an indication that a packet was received intact and does not need to be resent.
addressing

Anonymous FTP -- See FTP and FTP Server.

ANSI -- American National Standards Institute. They produce standards for everything from motorcycle helmets to toilet fittings to computer hardware and software. A common ANSI standard in computers is the ANSI standard terminal. Most modern systems supporting terminals from multiple vendors support ANSI terminals. The Amiga console is ANSI terminal based. The current standard for the 'C' programming language is also referred to as 'ANSI' C.

Application -- A program which directly does something for a human user. A network, application, for example, may provide for file sharing, file transfer, remote login, etc. Other network software, such as a protocol stack or SANA-II driver, does not directly provide any user services.

Application Layer -- The seventh layer in the ISO/OSI model. Provides network services to users. See OSI and applications. Archie -- An Internet application which makes it easy to find freely redistributable files which match a string in the filename or a description.

Architecture -- The design plan. The OSI model, for example, could be used as an architecture for a some protocol stack. Archive -- Usually a group of files, often compressed. Files are usually made into archives for distribution. Hard drive backups are also sometimes called archives. See also: freely redistributable.

ARP -- Address Resolution Protocol. Used for converting network addresses to physical addresses on Ethernets with TCP/IP.

ASCII -- American Standard Code for Information Interchange. The code most computers use for representing characters -- letters, numbers and symbols. Technically, ASCII is a particular 7-bit code, but in typical use, a full 8-bit character set is called ASCII. The meanings of many of the codes higher than 128 can vary from computer to computer.

Asynchronous -- Literally, in different times. In software or human communications, it means that both ends aren't necessarily connected at the same time. Mail (including physical and electronic mail) is a good example of human asynchronous communication. In hardware, it means that two connected circuits aren't necessarily kept in step with each other. See also: synchronous.

Backbone -- The large main network at the center of an internetwork. A company might have a fiberoptic backbone with Ethernet going to individual PCs and workstations. The Internet no longer has a single backbone, it actually has many which are maintained by various service providers and other entities and are interconnected in complex ways.

Bandwidth -- The width of a network "pipe." Determines how much data can be sent in a given amount of time. Compare with latency.

Baud -- The electrical signalling rate of a communications line. At one time, most modem communications happened with Baud rate and BPS equal. Baud is frequently (mis-)used interchangeably with BPS. Technically, high speed modems generally have Baud rates much lower than their BPS rates. Most people mean "BPS" when they say "Baud." See also: BPS and CPS.

Baud Barf -- Strictly speaking, the junk you see on your screen if you set your terminal to the wrong speed for the connection you make. Actually, many modern modems will convert speeds such that you don't ever see this. The term is also used to refer to random characters generated by errors from bursts of line noise (again, something made less common with modern error-correcting modems).

BBS -- A computer Bulletin-Board System is a computer system used for exchanging public and private messages and files between people. Some BBSs provide additional services such as databases, games and more.

Big-Endian -- See Byte Order.

Bis -- French for "second." Used to designate the second in a family of related standards, as in "v.32bis."

BPS -- Bits per second. Usually the number of bits of data a communications link is capable of transmitting and receiving end-to-end in one second. Typically used for comparing theoretical hardware performance. See also: Baud and CPS.

Bridge -- a device that links similar networks to each other to allow devices on one network to transmit data to devices on another. See also: gateway, repeater and router.

Broadcast Packet -- A network packet addressed to all machines. This may refer to a hardware packet broadcast to the physical network or to an IP packet broadcast to a range of IP addresses (as determined by the sending station's broadcast mask).

Browser -- A WWW Browser is an application used for reading hypertext "documents." May allow the viewing of pictures or other multimedia data.

BSD -- Berkeley Standard Distribution. A flavor of Unix, including source code for much of the system. Particularly noteworthy for the extensive TCP/IP networking protocols and applications which have been used widely as the starting point for many other TCP/IP implementations (including those on the Amiga). Sun, Ultrix and many other commercial Unices started from BSD. An Amiga version of the BSD operating system, NetBSD has been around for a while, and is almost ready for prime time. If you are interested in Unix or are really interested in networking, it's worth looking into.

Bus -- In a computer, principal channels connecting major elements. As in Zorro-II bus or SCSI bus. In networking, usually refers to bus topology.

Bus Topology -- The layout of a physical network as a bus -- with two distinct computers as ends and each of the machines between being connected in a line.

Byte Order -- The format for storage or transmission of binary data. God intended big-endian byte ordering -- where the most-significant byte (bit) comes first. The M68k processor family and the Internet use big-endian byte ordering. In little-endian byte ordering, the least-significant byte comes first. Many stupid Intel processors use Little-Endian: See byte ordering.

Character Code -- he numeric value used to represent a character. ASCII is the most common mapping (to eight-bits), though others exist, and multi-byte UniCode is likely to become more common as international support for non-latin languages becomes more important.

Circuit-Switched -- A network which uses dedicated circuits to connect nodes and which can switch the circuits to connect different nodes. A computer with a single-serial port connected to a switcher which selects between several peripherals is like a circuit-switched network. Any of the peripherals can be used, but only one at a time. Phone lines are circuit-switched (though they may be used to connect to a packet-switched network). See also: packet-switched.

Class 1 -- The first standard interface to fax modems. Consists of 'AT' type commands for accessing the fax features of the modem. Not used directly by humans but by fax software.

Class 2 -- A new standard interface with 'AT' commands for fax modems. Much simpler than Class 1, and hence easier to write software for. Early Class 2 modems were released before the standard was finalized, and hence are not 100% compatible. Some software addresses those problems to work with modems which don't strictly follow the standard. Any new Class 2 modem should work with any Class 2 software.

Client -- A computer which will be getting services from another. For example, printing to a remote printer, accessing remote files, or allowing login to a remote machine. See also: server.

CNG -- CalliNG tone. The tone a calling fax makes to indicate to the receiver that the incoming call is from a fax machine.

Chat -- A sort of BBS citizen's band radio. Everyone participating in a chat can type lines seen by everyone else in the chat and can read all of the lines typed by everyone else. There are private (usually two-person) chats and multi-user chats, sometimes with multiple 'channels.'

Cheapernet -- A nickname for 10-Base-2 Ethernet.

Coax -- A type of cabling. Looks like what your cable TV comes in on.

Copper -- Usually network cable which isn't glass or coax.

CPS -- Characters per second. Usually the number of characters (usually bytes) actually transmitted and received end-to-end on a given communications link in one second. Typically used for measuring and comparing real-world performance. File transfer rates of 1600 CPS on a 14.4kbps connection is usually considered quite good.

Data Link Layer -- The second layer of the ISO/OSI model. On the Amiga, usually some combination of the network hardware and SANA-II driver. See OSI.

Datagram -- A logically discrete encapsulation of data to be sent over the network. Contrast with packet.

Distinctive Ring - A service provided by your local telephone company whereby more than one telephone number is allocated to the same line. Calls to different numbers create different ringing patterns.

Duplex -- controls how a terminal displays locally typed characters. With half-duplex, the terminal displays all characters typed onto the screen when they are typed. With full-duplex, the only characters displayed are those sent from the remote host, so the remote host echos keyboard input to be displayed locally. Most connections are full-duplex because it allows flexibility (passwords don't have to be displayed as they are typed, for example). If you and a friend connect with terminal programs and modems, use half-duplex to see what you are typing.

Electronic Mail -- See: email.

Envoy -- A peer-to-peer networking software package with network API developed by Commodore and sold by Intangible Assets Manufacturing.

Email -- Electronic mail. A means of sending messages between people electronically. Basic email supports only ASCII text, but some email systems (MIME, for example) also support sending binaries, sounds, pictures, etc. While most BBSs and online services provide limited email services, being able to send and receive Internet email is much cooler, and is available with some BBSs and many online services.

Export -- To make a network service available from a particular machine. To let someone else access a drawer on your harddrive over the network is to export that drawer.

FAXX -- A standard IFF form for fax data. A 3.0 Datatype exists for this form, with which Multiview can display standard Amiga fax files.

FDDI -- Fiber Distribution Data Interface. A standard for network hardware in the same way that Ethernet is a standard for network hardware. FDDI uses glass and operates at 100mbps. With repeaters at least every 2km, it is limited to approximately 200km total length.

Fiberoptic Cable -- Also called 'glass' or just 'fiber.' Very fine strands of glass which carry light over long distances. Modulated to transmit digital data, fiber has a much higher bandwidth than coax or copper.

File Server -- A computer which makes files available to other computers through a network filesystem. Sometimes called a disk server. Some software (i.e., Netware) requires that file servers be dedicated. Even when using more flexible software, file servers in networks with more than a few computers are usually dedicated for performance reasons. Should not be confused with an FTP Server.

Finger -- a program on many Unix systems and on Internet-connected systems which allows one to check the status of a particular user: when last logged in, etc. Some users include humorous, biographical or other information in their ".plan" printed in response to a finger. Some fictitious users exist only to be fingered and display various information.

Flaming -- Ad hominem arguments. Attacking the person rather than their position. Often degenerating into simple (but verbose) name calling. Flaming is common in electronic communications, perhaps because many people forget that online messages should be held to the same standards of civility as face-to-face communications.

Flow Control -- how a computer and a modem or other peripheral start and stop the movement of data (as when a buffer is filled). The two common types of serial flow control are XON/XOFF (a software solution) and RTS/CTS (a hardware solution using special serial port pins and requiring a cable capable of hardware flow control).

FTP -- File Transfer Protocol. The standard Internet application to get files from one place to another. TFTP is a Tiny version. NcFTP is a version with a nice user interface and a port is included with AmiTCP Release 3. See also: FTP Server.

FTP Server -- A system which has files available to get via FTP. Since many systems on the Internet do run FTP server software, the term is usually applied in the context of Anonymous FTP servers. These servers contain freely redistributable software or information usually accessed with the username "anonymous" and the password "user@domain.name."

Gateway -- a device that connects networks that use different protocols. In effect, it translates between the protocols so that devices on the connected networks can exchange data. See also: bridge, repeater, and router.

Glass -- see Fiberoptic Cable.

Gopher -- An Internet resource locator. Browsing through Gopher menus lets you find a wide variety of resources on many hosts by subject rather than by application and location.

Graffiti Wall -- A feature of some BBSs which allows the posting of short (usually one line), often anonymous, messages to a small circular buffer (usually about 25 lines). The contents of the buffer are usually displayed to everyone at log out or through a menu selection.

Group 3 -- The current standard for fax devices. All the products mentioned in this article are for Group 3 fax. Anyone who gives you a fax number without indicating otherwise is probably giving you the number to a Group 3 fax.

Home Directory -- A directory owned by a particular user in which that user's files are stored by default. Normally, users cannot write or delete files in other user's home dirs. Typically, a user can control whether other users will be allowed to read the files in her home directory (and a user can, if she really wants to, even make other users able to write or delete files in her home dir).

Home Page -- A top-level Web page on a certain subject.

Hop -- The distance between two gateways. When an internet packet traverses a route, each network that it crosses is a hop.

Host -- A computer on a network. Also refers to a computer that multiple terminals are attached to (like some BBSs or online services). Some people call network hosts "nodes."

Host Name -- The name humans use to refer to a given computer on a network.

Hub -- The central device in a star topology network. An Amiga with a multi-serial card can serve as a hub for a serial-port network. 10-Base-T Ethernet uses hubs which are usually stand-alone devices.

IMAP -- Interactive Mail Access Protocol. A standard TCP/IP protocol for allowing email to be read remotely. This is a preferable solution to POP, but POP is more widely implemented and available than IMAP. See also: SMTP.

Import -- To connect as a client and to bring in a network service. When a network filesystem is mounted, it is said to be imported.

InfoBahn -- A better (but less than perfect) name for the Information Highway. At least it has an international flavor and isn't likely to be limited to 55.

Information Highway -- An unfortunate turn of phrase. While it is nice to have a term which refers to the online world generally, the hype and technical incorrectness of the general media seems to ruin most of what they get their hands on. Among other things, the term leads to many poor metaphors.

internet -- [note the lowercase 'i'] A network made up of smaller, physically distinct networks which have been joined. The smaller networks might have similar or dissimilar hardware. For example, an internet could be composed of two Ethernets, or of an Ethernet and an ARCNet.

Internet -- [note the uppercase 'i'] The huge world-wide network made up of hundreds of thousands of smaller networks, all connected, running the TCP/IP protocol suite, and sharing certain common applications. See also: TCP/IP.

INU -- Abbreviation for InterNet Utilities. A freely redistributable Amiga software package by Michael B. Smith. Includes NNTP and SMTP.

IRC -- Internet Relay Chat. The world-wide Internet equivalent of a BBS or online service chat mode.

IP -- Internet Protocol. The most basic protocol of the TCP/IP protocol suite.

IP Address -- See IP Number.

IP Number-- An IP number is the network address for a host. Usually expressed by humans in dotted-decimal notation (i.e., 128.252.135.4), they are really just 32-bit numbers.

ISO model -- A theoretical model from the International Standards Organization of how networking protocols should be split up into seven layers. No real working protocols follow this model exactly, despite the fact that nearly every networking text refers to the ISO model. See also: OSI.

LAN -- Local Area Network. A high speed network which operates over short distances. Ethernet is a good example. Serial links can't constitute a LAN because of their low speed. A simple LAN is made up of a single physical network, though many larger LANs are internetworked.

Little-Endian -- See Byte Order.

Log In -- The act of entering a system. This usually consists of entering a name and password. It may include starting a terminal program, dialing a remote system, connecting, then entering a name and password.

Login -- A user name. "What is your login?" is another way of asking "What is your user name?"

Mainframe -- Also referred to as 'big iron.' A large computer designed for data processing. The prototypical mainframe is the large IBM system. See also minicomputer.

MBPS -- Million Bits Per Second. See BPS.

Microcomputer -- Generally, a desktop computer system.

Minicomputer -- Systems designed for multiuser general computing. The DEC Vax is the prototypical mini. See also mainframe and microcomputer.

Modem -- MODulator DEModulator. Converts digital computer signals (generally from a serial port) into audio signals to be transmitted over phone lines and then converted back into computer signals.

MUD -- Multi User Dungeon. A category of multi-player interactive game. There are several MUD programs, and many distinctive instances of each. Sometimes used for non-game applications since they provide facilities for complex interaction between people and an artificial environment. A poor-man's virtual reality.

Multiplexing -- To multiplex is to run multiple signals over a single line simultaneously.

Nack -- Short for negative acknowledgment, an indication the data was received but corrupted and must be resent. Most network protocols don't transmit nacks -- corrupted packets are tossed, and if an ack is not received for a given packet within a given time, the packet is resent.

Netrek -- a 16-player network video game of interplanetary warfare. Typically using mice or keyboard for input, players control starships which can attach each other in an arcade-like sequence (a la Space War), travel across a galaxy on a strategic map and transport armies to control planets. While there were still Software Engineers at Commodore's now abandoned West Chester facility, many played netrek every Tuesday night.

Network -- A collection of individually-controlled computers, printers, modems and other electronic devices interconnected so they can all communicate with each other. Networks also include all the software used to communicate on the network and the wires, cables, connector modules and other hardware that make the physical connections.

Network Layer -- The third layer of the ISO/OSI model. That part of a network protocol which handles Addressing and Routing. See OSI.

Network Surfing -- Finding data, files, or other resources on the net, sometimes starting with a purpose, but often following leads to interesting but completely unrelated resources. Gopher and WWW make surfing much easier and more efficient than it was previously.

News -- UseNet (and now Internet) message system consisting of thousands of subject groups (newsgroups) and daily megabytes of messages posted from machines around the world.

NFS -- Network FileSystem. A standard created by Sun Microsystems for sharing harddrives over TCP/IP networks (there is now a transport-independent version, but TCP/IP is still the most used).

NNTP -- Net News Transfer Protocol. A TCP/IP standard for exchanging UseNet news through TCP/IP rather than UUCP. It also provides services that allow easy implementation of software for a user to read news remotely, without moving all messages to the user's local machine.

Node -- Sometimes used interchangeably with host, sometimes referring to machines connected to FidoNet.
Node Number -- A loose term sometimes referring to a FidoNet

address, sometimes to an IP number, sometimes to some other address.

Null-modem -- An adapter which crosses certain lines on a serial cable. A null-modem cable is one constructed with the same crosses rather than being wired straight through. Two computers whose serial ports are connected via null-modem can communicate with each other in the same way that they would communicate via a standard modem. For example, a terminal program can be run on each machine to allow users to type messages to each other or to transfer files.

Optical Fiber -- See Fiberoptic Cable.

OSI -- Open Standard Interconnect. A suite of internet protocols. Also, a brain-dead attempt to replace TCP/IP with a suite of protocols steeped thoroughly in bureaucracy and other results of large international committee meetings.

Packet -- The unit of data sent across a (packet-switched) network. Usually an arbitrary part of a datagram or stream. Packet-Switched -- A network which uses a single cable to share communications between many different devices. Many different "conversations" are carried by the cable simultaneously, and a given computer might be connected to several other. All current Amiga LANs are packet-switched.

ParNet -- a kludge which allows two Amigas to connect using parallel ports. It is faster than using a serial port and cheaper than buying real network hardware. It has the disadvantages of using some lines shared by the serial port and of keeping one from using a parallel-port printer.

Physical Layer -- The first layer of the ISO/OSI model. Consists only of networking hardware such as Ethernet or RS-232. See OSI.

Ping -- a TCP/IP application which sends a packet to a remote machine requesting a return packet. Named after the noise made by active sonar. It is used to determine if a remote machine is up and reachable, as well as to determine the latency and other characteristics of the network connection to the remote machine.

POP -- Post Office Protocol. A standard TCP/IP protocol for moving email from a mail server to a mail client. Mail is addressed to a user on the server, but may eventually be delivered to the user on the client. This is preferred on most Amigas, because many Amigas are not always running to receiving mail and are not usually backed up as well as the servers. See also: SMTP and IMAP.

PPP -- Point-to-Point protocol. A standard for networking connections on serial hardware. Most often used with TCP/IP, is flexible enough to support other protocols (simultaneously even). The Amiga implementation currently supports only TCP/IP.

Presentation Layer -- The sixth layer in the ISO/OSI model. Converts data formats. See OSI and byte-order.

Print Server -- A network printer system to which clients may send print jobs. Sometimes a printer with a network interface, often a computer and printer connected to the network.

Protocols -- A set of procedural rules for information exchange over a communication medium. These rules govern the content, format, timing, sequencing, and error control of messages exchanged in a network.

Protocol Stack -- The sum of many protocols at different levels used in a network, usually not including application protocols. See also: protocol suite.

Protocol Suite -- The sum of protocols used with a networking package. The usual suite of TCP/IP protocols includes ARP, IP, ICMP, TCP, and UDP, as well as FTP, Telnet, finger, and others. Note that the applications are definitely part of a protocol suite. See also: protocol stack.

Repeater -- a device that extends the maximum length of cable in a single network, so that the network can be expanded. See also: bridge, gateway, and router.

RoboSport -- A great network game. Originally released for the Mac using AppleTalk. The Amiga port was released before the existence of Envoy, and only supports serial ports (for two-player) and AS225r2 (for four-player). After seeing the Mac version over AppleTalk, the author did a lot of fast talking to ensure that the port would have AS225 support.
Route -- The path a packet takes between hosts.

Router -- a device that connects similar networks to each other. A router receives data transmitted from other nodes and retransmits it to its proper destination over the most efficient route; this route may include several routers, each forwarding the data to the next. See also: bridge, gateway, and repeater.

Service -- The application made available by a server over the network to client machines.

Server -- Any machine which makes available to other machines on the network resources or data. In a client/server network, such as Netware, only dedicated machines running obnoxiously expensive software may be servers. In a peer-to-peer network such as Envoy, any machine may act as a server and need not be dedicated to the task.

Session Layer -- The Fifth layer of the ISO/OSI model. Manages the sequence of interaction between devices. See OSI.

Silent Answer -- A feature of Supra modems that allows them to "listen" for a CNG tone before generating a carrier tone (screech). Works in combination with an answering machine to allow incoming fax and voice calls on the same line. Most fax machines offer a similar feature, and fax switches are based on this feature.

SLIP -- Serial Line Internet Protocol. An unofficial but widely used method for running TCP/IP over serial lines (especially dial-up lines). See also PPP.

SMTP -- Simple Mail Transfer Protocol. The standard TCP/IP protocol for mail exchange between systems. It is not designed as an interface to a mail reader. Most Amigas ought to be running a protocol such as POP or IMAP rather than SMTP.
Socket -- In networking software, an application programming interface to a protocol stack. Usually refers to Berkeley sockets, one standard interface to TCP/IP (and, less commonly, other protocols) under Unix. Is used on the Amiga in AS225 and AmiTCP.

Spamming -- The act of posting a message in many, many message groups with little or no regard for whether the message is relevant to the topic of the message group.

Squirel -- A self-propelled short-circuit.
(We're talking about the creature here, not to be confused with the Oregon Research Squirel SCSI controller, which is a fine product.)

Standards -- In networking, standards make the world go 'round. While proprietary file formats and interfaces may be OK for word processors or spreadsheets, they don't fly in most networks. If every hardware manufacturer's network card could only work with network cards from the same manufacturer, or if email could only be sent between machines of the same type running the same program, we'd all go crazy. A standard specifies exactly how a piece of hardware or software is to behave. Hardware and software developers use standards to create implementations (cards or programs) which are compatible with all other implementations of the standards. At least, that is the theory. In practice, developers sometimes make mistakes such that they aren't really compatible. Further, it is often said that "the nice thing about standards is that there are so many to choose from." Some developers tend to do this more often than others, so look out. Other developers (like those headquartered in Bellevue, WA and in Provo, UT) tend to declare their products "industry standard" regardless of whether anyone else has done anything compatible or whether a specification for the standard was released in advance.

Star Topology -- Network cabling configuration in which all connections from workstations are to a central hub. 10-Base-T Ethernet uses such a topology.

Stream -- Data which doesn't neatly fit into discrete units. A login session is a good example. Contrast with datagram.

Surfing -- See Net Surfing.

Synchronous -- Literally, at the same time. In software or human communications, it means that both ends are connected in real-time or near real-time. A telephone call or a talk session are good examples of human synchronous communication. In hardware, it means that two circuits are kept in step with each other. See also: asynchronous.

Sysop -- The person who runs a BBS is usually called a System Administrator or Sysop. Sometimes the person who runs an online service or a section in an online service. See also: system administrator.

System Administrator -- The person (or group of persons) who maintains a system. Sometimes called root, a sysop, a sysadmin, postmaster, etc. Most system are underpaid and underappreciated. If you have a problem on a system, you'll have to get the System Administrator to help you. Most are extremely knowledgable. Hence, it is worth being nice and getting on the good side of any sysadmin's you come into contact with.

T -- An adaptor with three connectors. In networking, usually having two BNC female connectors and one BNC male connector. The male connector is connected to an Ethernet or ARCNet adaptor, while each of the other two ends have either a terminator or a cable to another computer.

TCP/IP -- Strictly speaking, Transmission Control Protocol (a reliable stream service) running on top of Internet Protocol. Generally, it refers to a suite of network and application protocols including TCP, IP, UDP, ICMP, Telnet, FTP, and others. TCP/IP is used to create heterogeneous LANs and to connect to the world-wide Internet. See also: Internet.

Telnet -- The standard TCP/IP application for remote login. Also useful for accessing various text-based services via TCP/IP. Similar to rlogin.

Terminal -- A device for interfacing a user with a computer, usually a standard keyboard and an alpha-numeric display unit with a serial connection to a large shared computer. See also: terminal emulator.

Terminal Emulator -- A software program which allows a computer to act as a terminal. See also: terminal.

Terminal Settings -- A set of parameters including terminal (or terminal emulation) type (i.e., VT100 or ANSI), baud rate, duplex, flow control, etc. See also: terminal.

Terminator -- Usually an electronic device place at the ends of an electronic bus. Ethernet terminators are 50 ohm resistors which must be placed at each end of a thin Ethernet network. ARCNet terminators are 95 ohm resistors which must be placed at each end of a coaxial ARCNet. A T-1000 Terminator is used to eliminate carbon-based network problems (i.e., Mark Barrett).

Thinnet -- A nickname for 10-Base-2 Ethernet.

Token Ring -- A type of networking hardware. IBM Token Ring is not available for the Amiga.

Topology -- the way cables are physically laid out in a network. Often dictated by the type of hardware used. See bus topology, start topology, and ring topology.

Traffic -- Data moving over a network. When the traffic nears the bandwidth of the network, jams occur.

Transceiver -- Often referring to an Ethernet Transceiver: a hardware device which converts one type of Ethernet connection into another. For example, to convert an AUI port into a 10-Base-2 or 10-Base-T connection.

Transport Layer -- The fourth layer of the ISO/OSI model. Controls the continuity and reliability of communications. See OSI.

Twisted Pair Cable -- The most common form of copper. 10-Base-T Ethernet uses twisted-pair, but 10-Base-2 is a more common flavor in existing installations.

Unix -- An operating system. Actually, several related operating systems which aren't entirely compatible with each other. One of the most widespread multi-user systems, Unix systems are those you are most likely to run into on the Internet. The Amiga shell and Unix shells are often very similar, and basic tasks are carried out in the same way. Some command names are different: ls=dir, mv=rename, cat=type, rm=delete. See also: BSD.

Unreliable -- A network protocol which doesn't guarantee the delivery of packets, much less that those packets which do arrive will not be corrupted. UDP even has unreliable in its name (OK, it's really User Datagram Protocol, but it could be Unreliable).

User authentication method -- Any procedure used by a server and workstation by which the server may be convinced of the user's identity. Kerberos is a sophisticated example. See also: account and password.

VT100 -- A common member of the DEC family of terminals. So common that all modern systems supporting terminals from multiple vendors support the DEC VT100.

WAN -- Wide Area Network. A network spread out over a large geographic area. Special WAN hardware makes high-speed long-distance network links possible. Standard voice-grade modems make cheap but slow WAN links possible. Contrast with LAN.

W3 -- See WWW.

Web -- See WWW.

WWW -- The World Wide Web. Refers to both a specific Internet application and to the huge hypertext document created by it (there may be more than one, but it sure seems like they are all connected). The client applications used to browse the Web usually allow most kinds of Internet applications to be used from within the browser (common clients include WWW, Lynx, Mosaic and Cello). The Web is growing at an enormous rate and contains detailed information on a wide variety of topics. Also called W3 or "the Web."

Zone -- An AppleTalk equivalent of an Envoy realm.

Get More Information and Stay Up-to-Date

Check out our web page: http://www.iam.com. We've got information on our full line of products, links to other Amiga sites and much more.

Or, add yourself to our mailing list. You'll hear about updates to this book and get more information about IAM's current and future products. If you have a stable email address, please give us that, otherwise please give us your snail mail address. Send it to: **registration@iam.com** or to our snail mail address.

For a list of products available and other information, mail the IAM infobot at **info@iam.com**. As of this printing, products published by IAM include DiskSalv4 disk utility software, The Deathbed Vigil video tape, the game MegaBall4, Amiga Envoy software, and more.

Get Disks

If you have trouble obtaining freely redistributable software, order a current disk set from IAM. Disks include current versions of AmiTCP (demo), AmiTCP Utilities, AS225r2 Utilities, Virus Checkers, Envoy Utilities, Terminals, General Utilities (dearchivers, etc.), and SANA-II Specs and Drivers (includes SLIP and PPP). Eight disks for $27+shipping and handling. (Note that some items are shareware and will require you to pay a registration fee to the author if you use them.)

Ordering Information

For all orders, write to **sales@iam.com**, or to:

Intangible Assets Manufacturing
828 Ormond Avenue
Drexel Hill, PA 19026-2604
USA

Phone Orders: +1 610 853 4406 (orders only)
Fax Orders: +1 610 853 3733